IMAGES
of America

WEST MEMPHIS

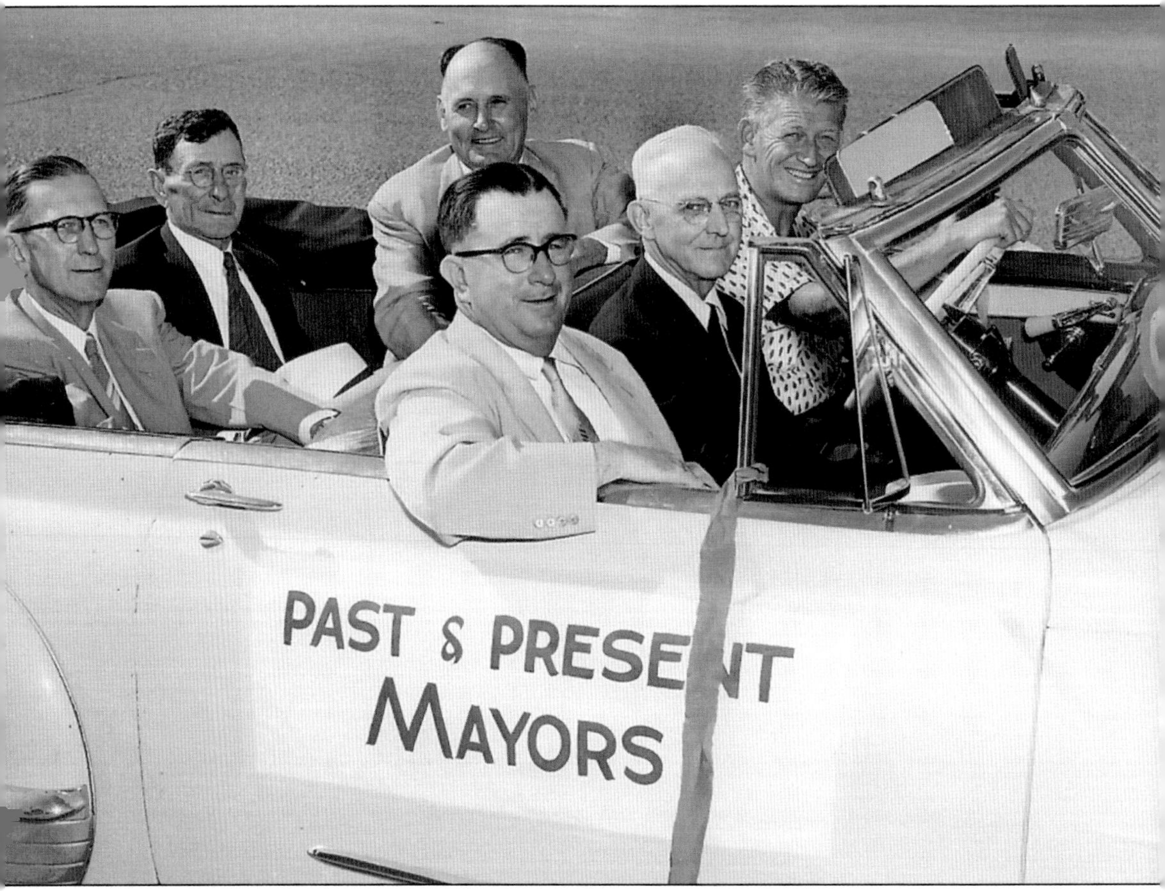

Although the Arkansas General Assembly approved an earlier incorporation act in 1923, that measure became null and void, as a required election was not held within a 30-day period. West Memphis was officially incorporated four years later. Celebrating the 25th anniversary of incorporation in 1952 are, from left to right, the first five mayors of West Memphis: (front seat) Melvin Dacus (1944–1952), William H. Hundhausen Sr. (1932–1944), and driver James G. Moore; (backseat) William Fordyce (1952–1954), Zack T. Bragg (1927–1930), and Marshall B. Currie Sr. (1930–1932). (Courtesy of the Mississippi Valley Collection at the University of Memphis.)

On the Cover: Mound City, photographed during the Great Flood of 1912, was once an active settlement along the Mississippi River before it naturally changed its course in the late 19th century. The area, a forerunner to West Memphis, was named after the numerous American Indian platform mounds located there, some of which are still visible today. On April 27, 1865, immediately north of Mound City, the worst maritime disaster in US history occurred when the steamship *Sultana* exploded, resulting in approximately 1,700 fatalities. Mound City and its vicinity have since been annexed to the city of West Memphis. (Courtesy of Memphis Public Library.)

IMAGES
of America

West Memphis

Michael A. Beauregard

ARCADIA
PUBLISHING

ISBN 978-1-4671-1116-4

Published by Arcadia Publishing
Charleston, South Carolina

Printed in the United States of America

Library of Congress Control Number: 2013940586

For all general information, please contact Arcadia Publishing:
Telephone 843-853-2070
Fax 843-853-0044
E-mail sales@arcadiapublishing.com
For customer service and orders:
Toll-Free 1-888-313-2665

Visit us on the Internet at www.arcadiapublishing.com

To the past and present citizens of West Memphis
who are responsible for their city's history

Contents

ACKNOWLEDGMENTS

The unique images contained in this work were selected from various collections. Ed Franks and his staff at the University of Memphis Special Collections Department provided great assistance with their holdings, and the staff at the Memphis and Shelby County Room at the Memphis Public Library were extremely helpful with their photographic collections. The following organizations and individuals provided additional photographs: West Memphis Chamber of Commerce, the Library of Congress, Seville General Archives of the Indias, Knox County Library, First Presbyterian Church, Holy Cross Episcopal Church, Trinity Baptist Church, Malco Theatres, Vincent Astor, Danny Craft, Loretta Dale, Michael Finger, Dale Franklin, Dixie Ball Gordon, Kent Hale, William H. Hundhausen Jr., Pat Magruder, Frank and Kay Martin, Jeannie B. O'Toole, Alfred Saig, Michael P. Sims, Murphy Smith, and Bonnie Waller.

The following people are recognized and thanked posthumously for their contributions: Virginia Forman, William L. Johnson, Dorothy Ward, and in grateful acknowledgment of Margaret Woolfolk, who pioneered the research and documentation of Crittenden County history.

Unless otherwise noted, all images are from the Mississippi Valley Collection at the University of Memphis.

Introduction

West Memphis, Arkansas, will always be known as "the Wonder City" due to its founding from unspoiled forests to its incorporation as a burgeoning town, all within a single generation of the early 20th century. Situated alongside the Mississippi River in an area that once witnessed annual flooding, West Memphis was conceived in an extremely challenging region for a town to properly develop and prosper. The early settlers who arrived in this area of Crittenden County, located west of Memphis, Tennessee, were drawn to the location for its old-growth hardwood forests and soon began lumbering establishments. During the late 1800s and early 1900s, the area that would later give rise to the city of West Memphis was a vast region of timber and swamps with very few cleared areas for farming. The swampy conditions and untamed environment hindered any early attempts to develop this area, in spite of its proximity to the river and downtown Memphis. Roads were nearly nonexistent at this time, and travelers were forced to use ferries to transverse from Tennessee to Arkansas before the first railroad bridge was constructed in 1892.

Lumberyards and sawmills quickly emerged, and those companies took advantage of the railroad lines that had been established for shipping products across the country. Within a very short time, the lumber industry dramatically changed the landscape of the area. The forests were cleared, and the remaining cutover lands were drained for further land use. Beginning in the early 1900s and continuing until the 1920s, a permanent levee system was constructed by the newly formed St. Francis Levee District to protect the region from seasonal floods. Ditches and drainage canals were created to help drain the swamps and help control future flooding. By the 1920s, the region had been transformed from dense hardwood forests to rich, fertile farmland. Aided by the newly constructed levee and the establishment of two federal highways in 1917, the future city of West Memphis soon developed along these routes and was an incorporated city by 1927. Before West Memphis came into fruition, there were a few early settlements in the vicinity that are considered as its forerunners. While West Memphis developed independently from these settlements, their past is important to the city's future development.

The Spanish, who had controlled lands west of the Mississippi River since 1763, established a fort in 1797 in this area named Campo de la Esperanza, or Field of Hope. The site of this fort today is immediately north of Interstate 40 from the entrance into Arkansas from Memphis. The Spanish governor of the territory sent Benjamin Fooy, born in Holland around 1759, to this locale in 1792 as a mediator with the American Indians. Fooy settled in the area and was appointed military commandant of Campo de la Esperanza under Gen. Augustine Grandee. In 1801, the Spanish territory west of the Mississippi reverted back to France. Two years later, the French sold this territory to the United States in the infamous Louisiana Purchase under Pres. Thomas Jefferson.

Following the withdrawal of the Spanish from Campo de la Esperanza, Benjamin Fooy established himself on the more than 600 acres he had received through Spanish land grants. Around 1804, the location that was once Campo de la Esperanza received its anglicized name of Hopefield. By

1820, Hopefield Township had approximately 500 residents. Hopefield was the second permanent settlement in the state of Arkansas (behind Arkansas Post) and the first settlement in the area that would later become Crittenden County. Fooy remained in Hopefield Township for the remainder of his life and served as a federal magistrate and a regional judge. By all accounts, Benjamin Fooy was a well-respected individual and greatly admired by citizens in both Arkansas and Tennessee. He died in Hopefield in 1823, just two years before the establishment of Crittenden County on October 22, 1825, from territory formerly included in Phillips County.

On February 8, 1859, Hopefield was officially incorporated by an act of the Arkansas General Assembly. Its popularity as a ferry landing and railroad terminal caused such an increase in businesses and population that moving the county seat from Marion to Hopefield was briefly considered. The Memphis & Little Rock Railroad (M&LR) was opened in 1858 from Hopefield to Madison, in St. Francis County, and was the first functioning railroad in the state of Arkansas. Another benefit of the town's location was its proximity to the beginning of Military Road in Crittenden County. The first federal road in the state of Arkansas, Military Road's construction began in 1824, and by 1826, the road extended through Mound City to Marion. Within five years, the route was completed to Little Rock, with additional improvements to be made in subsequent years. By 1831, a stage and mail route along Military Road was established between Memphis and Little Rock. Beginning in 1832, the road was used as the westbound route for the forced relocation and movement of American Indians, mainly the Creek tribe from Alabama, following the Indian Removal Act of 1830. Military Road was also used by soldiers and army caravans involved in the Mexican War and Civil War. For the remainder of the 19th century, Military Road was especially important to thousands of pioneers traveling west, and it remained the primary western route from Memphis until Highway 70 was created in 1917.

During the Civil War, Hopefield witnessed considerable raids and attacks by Confederate assailants against Union ships along the Mississippi River. This activity had become so frequent that, on February 19, 1863, by orders of Maj. Gen. Stephen Hurlbut, the entire town was burned. Witnesses in Memphis described how the little white houses with green shutters became smoking ruins. This included all homes and businesses, the church, the train depot, and livery stables. The residents of Hopefield were given one hour's notice of the fate of their town in order to save their personal belongings. One of the rare surviving items from the town's destruction is the Hopefield Methodist Church Bible, currently preserved and displayed at the Crittenden County Museum in Earle.

After the burning of Hopefield, the town reemerged as an important river venue due to its strategic location for commerce. Its reemergence was halted by the Great Yellow Fever Epidemic of 1878, which severely crippled Memphis and its vicinity with over 5,000 deaths and the flight of a majority of its remaining citizens. This drop in population kept Hopefield from returning to its former prominence. By the turn of the century, Hopefield was known by Memphians for its entertainment venues, including boxing rings and saloon halls. However, it was never able to regain its commercial importance, primarily due to the rerouting of the railroad with the opening of the Great Bridge at Memphis.

In 1892, the Great Bridge, later known as the Frisco Bridge, officially opened and was the first bridge constructed over the Mississippi River, south of St. Louis. Prior to its construction, freight cars transited the river on ferries from Memphis and were unloaded onto a ramp in Hopefield. From the ramp, the freight cars were reassembled behind and pulled by an Arkansas side locomotive stationed at a roundhouse. Since the bridge was located south of Hopefield, the train line was relocated as well, and the town lost its former rail traffic. In addition, the opening of the Frisco Bridge rendered Hopefield's ferry operations obsolete. The severing of Hopefield from its original rail and river traffic was only the beginning of its fate. The town was perpetually doomed when the levee system was created, leaving the area to become part of the Mississippi River floodplain. After the Great Flood of 1912, the few remaining structures of the town washed away. Today, Hopefield is only a memory, the former location of which lies beneath Interstate 40 where the Hernando de Soto Bridge enters Arkansas.

Below the Hopefield site, along the river immediately south of the Frisco Bridge, a small unincorporated community was the first site to receive the name West Memphis. This area was planned out in 1884 by Arthur, Frank, and Robert Vance, who were the third generation in their family to own this land. In 1883, the railroad had been completed to this location by the Kansas City, Fort Scott & Memphis Railroad. At this juncture, train cars were ferried from Memphis and assembled behind locomotives, in the same fashion as Hopefield. With a population of 200 residents in West Memphis, a post office was established in 1884, and during the 1880s, several more establishments were built, including a hotel, school, several boardinghouses, two sawmills, and three general stores. It was also the site of the West Memphis Amusement Park, located along the river to the immediate north of the Frisco Bridge, which entertained Memphians with rides, dances, and picnics during the 1880s and 1890s. After the completion of the Great Bridge and the construction of the levee farther west, the first West Memphis suffered the same fate as Hopefield, with the rerouting of rail traffic and the creation of the Mississippi River floodplain by the new levee.

Another nearby community that predated the incorporated city of West Memphis was Hulbert, located southwest of the original city limits of West Memphis. Hulbert was never an incorporated town, and the city of West Memphis annexed the area in 1955. This community was most likely named after William R. Hulbert, who owned substantial lands in the vicinity. Hulbert acquired these lands in the 1820s directly from the US government for the $1.25 cash price per acre based on the 1820 Land Act initiative, having been discounted from the previous $2 per acre credit rate from the original 1804 Land Act. The area had been called Hulbert since the 1830s and received a post office in 1838 for a brief period before being reestablished later in 1900. The railroad was built through the Hulbert area in 1858 as part of the first segment of the Memphis & Little Rock Railroad. In 1908, another track was constructed from Hulbert to Marianna, Arkansas, and this site became an important juncture of two train lines. The first telephone system in the area was located in Hulbert, having been established there by the American Telephone and Telegraph Company in 1910.

In the same year, Harry Rupple Dabbs arrived from Memphis with a $500 loan to establish a store located among other retail establishments. Dabbs built a white clapboard building for his store in 1911; however, that structure was greatly damaged during the flood of 1912. In 1913, Harry Dabbs, along with his brother Edwin, constructed a two-story brick building facing the railroad tracks. Between 1923 and 1972, Dabbs Brothers store also housed the Hulbert Post Office. Although the store closed in 1975, Harry Dabbs retained ownership of the building for four more years.

The first school was built in Hulbert in 1914 but was not adequate to support the population growth of the area, including the future West Memphis. Eleven years later, a large three-story brick school south of Dabbs Brothers was constructed to serve students in grades one through twelve who lived in the area south of the Marion School District. Originally named Hulbert School, it was the only public school in the vicinity until a new high school was built on West Barton Avenue in the city of West Memphis in 1948. Following the completion of this high school in West Memphis, Hulbert School was renamed Dabbs Elementary School in honor of Harry Dabbs and served students in grades one through six until it closed in 1978.

The present city of West Memphis was an outgrowth of two early industries that formed the nucleus of the future town. Zack Taylor Bragg came to Crittenden County from Mississippi in 1905 to engage in the lumber business, and in 1914, he established his own sawmill on a dirt road leading to Marion, what would later become Missouri Street. Bragg's lumber mill was serviced by a railroad spur from the main railroad farther north. For this reason, for a short time, the area was called Bragg's Spur and Bragg City. During these early years, the region of this second West Memphis was marked by thick, virgin hardwood forests and swamps. It was reported by Bragg that black bears were still living in the vicinity as late as 1912. Having owned over 320 acres and buying the logging rights to thousands of neighboring acreage, Bragg was responsible for clearing nearly all the land that would become the future West Memphis. There were almost 100 workers at Bragg's mill in 1920, and as a result, housing and a few stores were soon established in the vicinity.

Two miles south of Bragg's Lumber Mill, a separate venture began in 1914 when William H. Hundhausen Sr. was sent from St. Louis by P.T. Bolz to inspect timber holdings. The report of the availability of quality timber combined with railroad and river access led to the establishment of Bolz Cooperage Company. This site included a sawmill and cooperage for barrel manufacturing and located on the south ends of Eighth and Ninth Streets. This area, south of the future Broadway, had been platted for homes and businesses with planned streets around 1911, but the Great Flood of 1912 discouraged any new growth. Thus, the establishment of the cooperage plant provided a considerable growth opportunity to a stagnant area. Workers and their families started a community that included a private school near the plant. Permanent houses began to appear, and stores were soon established to meet the needs of the new residents.

Prior to 1917, there were no major roads in the vicinity, as the nearest main route was Military Road, located more than five miles north toward Marion. Travelers to this area were either ferried to a landing on the Mississippi River near South Eighth Street or transited by train. The railroad lines were also used by horseback riders, pedestrians, and the occasional automobile, as it was the only cleared pathway to safely navigate through the thick timber and swamps between towns. In 1917, US Highway 70 was cleared between the levee and the western edge of the county. The following year, it was graveled to Lehi, Arkansas, and later concreted by 1926. US Highway 61 was also cleared north to Marion in 1917, with concrete laid within five years. These two major highways, which were later named Broadway and Missouri Street within the city limits of West Memphis, prompted exceptional growth for the area, as motorcar ownership increased and eventually became the preferred mode of travel. By the mid-1920s, with these crossroads firmly established and the completion of the main levee constructed to withstand major flooding, the communities that emerged from Bragg's Lumber Mill and Bolz Cooperage Company fueled the area with permanent residents, and in 1927, the City of West Memphis was officially incorporated with approximately 500 citizens.

Memories can only represent the past if they are recalled and communicated as they actually occurred. While historical narratives provide the context of the past, they are subjective and do not replicate each person's experience. In contrast, photographs provide an objective window from which one cannot only relate to images of the past, but they can also provide a broader perspective to the present as well as a glimpse of how the present will become the future. The photographs presented in this book offer a lens of West Memphis that will evoke historical connections that provide continuity between former and future generations.

One

Early History

Zack Bragg was one of the first permanent settlers in the area to become West Memphis. Bragg was originally from Utica, Mississippi, and in 1905, he moved to western Crittenden County to clear land for a lumber operation. In 1914, Bragg established his own sawmill operation along a railroad spur and a dirt path that would later become Missouri Street with the purchase of 320 acres at $17.50 per acre. With the logging rights he acquired, Bragg also cleared a majority of the adjacent properties. During this period, the area around Bragg's lumber company was referred to as Bragg City. Another early settler, William H. Hundhausen Sr., arrived in 1914 from St. Louis and was instrumental in establishing Bolz Cooperage Company, which started production the following year. Shortly thereafter, workers and their families formed a small community approximately two miles south of Bragg's sawmill, around Eighth and Ninth Streets.

By the early 1920s, local residents began to petition for incorporation. Originally, most people desired the name Bragg City. Ironically, it was Zack Bragg himself who opposed this name and was strongly in favor of the name West Memphis. His business rationale was later explained in the April 9, 1962, issue of the *Commercial Appeal* when he stated, "In those days Memphis was known everywhere for its good lumber. If the inspectors saw it was stamped from Memphis, they didn't even look at it a lot of times. So, I thought if I could get my sawmill place incorporated as a town with the name West Memphis, it would be a big help for the lumber's selling price."

In February 1923, the State of Arkansas passed an act to incorporate West Memphis, with the condition that an election for city officials would follow within 30 days. An election was never held, and the incorporation act became null and void. Based on the persistence from more residents, the Arkansas General Assembly passed another incorporation act for West Memphis in the spring of 1927, and the citizens elected Zack Bragg as their first mayor.

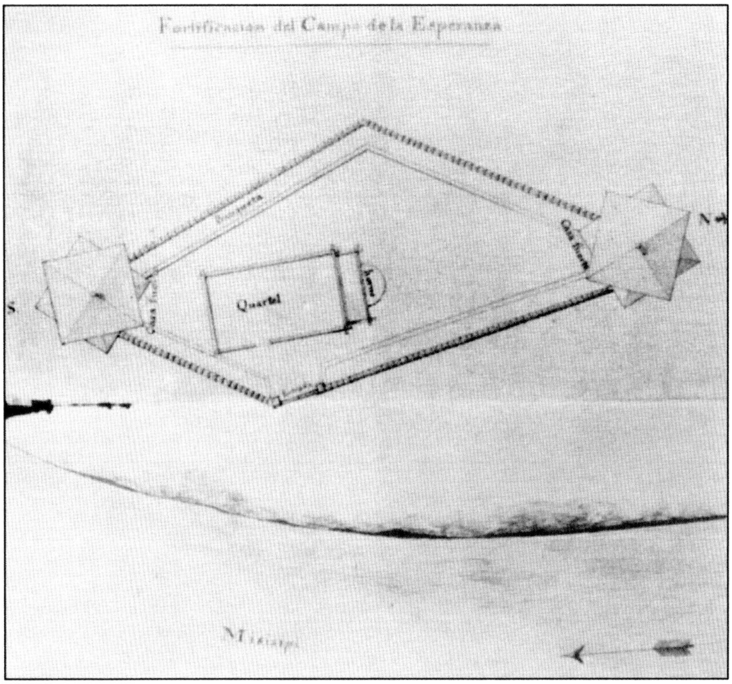

This 1797 drawing displays the layout of Campo de la Esperanza, or Field of Hope. It was in that year when the Spanish established the camp along the Mississippi River, opposite the future city of Memphis, Tennessee. Since the time of the Louisiana Purchase in 1803, the name of the area around the fort was anglicized to Hopefield. The site of the fort today is immediately north of the Hernando de Soto Bridge. (Courtesy of Archivo General de Indias, Seville, Spain.)

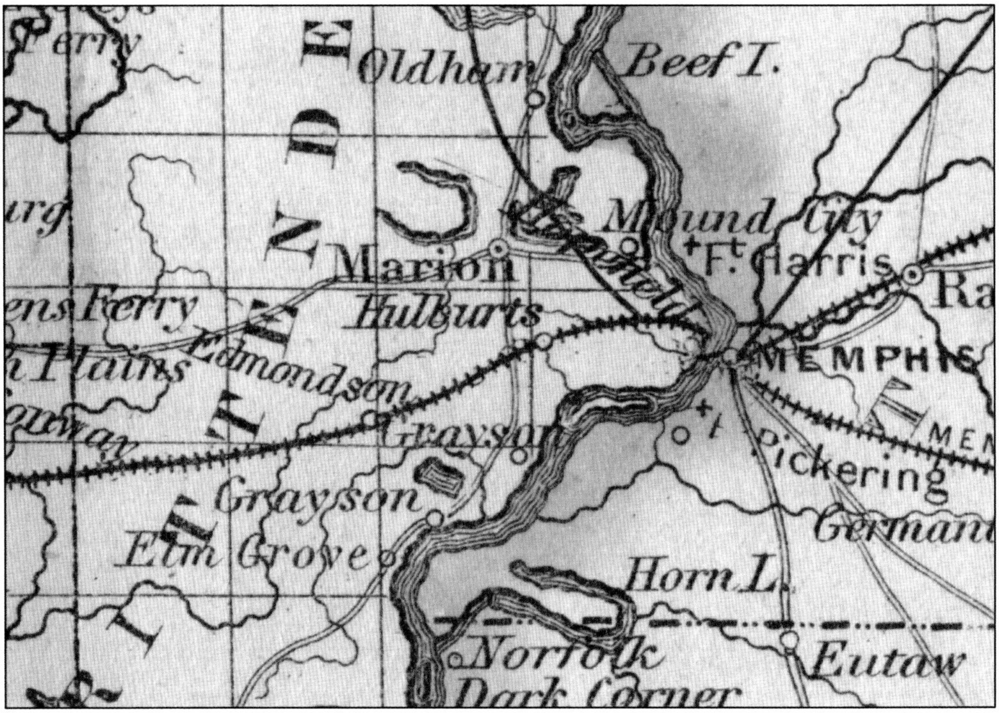

Crittenden County was established in 1825 and was named in honor of Robert Crittenden, the first secretary of the Arkansas territory. The original county seat was Greenock and later moved to Marion in 1835. This early Arkansas map from 1855 depicts the course of the Mississippi winding toward Mound City and above Hopefield before naturally changing its course and moving farther east in the late 1800s.

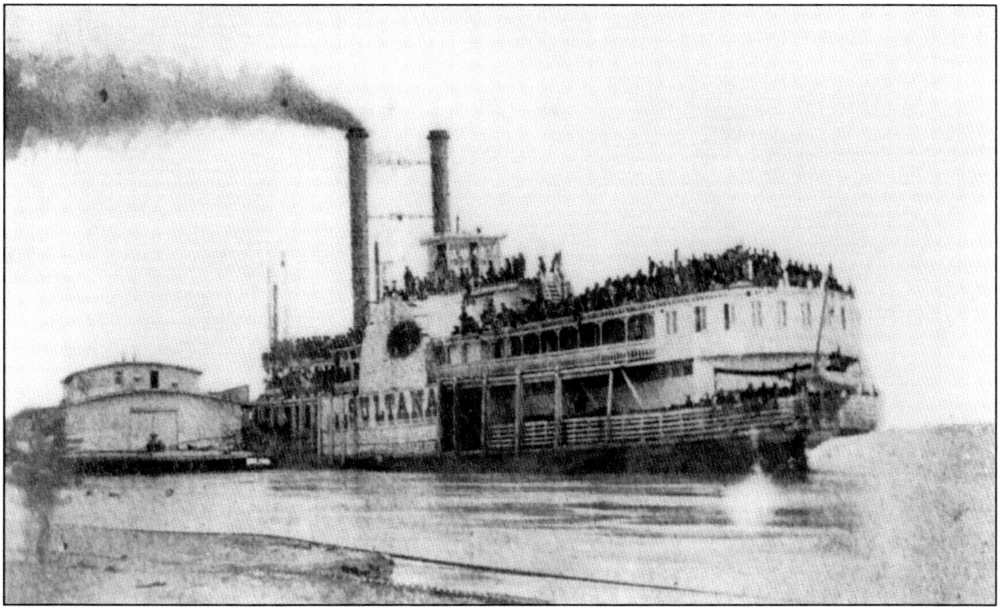

The deadliest maritime disaster in US history was the sinking of the steamship *Sultana* on April 27, 1865, directly north of Mound City. This photograph was taken the day the ship departed Helena, Arkansas, on April 25. The ship was overloaded with 2,400 passengers, most of whom were recently released Union soldiers from Confederate prison camps. Approximately 1,700 soldiers and civilians were killed when the boilers violently exploded and caught the vessel on fire. (Courtesy of the Library of Congress.)

Survivors of the *Sultana* frequently held regional reunions until the 1920s, as seen here at one in East Tennessee in April 1894. The last-known living *Sultana* survivor was Albert Norris of the 76th Ohio Volunteer Infantry who died in 1936. (Courtesy of the McClung Collection, Knox County Library.)

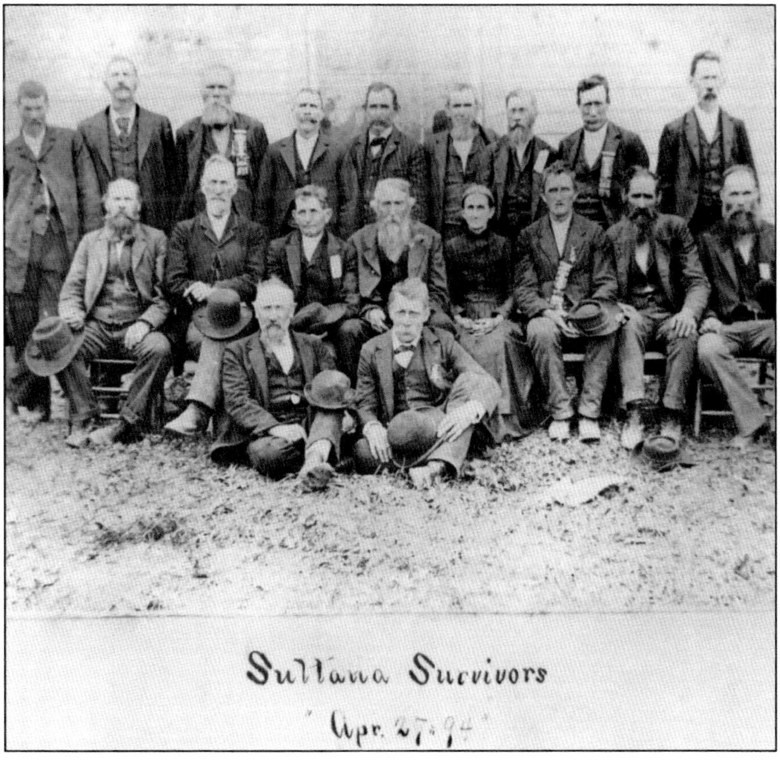

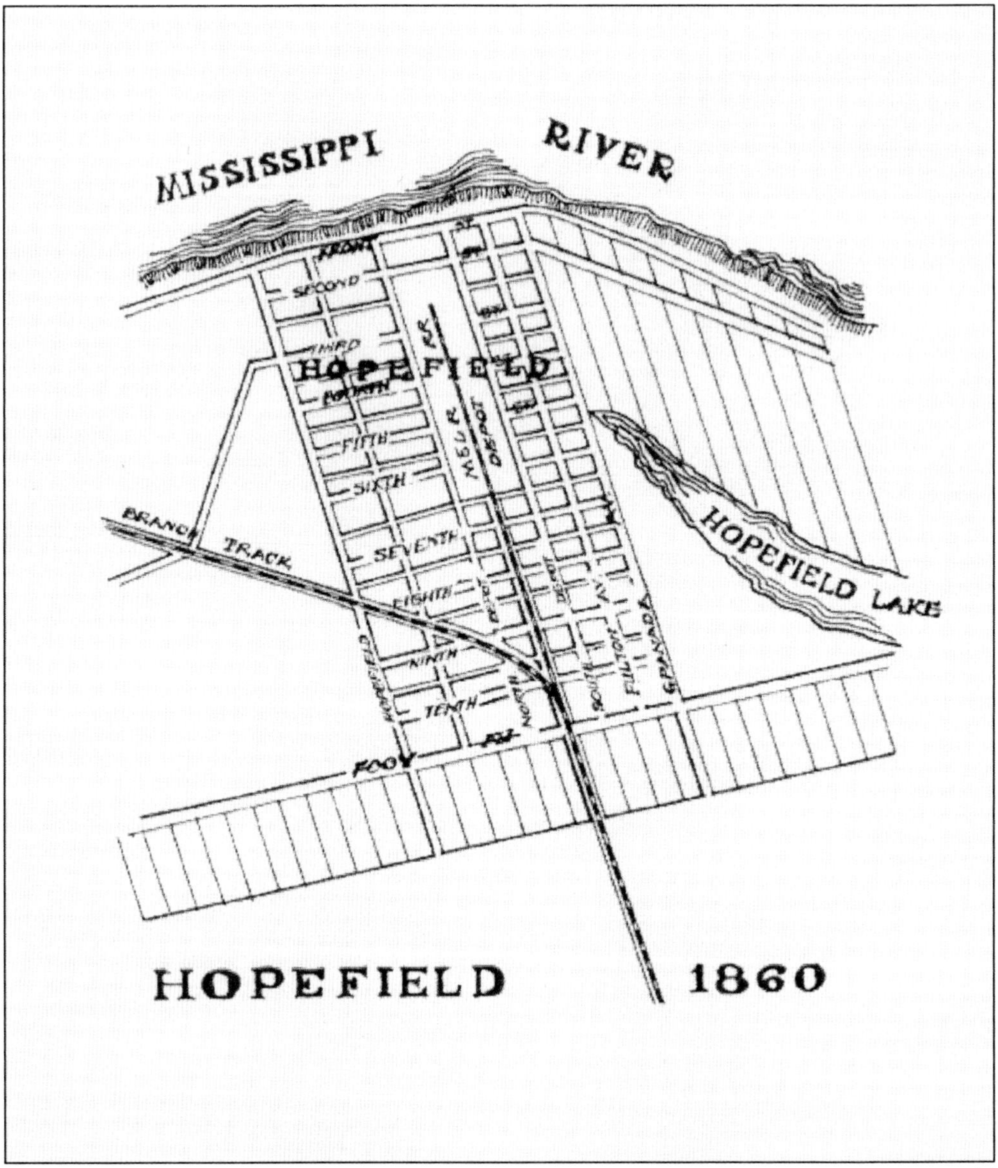

This illustration depicts the layout of Hopefield as it appeared in 1860. Downtown Memphis would have been located above the upper-right corner of this map. Hopefield became a prosperous town due to its location on the Mississippi River. In addition, it was also the starting point of Military Road and the Memphis & Little Rock Railroad. On February 19, 1863, Union troops burned the entire town in punishment for repeated Confederate guerilla attacks on Union ships. The town was soon rebuilt and became an important transportation hub for river and rail commerce. Its demise came after the railroad was rerouted and the main levee was constructed around 1900, leaving the town within the Mississippi River floodplain.

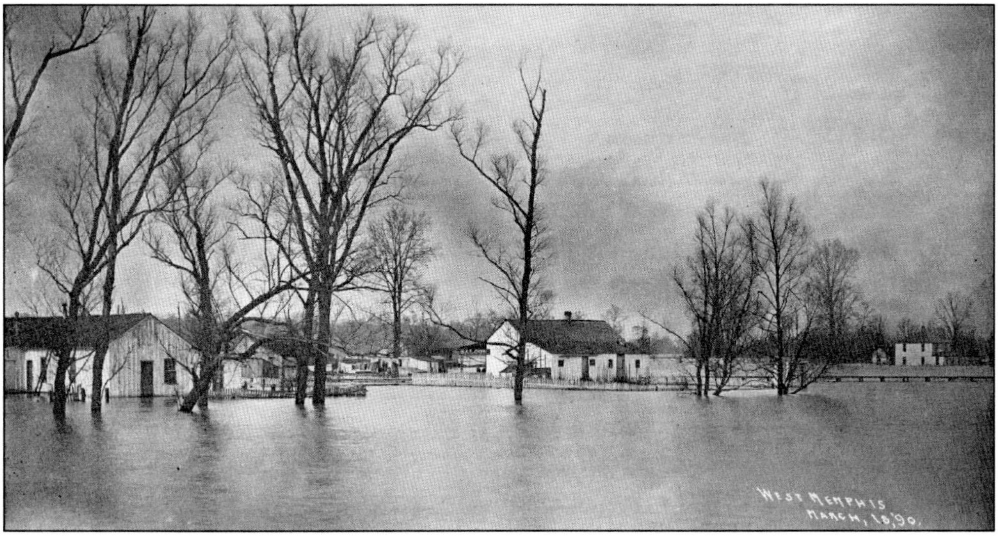

This photograph from 1890 is the only known image of the first settlement to bear the name West Memphis. A short-lived community, it began in the 1880s along the Mississippi River, immediately south of the present-day Memphis-Arkansas Bridge, and by 1900, the area was abandoned primarily because it, like Hopefield, became part of the Mississippi River floodplain.

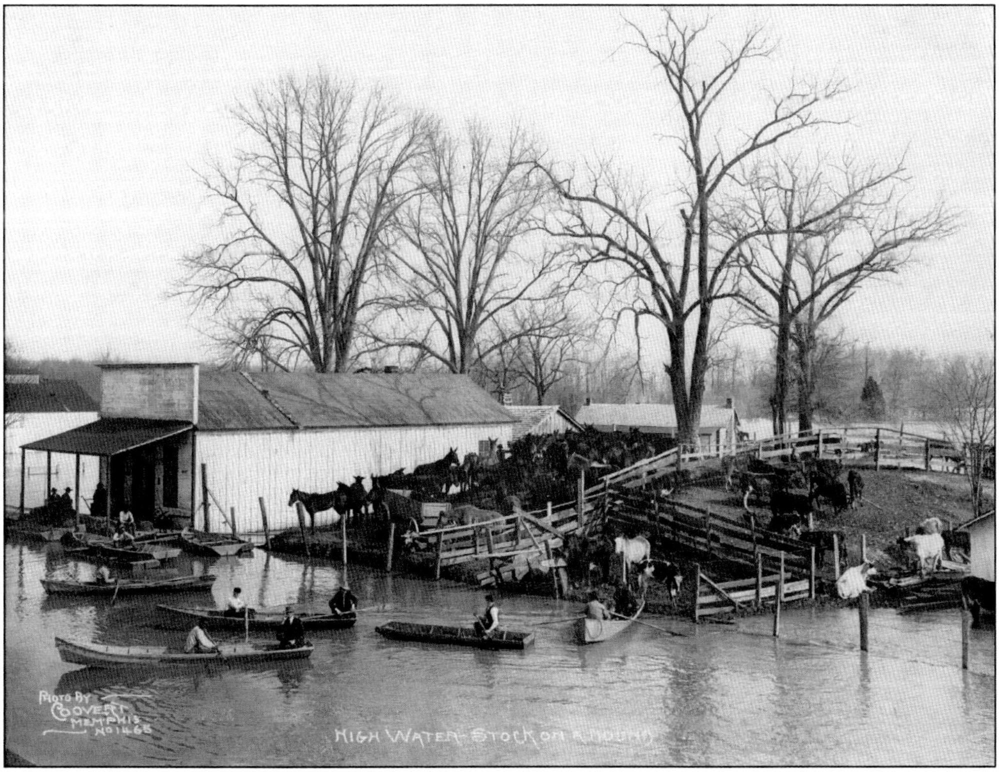

Named after the American Indian platform mounds found in the area by early settlers, Mound City was once a thriving settlement before the Mississippi River changed its course, leaving the town disconnected from the main channel. This photograph shows livestock taking refuge on one of those mounds during the flood of 1912. (Courtesy of Memphis Public Library.)

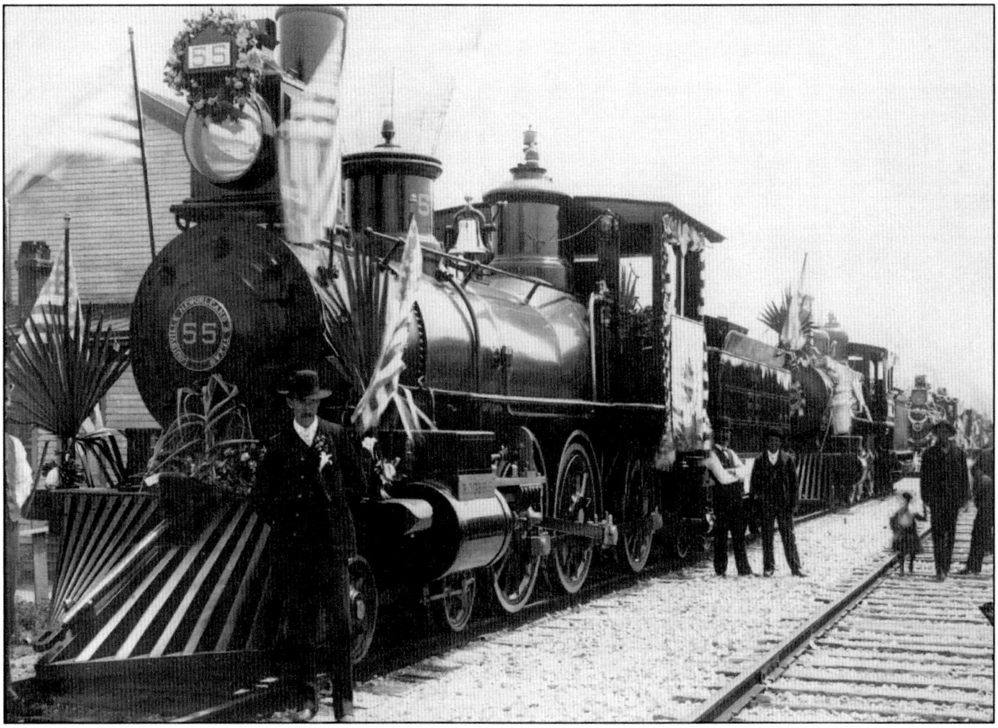

The Great Bridge, later named the Frisco Bridge, was the first to be built on the lower Mississippi River and the only bridge south of St. Louis when it opened on May 12, 1892. For its dedication, nine connected steam locomotives crossed from Memphis into Arkansas to test its strength. This bridge remained the sole structure in the vicinity spanning the Mississippi until the Harahan Bridge was completed in 1916.

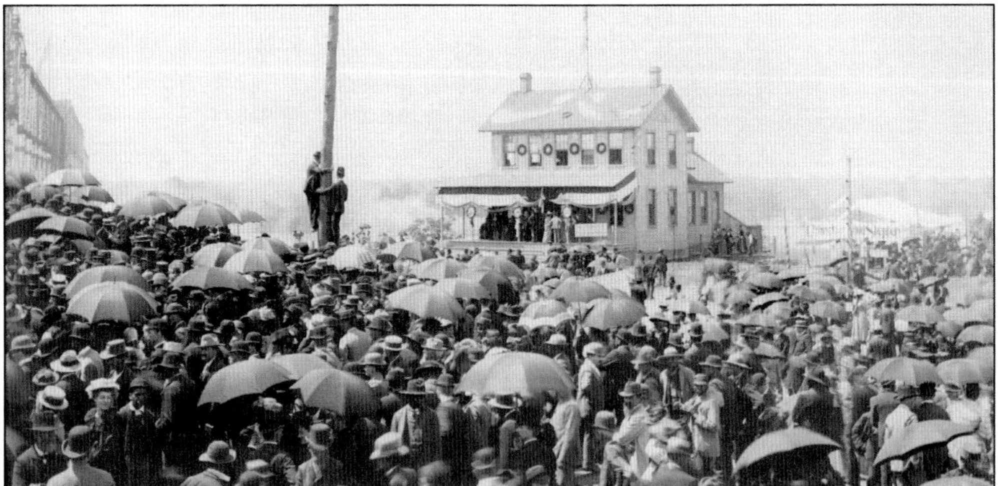

On May 12, 1892, over 50,000 people attended the dedication of the Great Bridge. After the locomotives crossed, the governors of Arkansas and Tennessee rode on flatcars that were pushed from both directions until they met in the middle of the bridge. The total bridge cost was $3 million, and at the time of its completion, it was the third-largest bridge in the world and the longest steel span in the United States. (Courtesy of Memphis Public Library.)

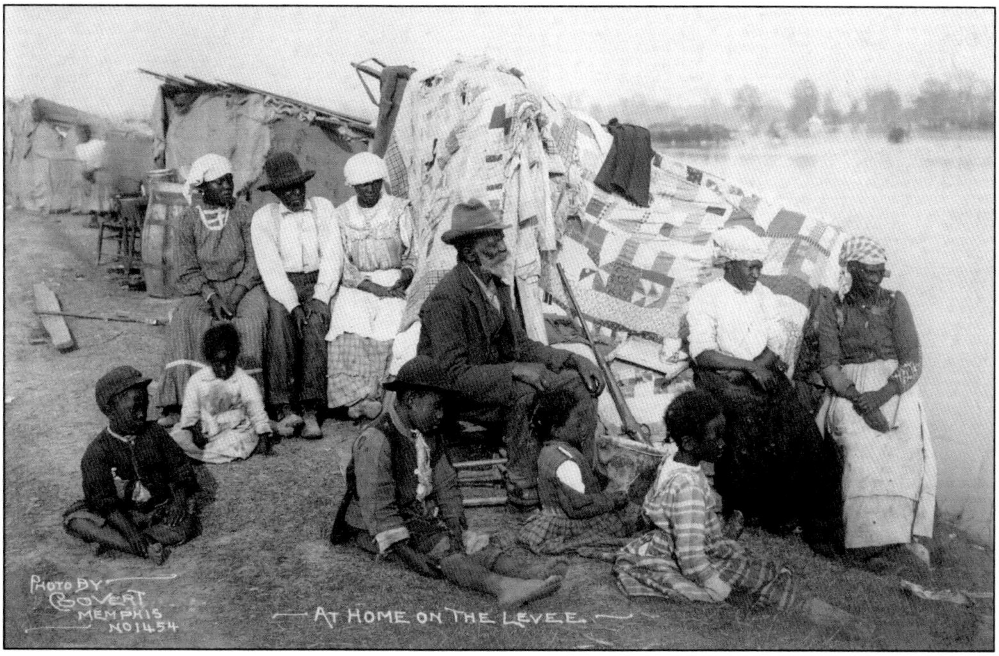

Due to several breaks, the Great Flood of 1912 breached the recently completed levee and flooded Crittenden County. With nowhere else to go, many sharecroppers took refuge atop the levee. Over the next 10 years, the levee was strengthened and raised to withstand future flooding. (Courtesy of Memphis Public Library.)

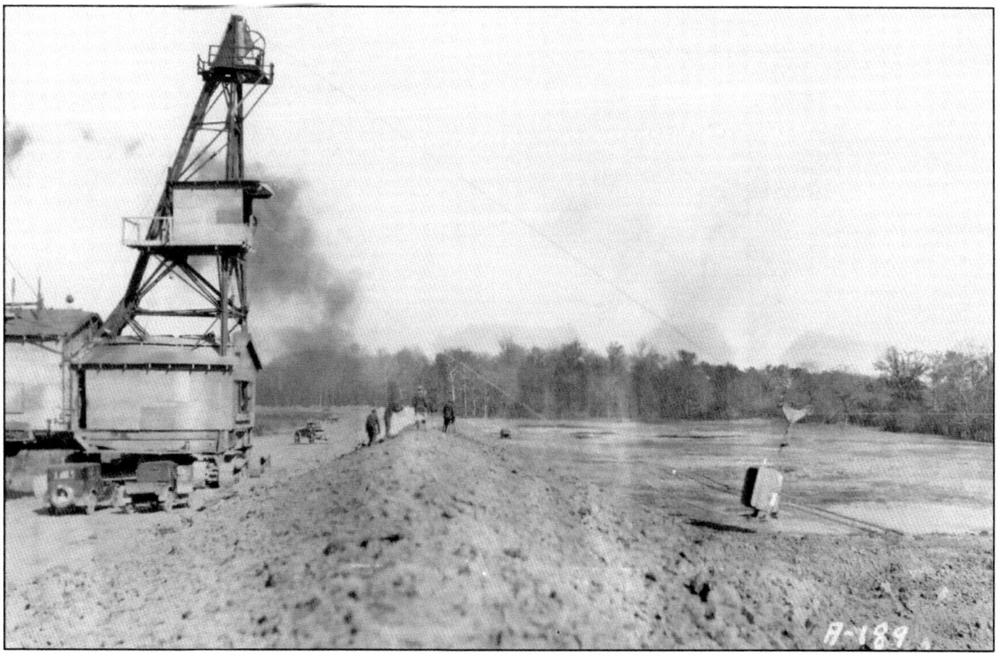

The St. Francis Levee District was established in 1893 and had constructed most of the levee system in Arkansas by 1905, with improvements following in subsequent years. The flood of 1913 was the last time that the levee broke or that West Memphis flooded from the Mississippi River. The strengthened levee protected Crittenden County from the Great Floods of 1927 and 1937.

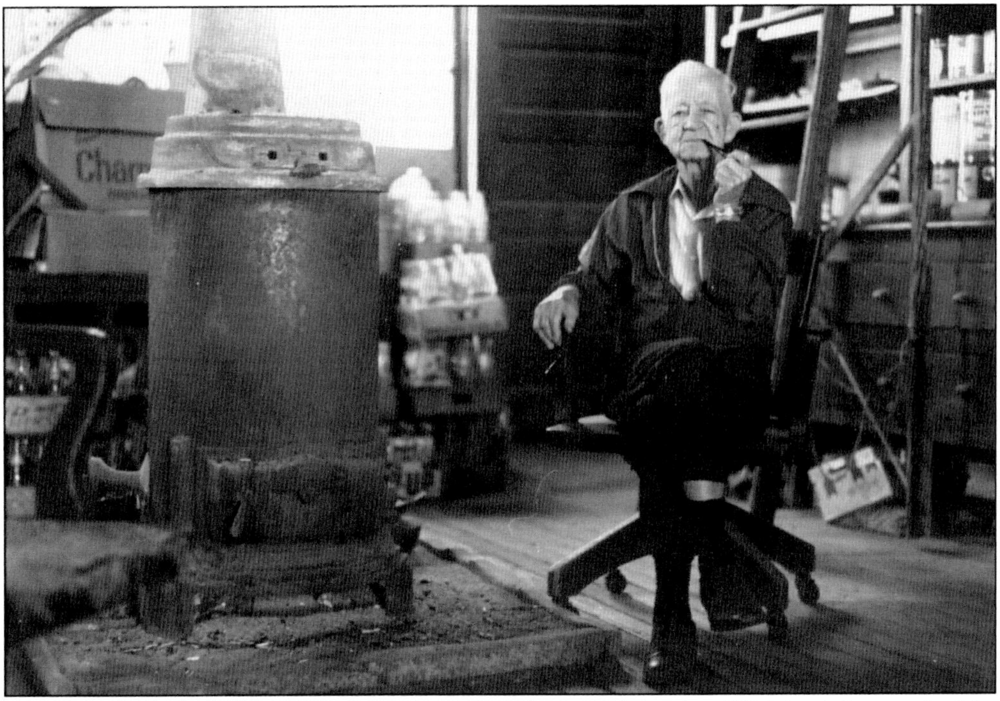

Harry Rupple Dabbs came to Hulbert from Memphis in 1910 with a $500 bank loan to build a general store. His first store suffered damage from the flood of 1912 and was rebuilt across the road the following year. Dabbs Brothers store operated in the same building from the time of its construction in 1913 until 1975.

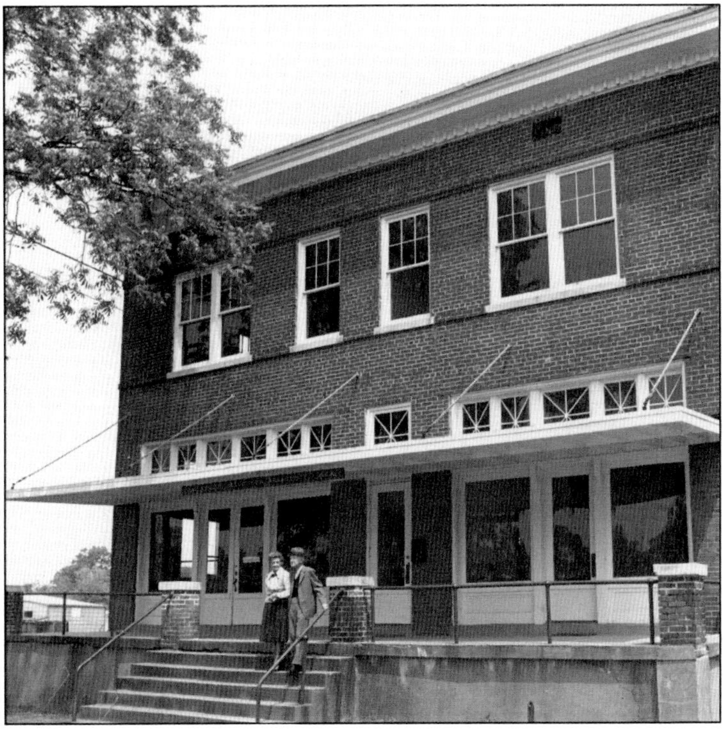

Dabbs Brothers store, shown at left with Harry and Kate Dabbs, was built elevated to protect it against possible future flooding. In addition to the store, a portion of the building served as a post office from 1923 until 1972. The store closed in 1975, and Patrick Kelly Magruder Sr. acquired the building four years later. Magruder, an architect, restored the interior and exterior of the structure, which has since been used as the office of PKM Architects.

Zack Taylor Bragg, born in Utica, Mississippi, in 1888, first came to Crittenden County in 1905 and worked for several logging establishments in both Crittenden and St. Francis Counties. In 1914, Bragg opened his own sawmill beside a railroad spur and along a dirt road, later named Missouri Street. He was primarily responsible for clearing the old-growth forests in the vicinity of the future West Memphis and became the first mayor after the city was incorporated in 1927.

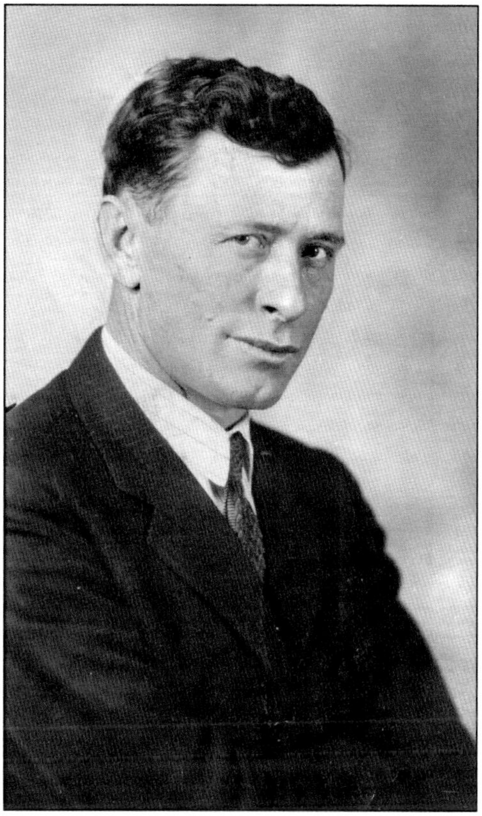

Bragg Commissary, photographed below in the late 1920s, was the center of activity around the sawmill. This building burned in 1937 and was replaced with a white two-story framed structure that served as the main office. The site of the old Bragg Commissary is where Pizza Hut is currently located on Missouri Street. In 1935, Aubrey P. Dacus purchased the sawmill operation, which continued as Dacus Lumber Company until 1972.

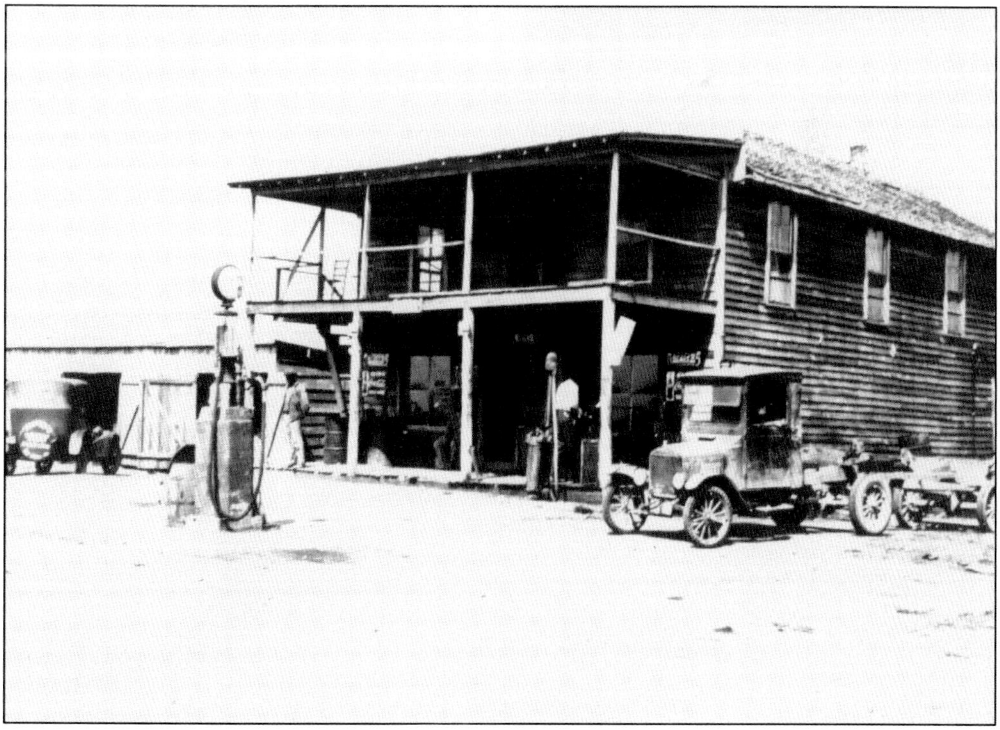

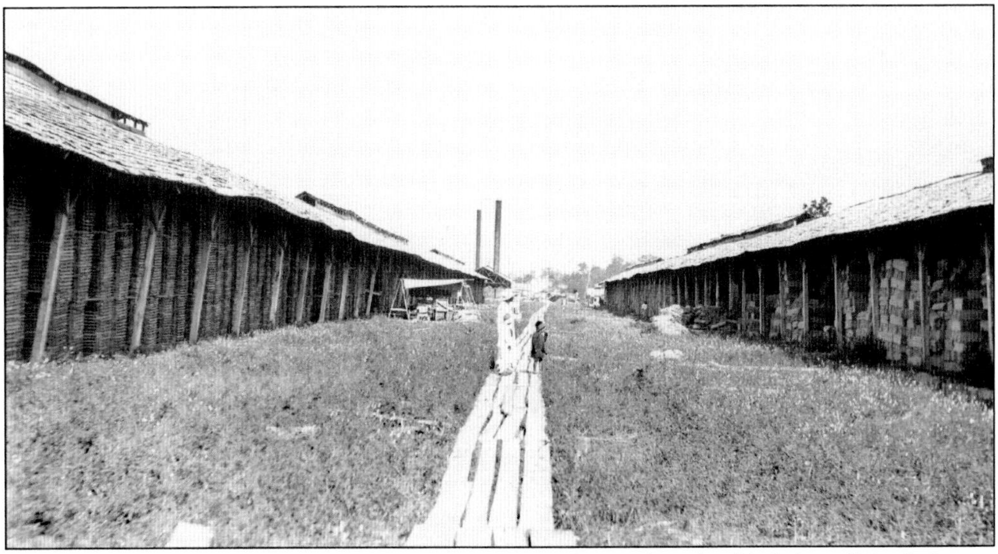

Bolz Cooperage Company started operations in 1915 on the south ends of Eighth and Ninth Streets and greatly contributed to the growth and development of the area. William H. Hundhausen Sr., who came from St. Louis in 1914, was the superintendent for the company until it closed in 1925.

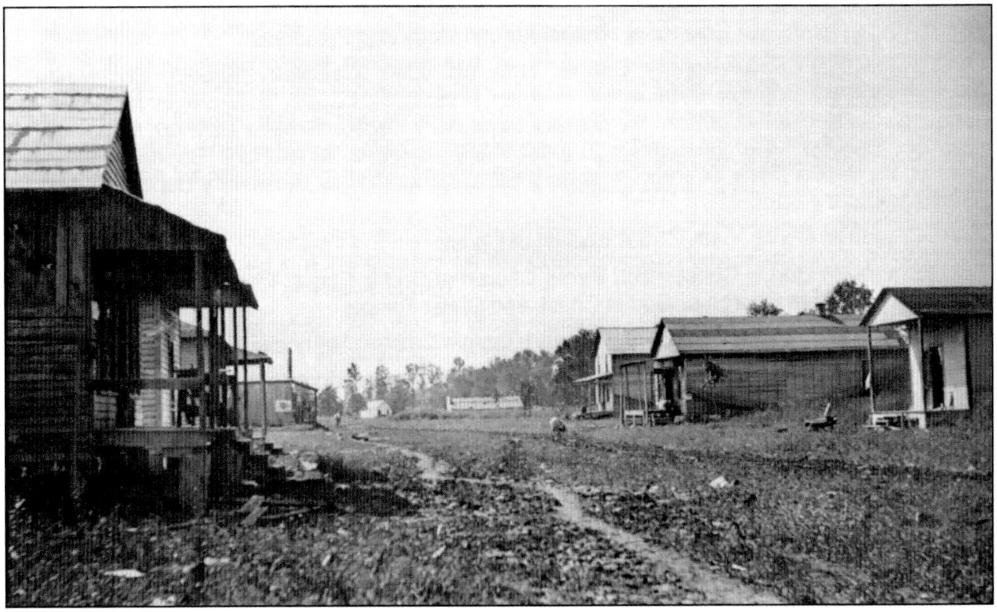

This photograph shows South Eighth Street in 1919. Most of the first stores and houses were built for workers of Bolz Cooperage Company and their families. Paved roads did not exist in the area until Highway 70, later named Broadway within the city limits, was paved in the mid-1920s.

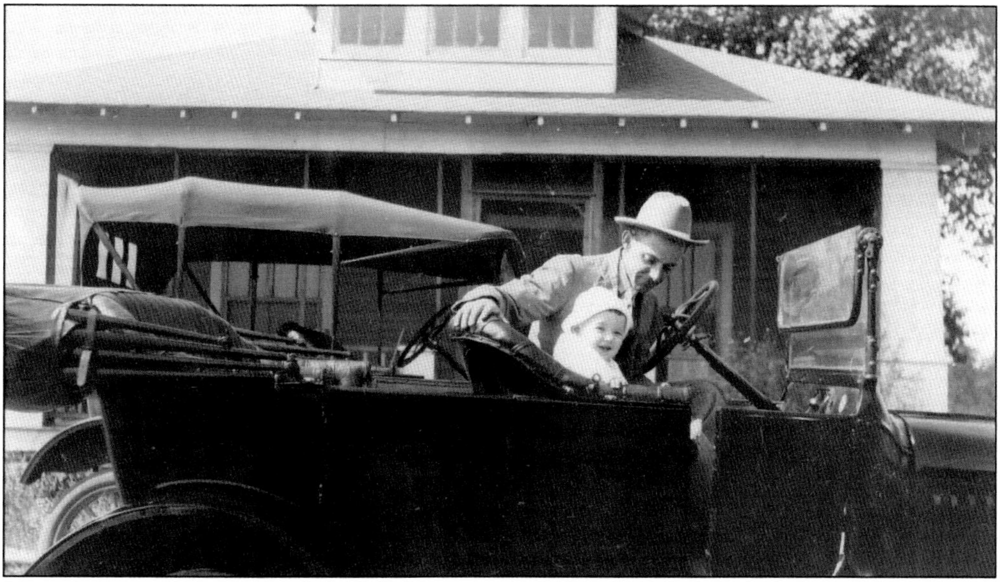

William H. Hundhausen Sr. later became the third mayor of West Memphis, serving for 12 years. He was the first registered automobile owner in the area and was forced to drive his Ford Model T on the railroad tracks to travel from West Memphis to Memphis when dirt roads became too muddy during wet seasons. He is pictured above with his son William H. Hundhausen Jr., who, in 1919, had the honor of being the first documented boy to be born in West Memphis.

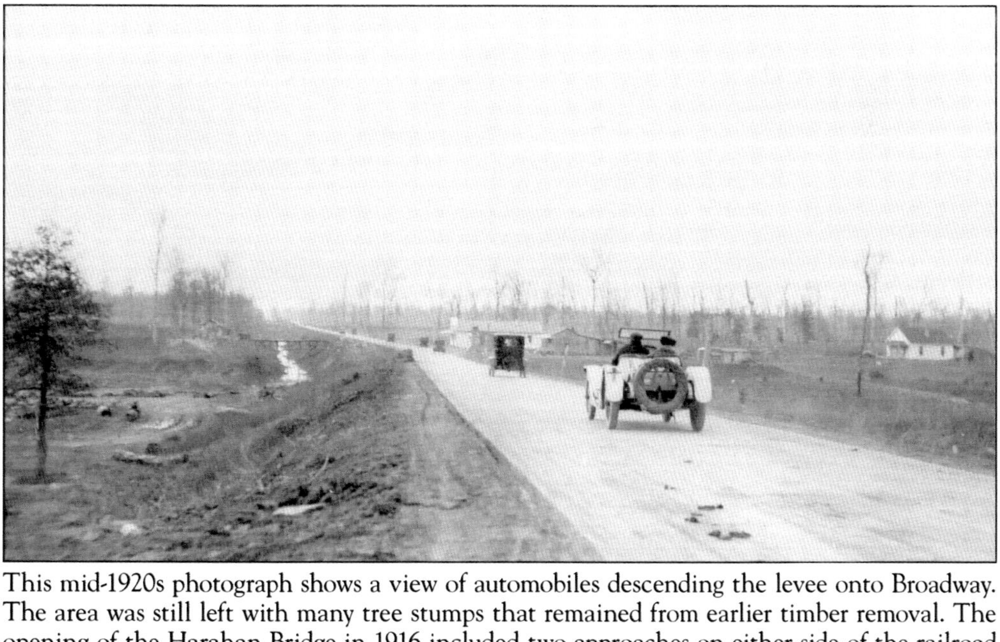

This mid-1920s photograph shows a view of automobiles descending the levee onto Broadway. The area was still left with many tree stumps that remained from earlier timber removal. The opening of the Harahan Bridge in 1916 included two approaches on either side of the railroad that were devoted to wagon and automobile traffic and that greatly increased traffic along the future Highway 70 through West Memphis.

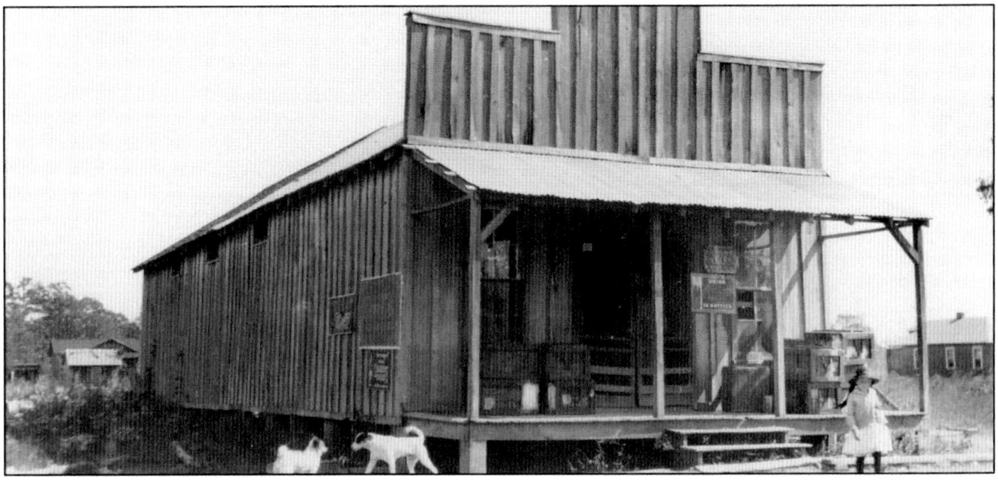

This photograph from 1918 depicts Stotts Grocery located on the corner of Madison and South Eighth Streets. At this time, the area around South Eighth Street contained the majority of retail establishments. Beginning in the early 1920s, more businesses began to be established along the newly created Highways 70 and 61, which were later named Broadway and Missouri Street within the city limits.

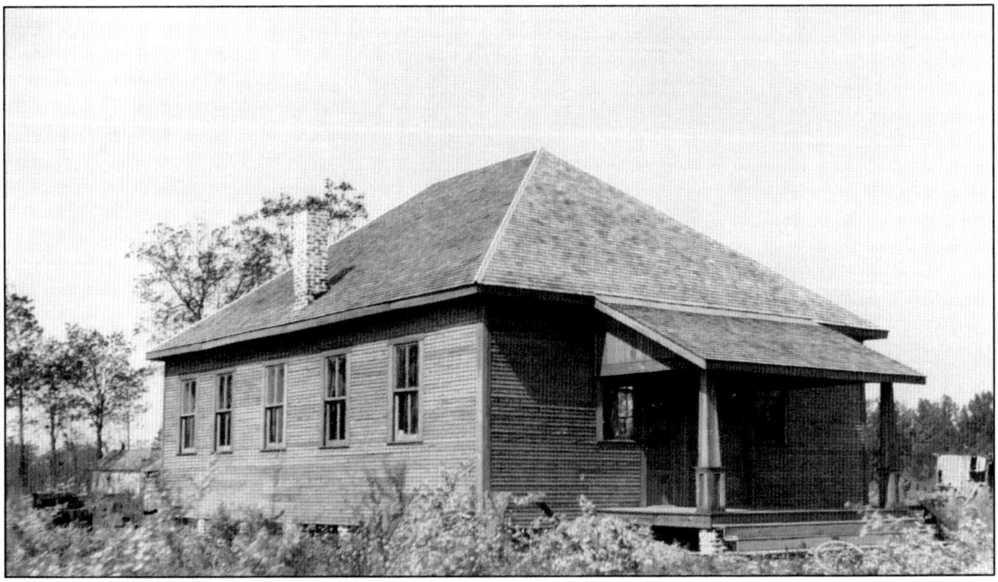

William H. Hundhausen Sr. established the first school in West Memphis, which was a private subscription school, around 1916 for children of the workers of Bolz Cooperage Company. The two-room schoolhouse was located on South Eighth Street, just north of the railroad. The school operated until 1925, when children in West Memphis started attending the newly built school in Hulbert.

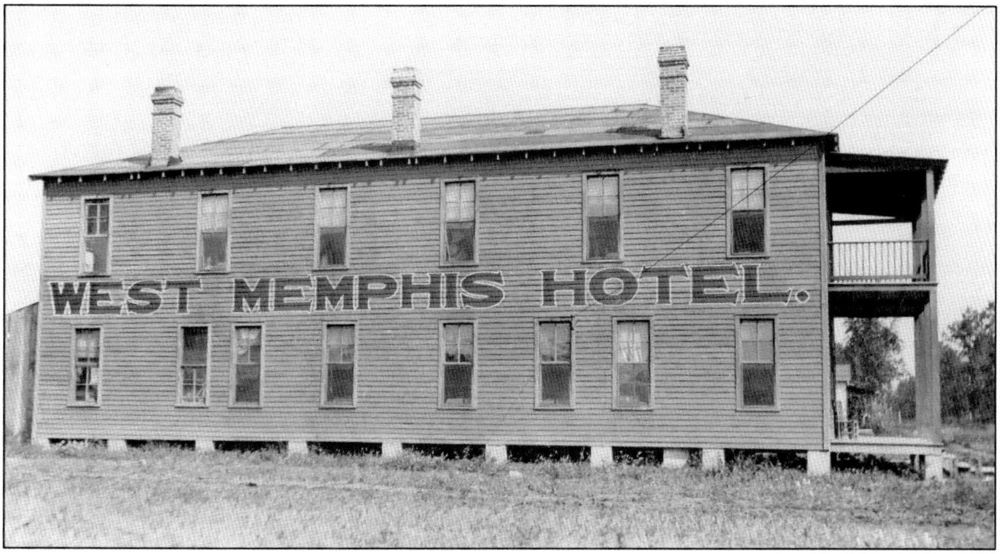

George Kendal built the West Memphis Hotel in 1916 on the corner of South Tenth Street and Jefferson Avenue. Kendal was also responsible for some of the earliest developments south of Broadway. He built approximately 25 houses on Tenth, Eleventh, and Twelfth Streets for employees of Bolz Cooperage Company.

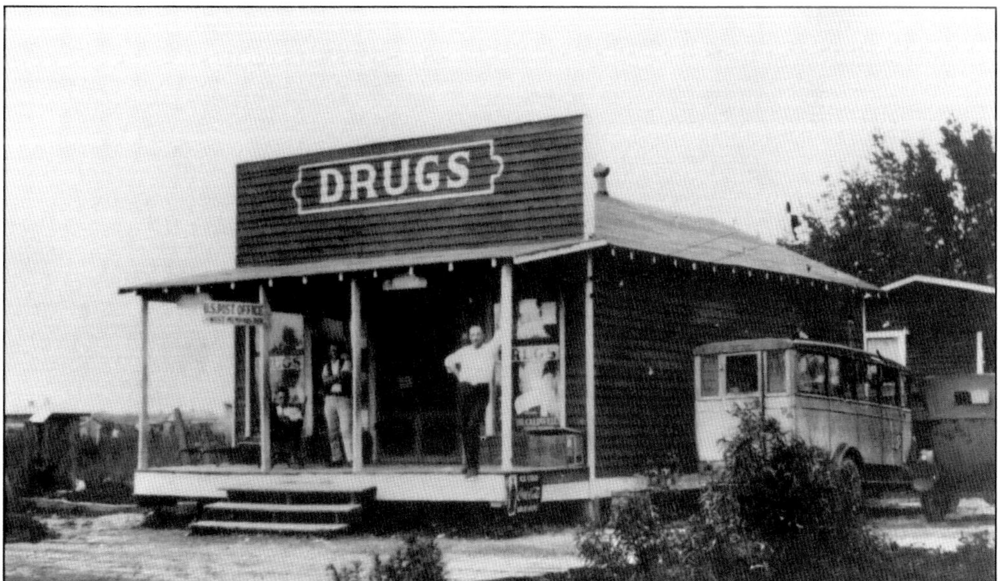

The first pharmacy in West Memphis was the Travaskas drugstore, which later became the Dodd drugstore. It was located on South Eighth Street, the epicenter of activity during West Memphis's early years. At one time, there were five independent pharmacies operating in the city.

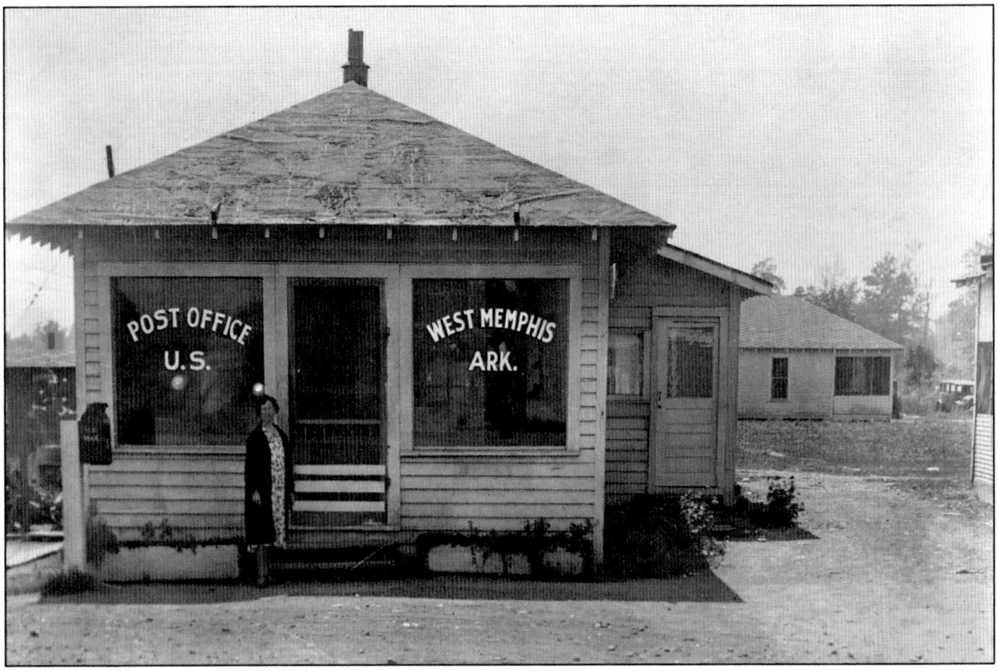

The post office in West Memphis was established in 1920, during a time when mail was still delivered on horseback. Isabelle Tice, who was the first schoolteacher in West Memphis, is shown here outside the post office in 1929 during her tenure as postmaster. The post office was housed in various locations until a permanent structure was built in 1957 on the corner of Missouri Street and Bond Avenue.

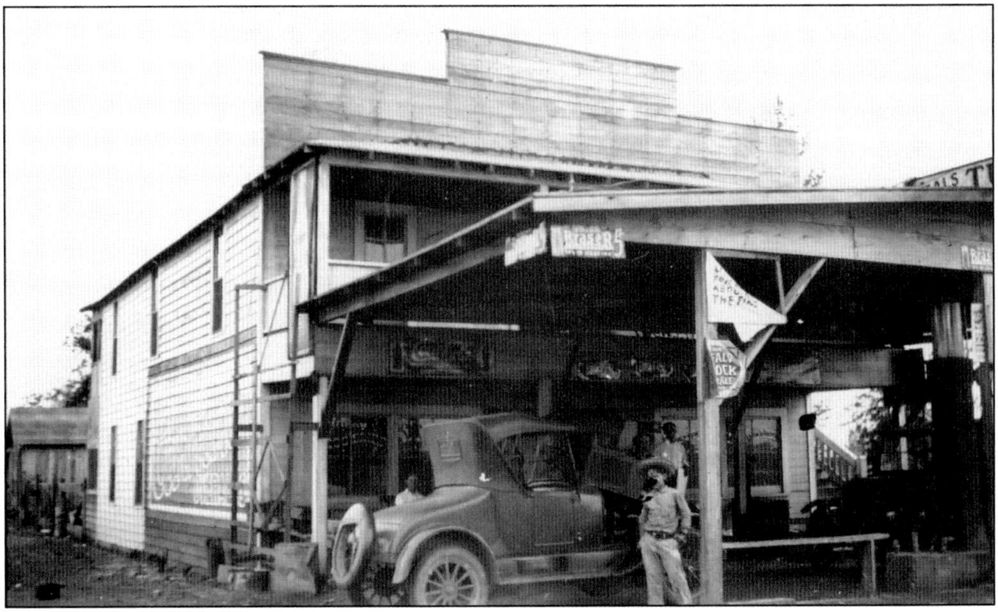

After Highway 70, also named Broadway, was cleared in 1917 and paved in the early 1920s, several service stations and cafés were established to cater to motorists and the occasional horse-drawn wagon. Pictured here is one of the earlier businesses that developed along Broadway during the late 1920s.

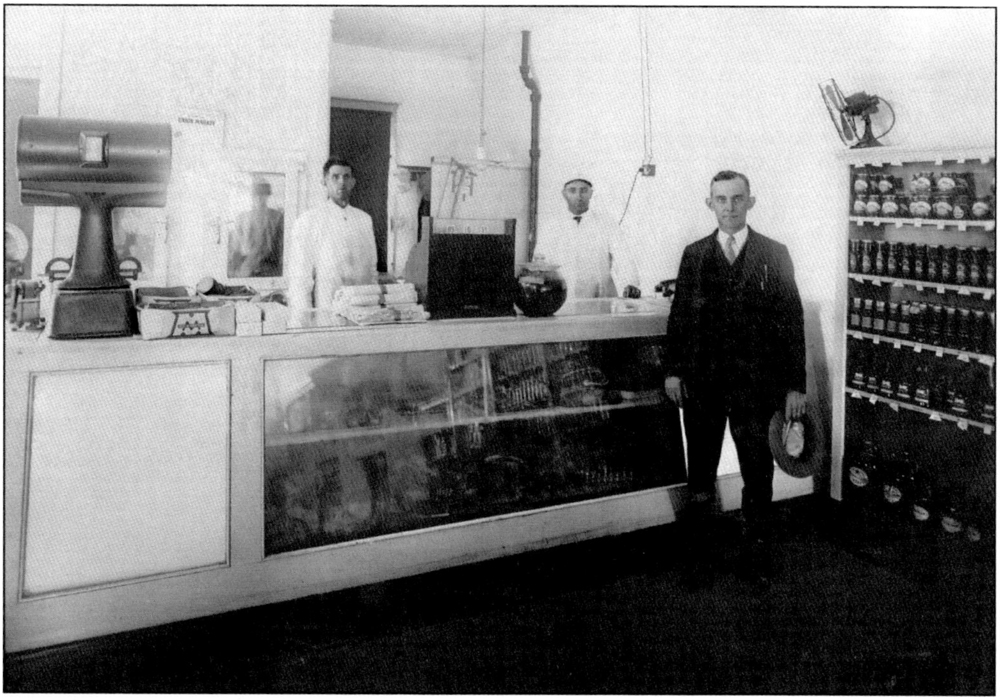

After the closure of Bolz Cooperage Company, William H. Hundhausen Sr. engaged in the grocery business and established a store at 106 Missouri Street. Pictured here on the far right is Hundhausen with his employees on opening day in 1925. (Courtesy of William H. Hundhausen Jr.)

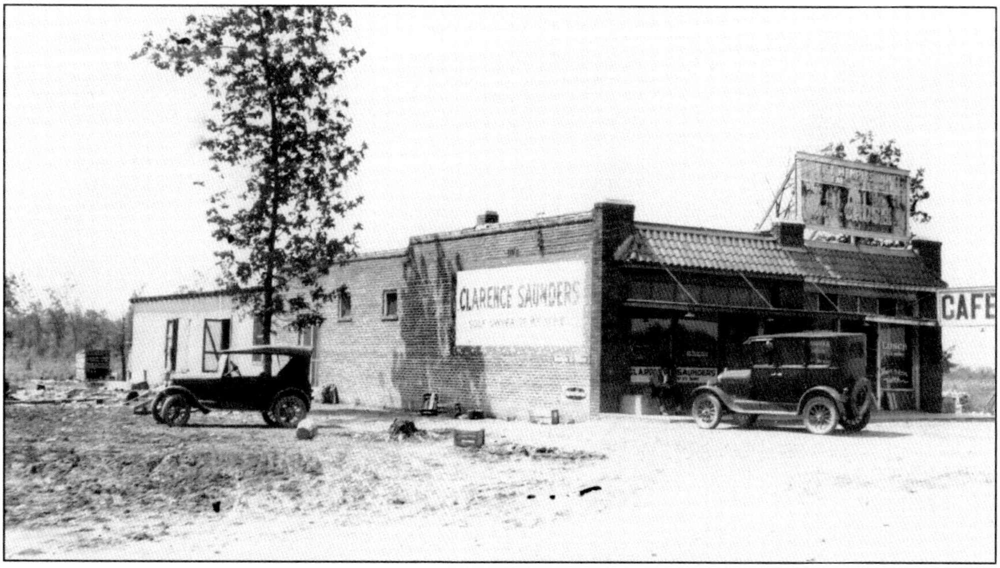

When William H. Hundhausen's store first opened, it operated under the franchise name Clarence Saunders Sole Owner of My Name, known to the public as the "Sole Owner" store. The founder of Piggly Wiggly, Clarence Saunders, established this franchise after those stores were liquidated due to bankruptcy in the mid-1920s. Later, Hundhausen's business operated as Hundhausen's Grocery until the 1960s.

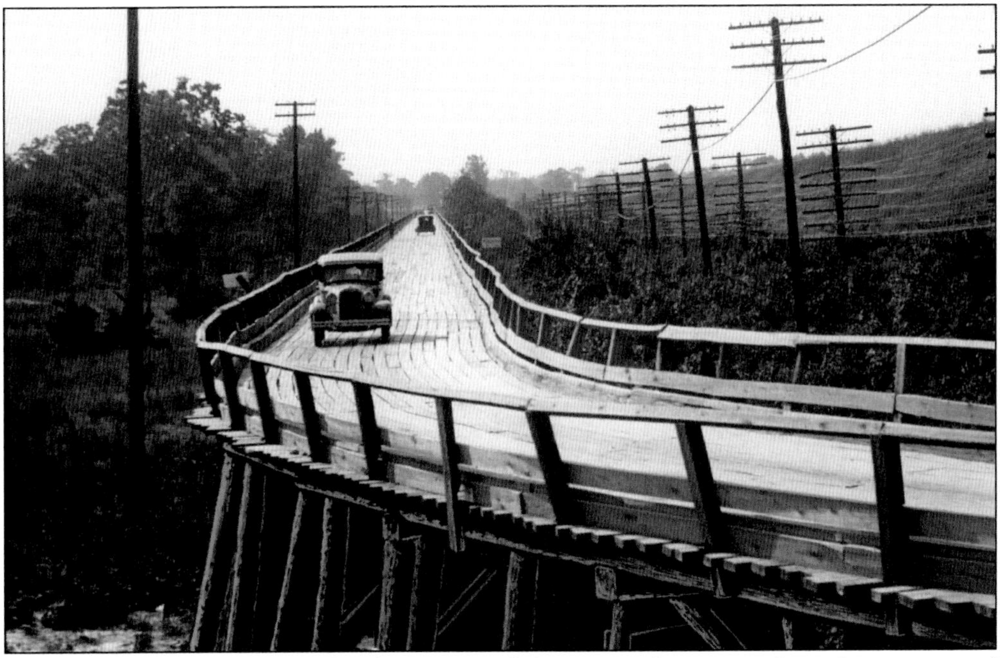

The Harahan Bridge was completed in 1916, and the two roadways on either side were opened to wagon and automobile traffic in 1917. A raised wooden viaduct, shown photographed here in 1929, was constructed between the bridge and the levee to elevate it from the annual flooding of the Mississippi River.

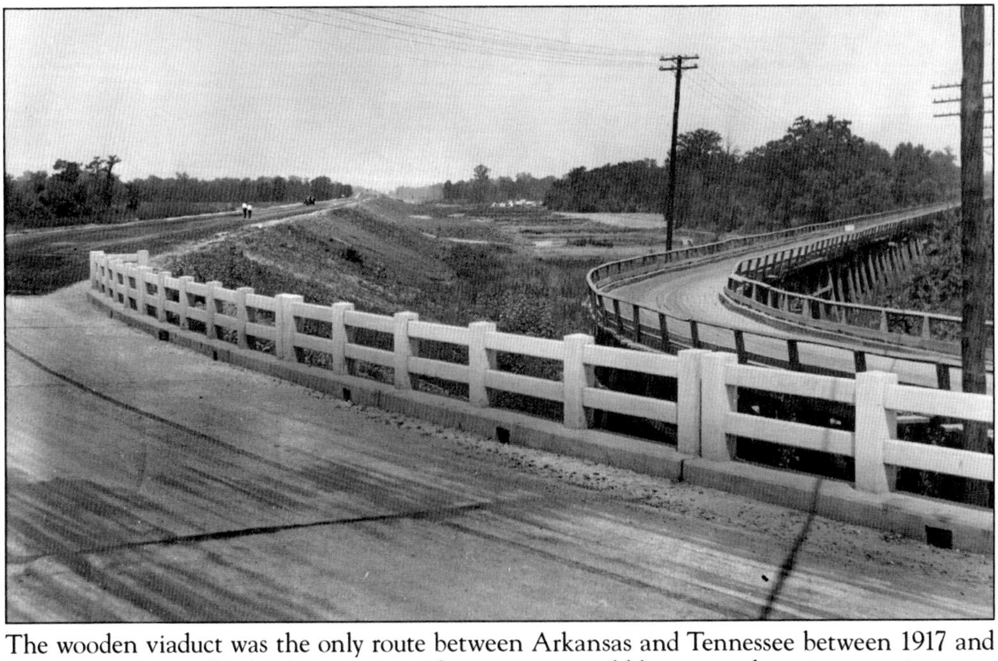

The wooden viaduct was the only route between Arkansas and Tennessee between 1917 and 1930. During river floods, driving across the structure could become a daunting experience, as high water would rise to the level of the wooden roadbed. In 1930, an improved roadway, shown in the foreground, replaced the viaduct. Interstate 55 roughly follows this same route and uses the Memphis-Arkansas Bridge that was completed in 1949.

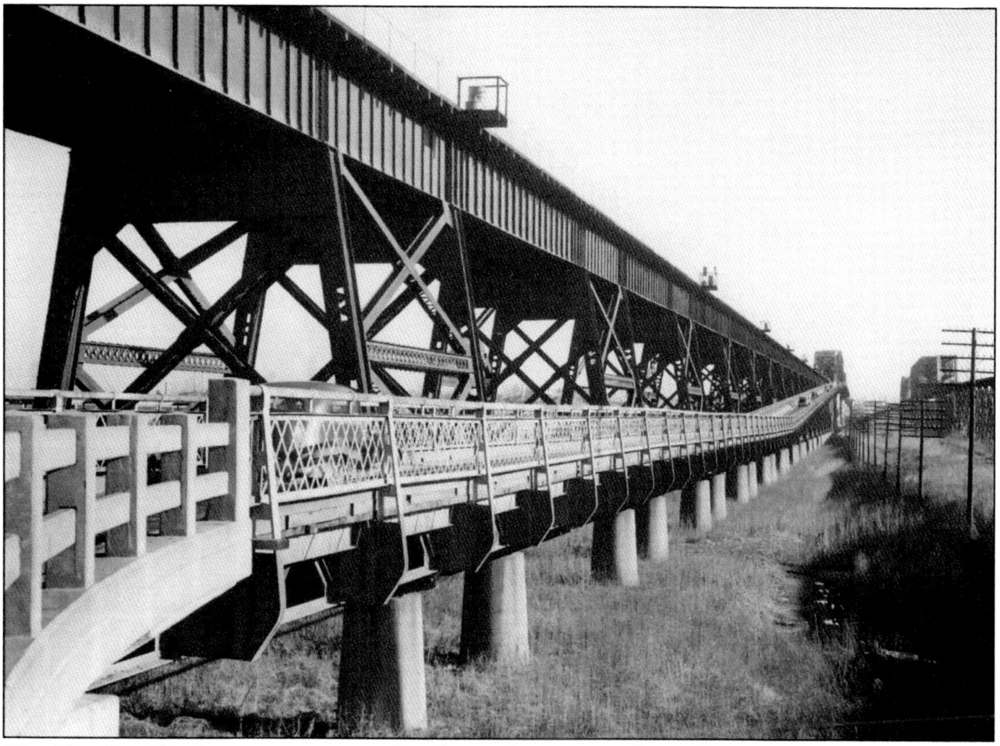

The Harahan Bridge was constructed with two lanes on either side of the main railroad track exclusively for wagons and automobiles. This photograph from the 1930s shows the eastbound approach from the Arkansas side.

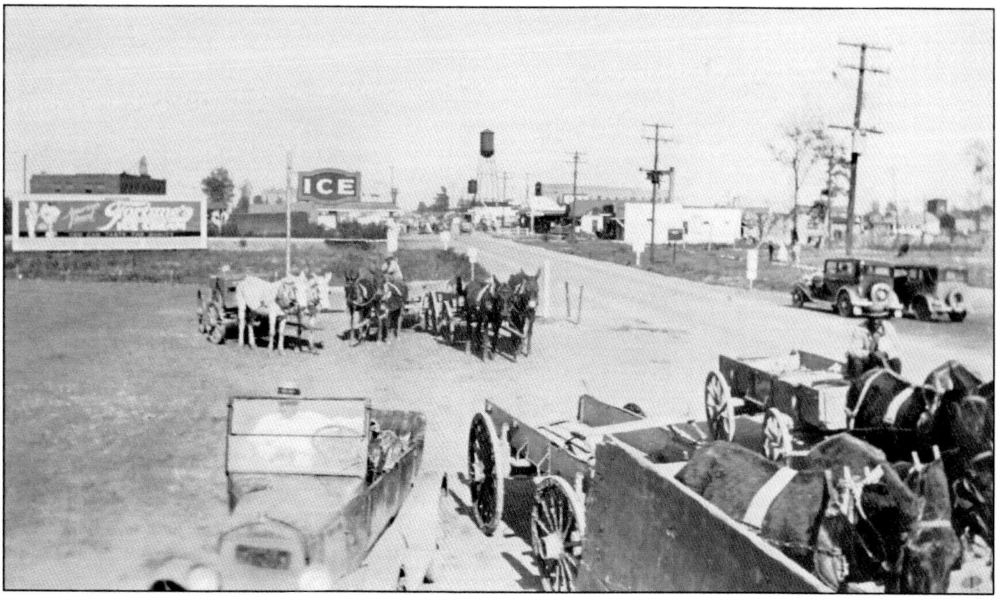

The Harahan Bridge helped usher traffic across the Mississippi River into Arkansas. This 1932 photograph was taken on Broadway looking east toward the railroad tracks. At this time, horse-drawn wagons were being phased out with the increasing popularity of automobiles. (Courtesy of Michael Finger.)

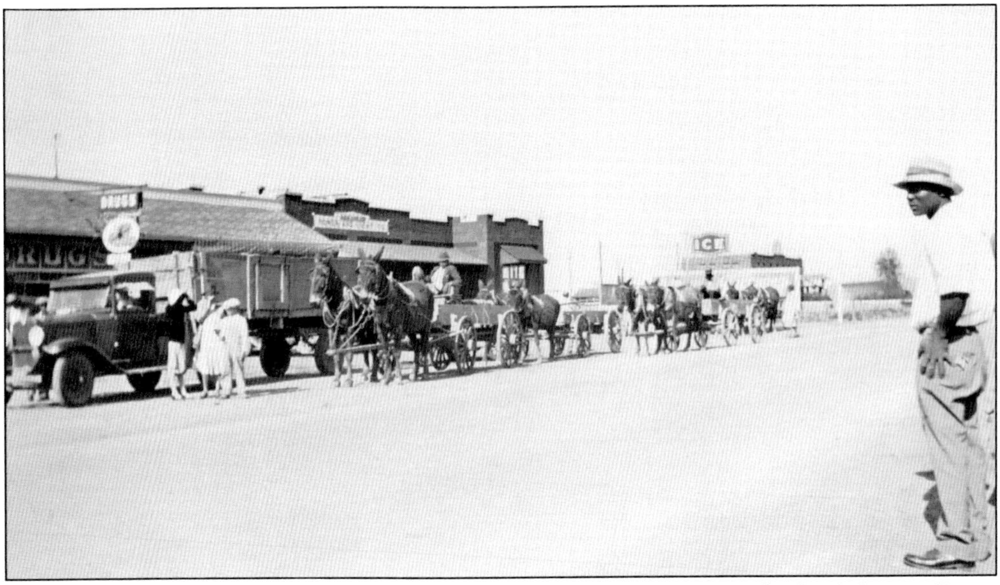

The building seen in the center of this photograph from 1932 was originally the Arkansas Power and Light Company. In 1942, the building was sold to Delta Ice and has been used as an icehouse ever since. The multistory structure seen in the distance was Broadway's first hotel, the West Memphis Inn. (Courtesy of Michael Finger.)

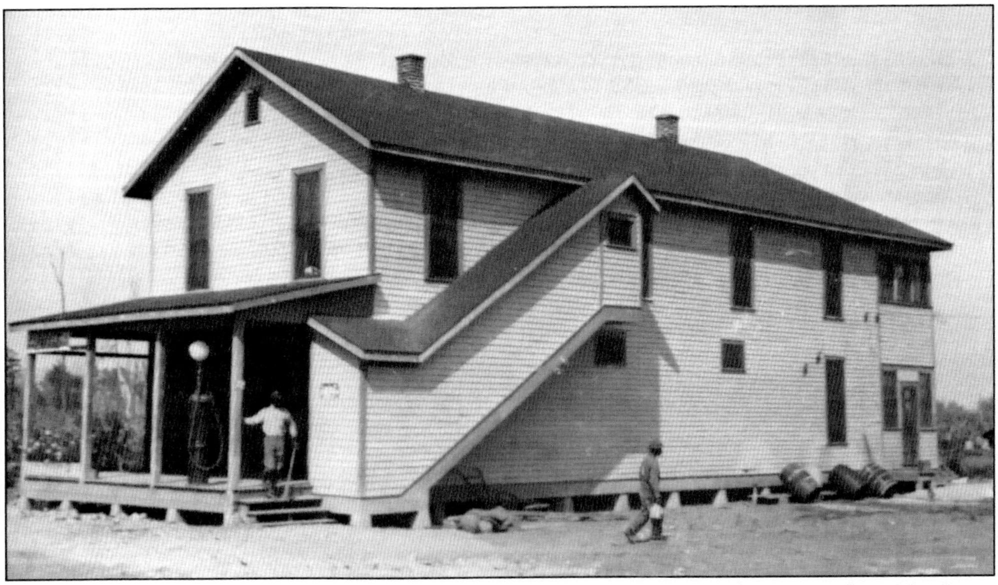

One of the first establishments on Broadway was Thompson's Gin and Mercantile. Miles Lane Thompson erected his wood-frame building for the store on the north side near the railroad tracks in 1920. In 1928, the store burned and was soon replaced with a brick structure now known as the M.L. Thompson Building.

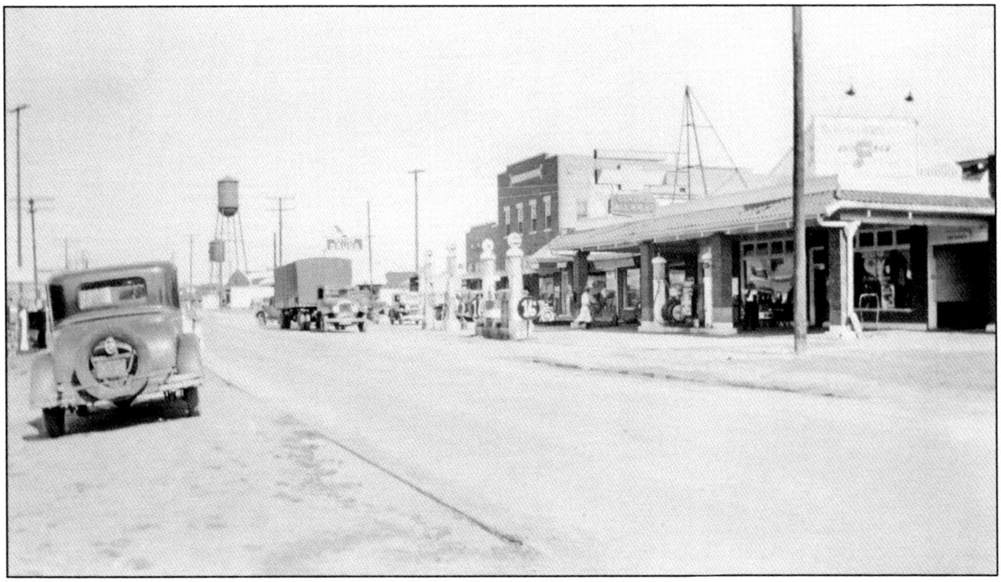

The 300 block of East Broadway was the site of the Bragg Building, shown in the background of this 1932 photograph. Many of the early buildings along Broadway provided retail space on the ground floor and residences on the second floor. The Bragg Building, as well as the future neighboring Broadway Building, was destroyed in a tornado in 1994, and the property has since been replaced with an auto parts store.

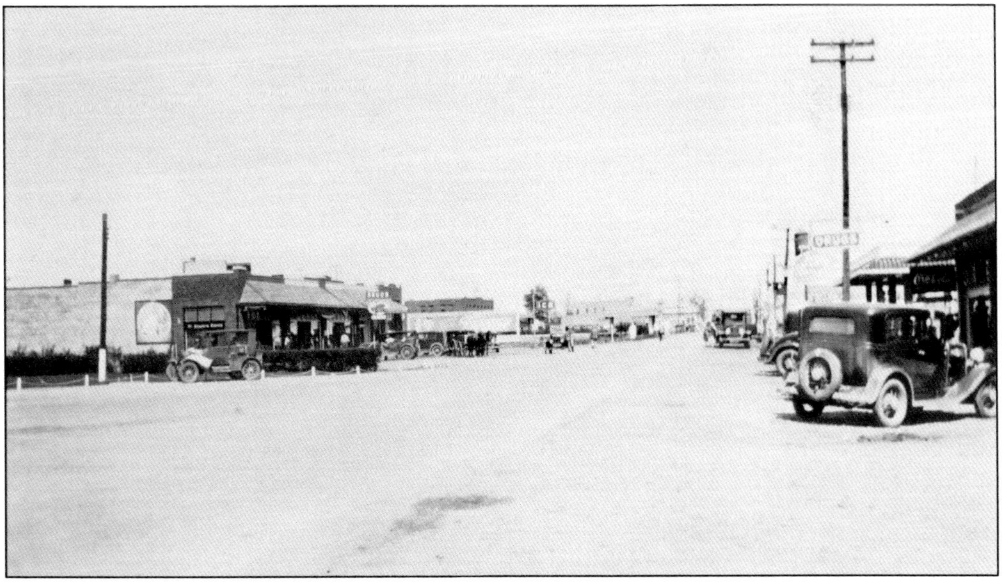

Broadway was once described as one of the longest main streets in the United States. The majority of businesses were established on both Broadway and Missouri Street not only because of the high volume of traffic, but also because these two streets were the only paved roads in West Memphis until the early 1950s. (Courtesy of Michael Finger.)

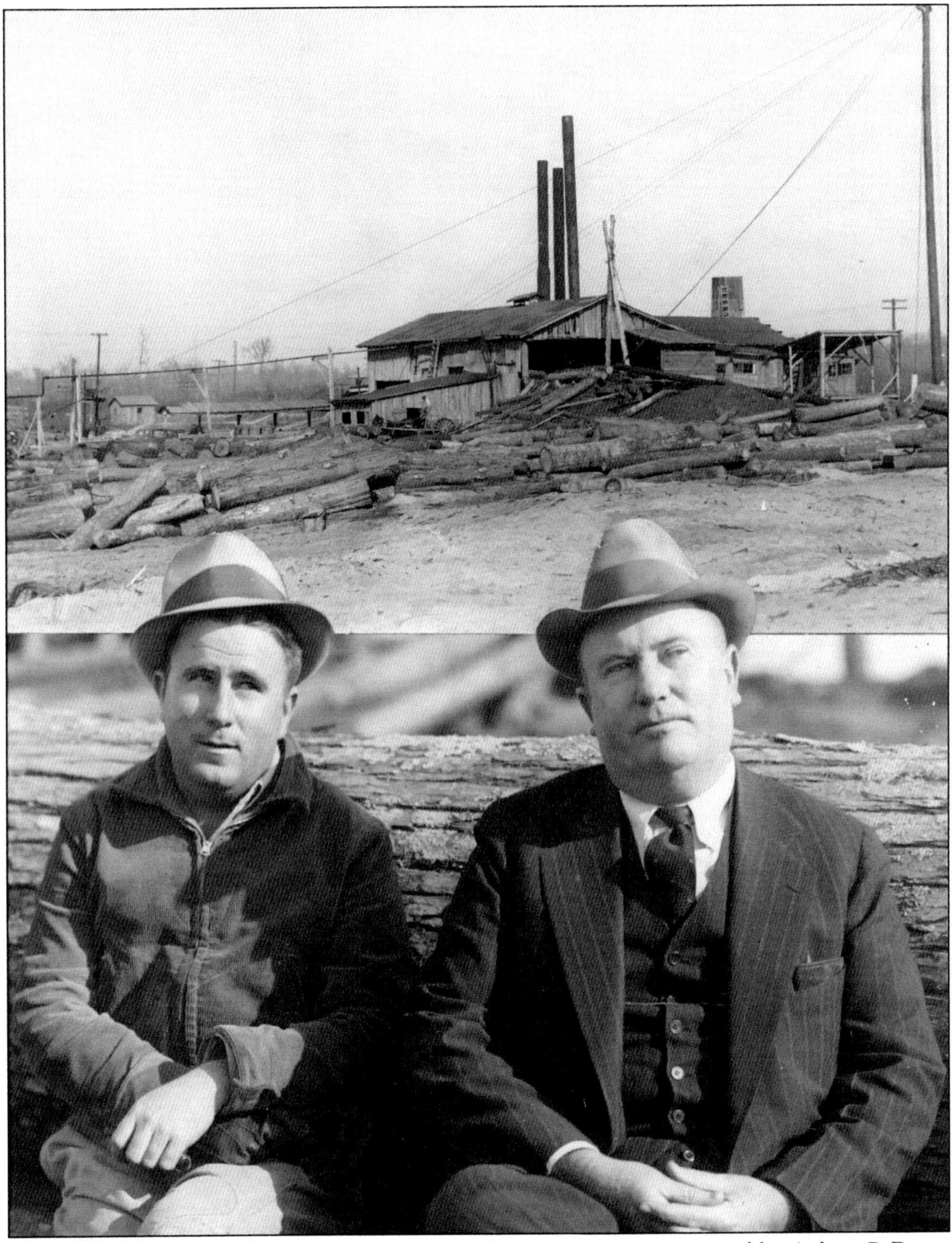

The mill established by Zack Bragg on Missouri Street in 1914 was acquired by Aubrey P. Dacus in 1935 and became Dacus Lumber Mill. After Aubrey Dacus's death, his son Melvin took over operations until the mill closed in 1972. Shown here in 1935 are Melvin (left) and Aubrey Dacus.

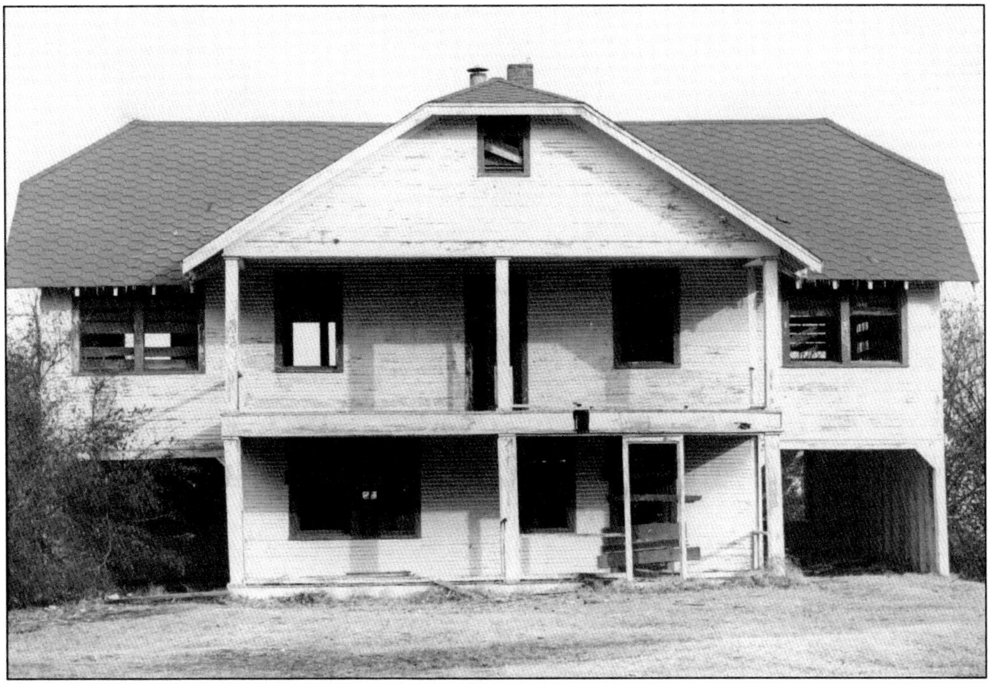

Aubrey Dacus originally owned this house, once located on the northeast corner of Roosevelt Avenue and Redding Street. In the early 1940s, Aubrey Dacus purchased Zack Bragg's house at 230 Cooper Avenue. The house on Roosevelt Avenue, pictured above, was razed in the early 1960s, and the site was later replaced with another house built by William and Thelma McAuley.

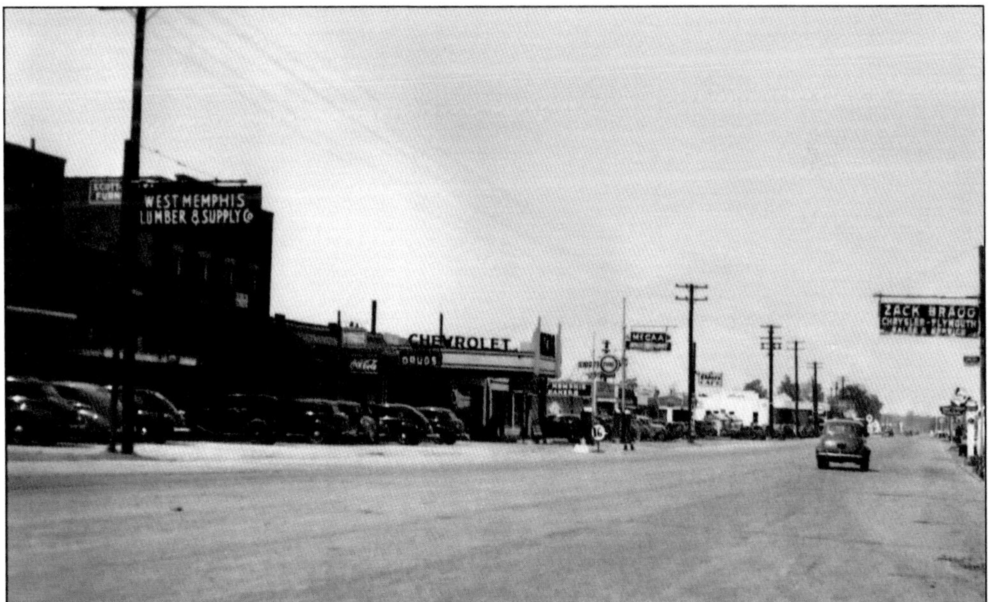

By the end of the 1930s, Broadway was the location of dozens of cafés and service stations. In addition, Broadway was also the site of several automobile dealerships. This 1939 photograph shows the Bragg and Broadway Buildings on the left and Zack Bragg's Chrysler Dealership on the far right.

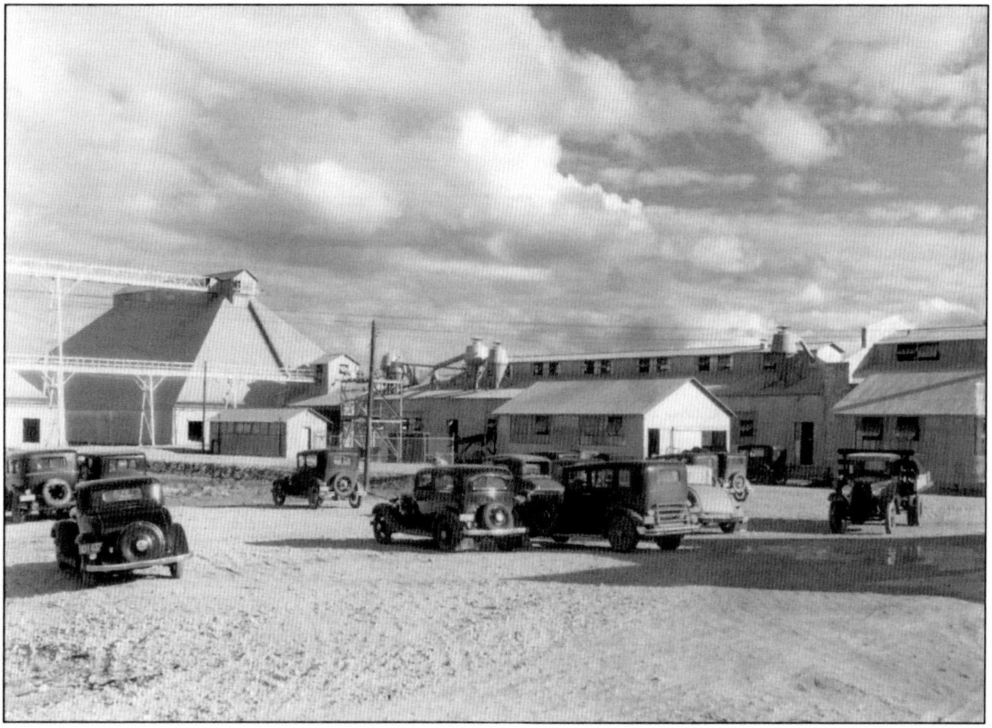

The West Memphis Cotton Oil Mill was located on the east side of Missouri Street between the 10 Mile Bayou and the Dacus Lumber Company. The facility included three large cottonseed houses along the railroad tracks that dominated the skyline of West Memphis. The majority of the buildings were torn down in the 1990s, and today, McCain Boulevard occupies a portion of the site.

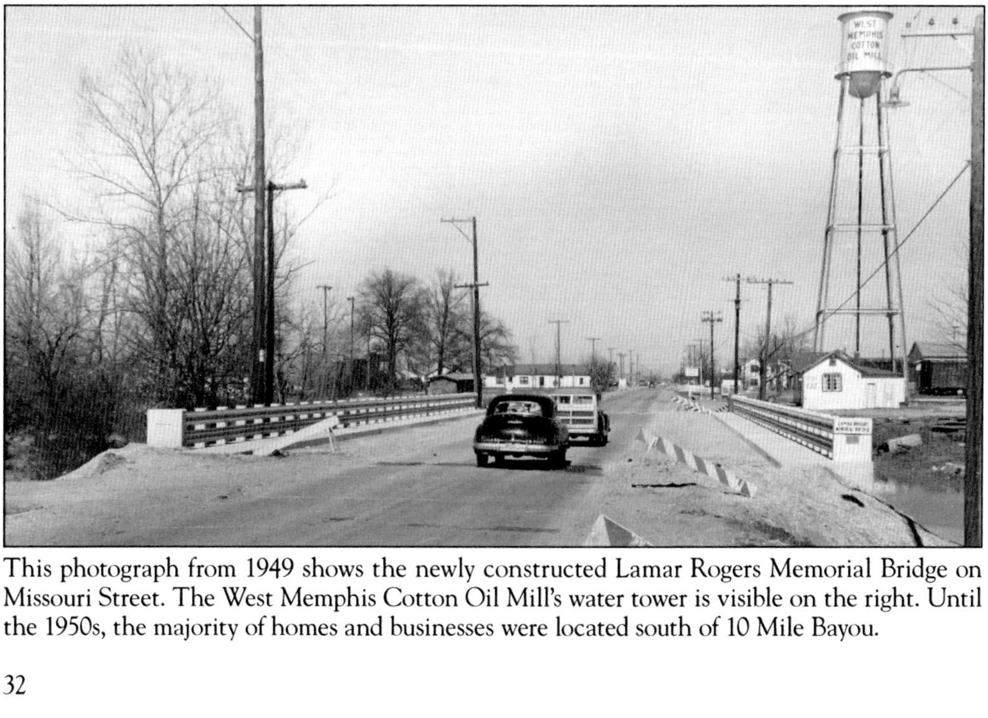

This photograph from 1949 shows the newly constructed Lamar Rogers Memorial Bridge on Missouri Street. The West Memphis Cotton Oil Mill's water tower is visible on the right. Until the 1950s, the majority of homes and businesses were located south of 10 Mile Bayou.

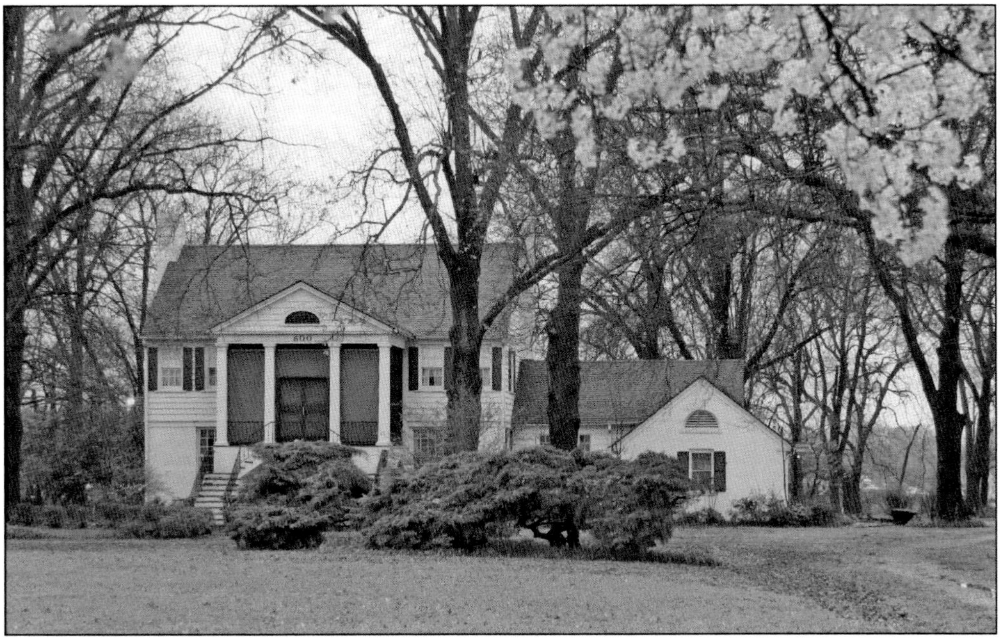

The Lawrie House, located on Seventh Street, was constructed in 1939 in the late Colonial Revival style and was once part of a working plantation. Landowner James Beck constructed the house as a wedding gift for his daughter Elizabeth Lawrie. In 1955, the Montgomery family acquired the property and would own it for the next 40 years.

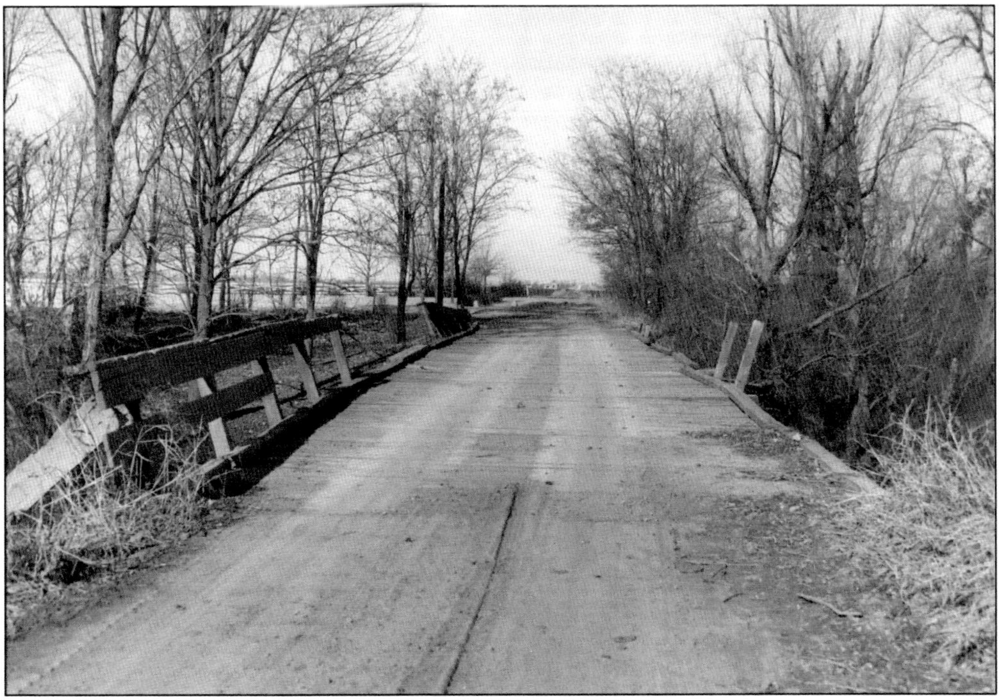

Until the early 1960s, the north portion of Seventh Street was a dirt road mainly used by farmers. This 1955 photograph shows Seventh Street looking north from 10 Mile Bayou. The Lawrie House is located just past the bridge on the left.

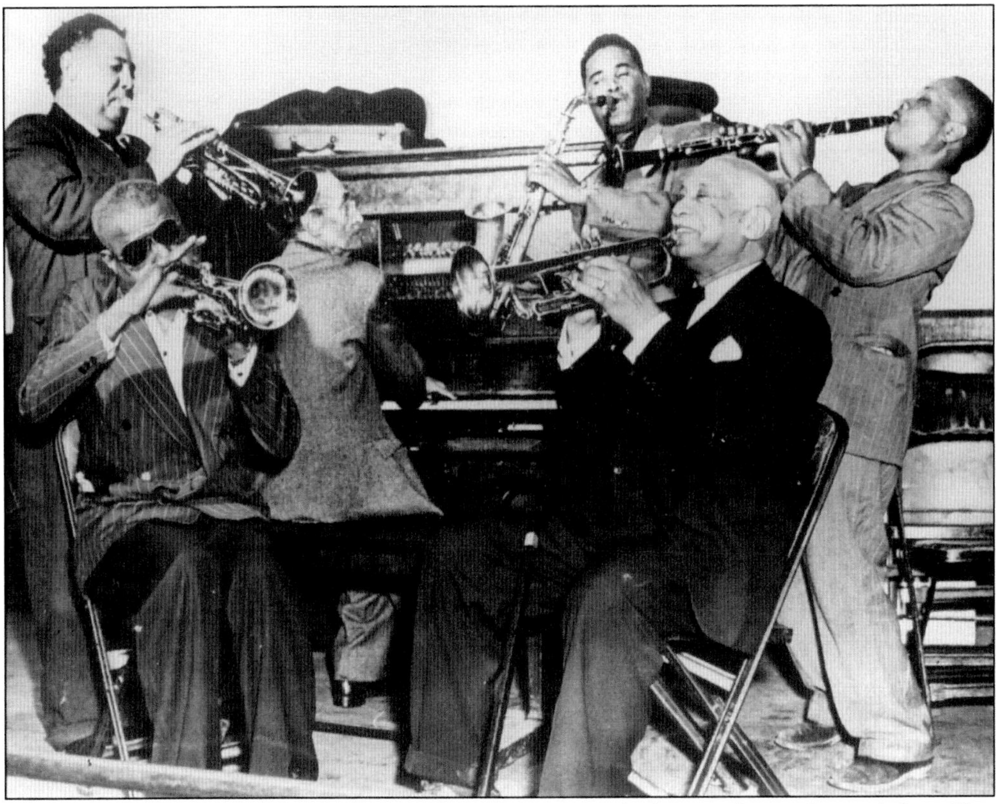

When Zack Bragg opened his first commissary, W.C. Handy (pictured seated at right) and his orchestra played for more than 100 guests, many of whom arrived by train. Early in the 20th century, commissaries were a staple of the working class, located across the South on farms and at principal places of business.

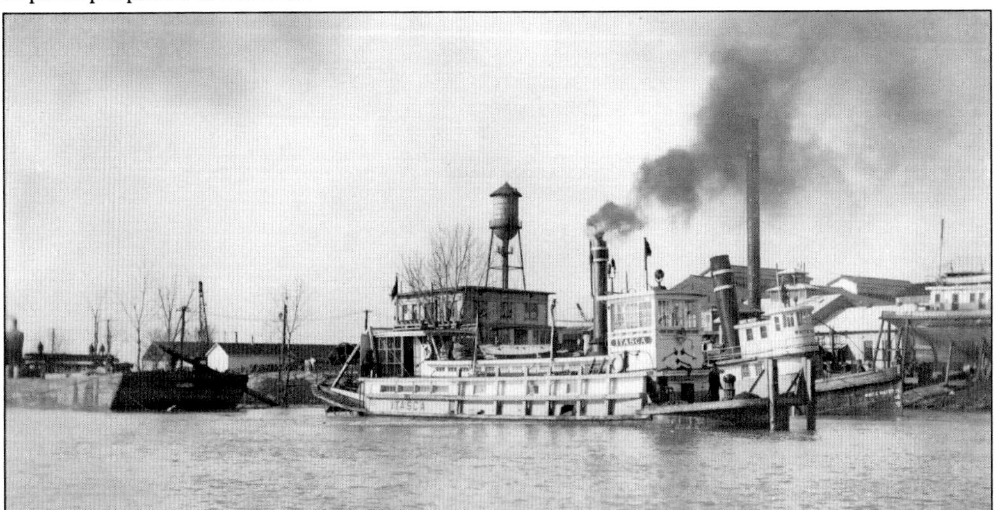

The Army Corps of Engineers established a depot along the Mississippi River between the levee and the Harahan Bridge in 1932. The entire site was enclosed within its own levee system to protect it from flooding since it was located within the floodplain.

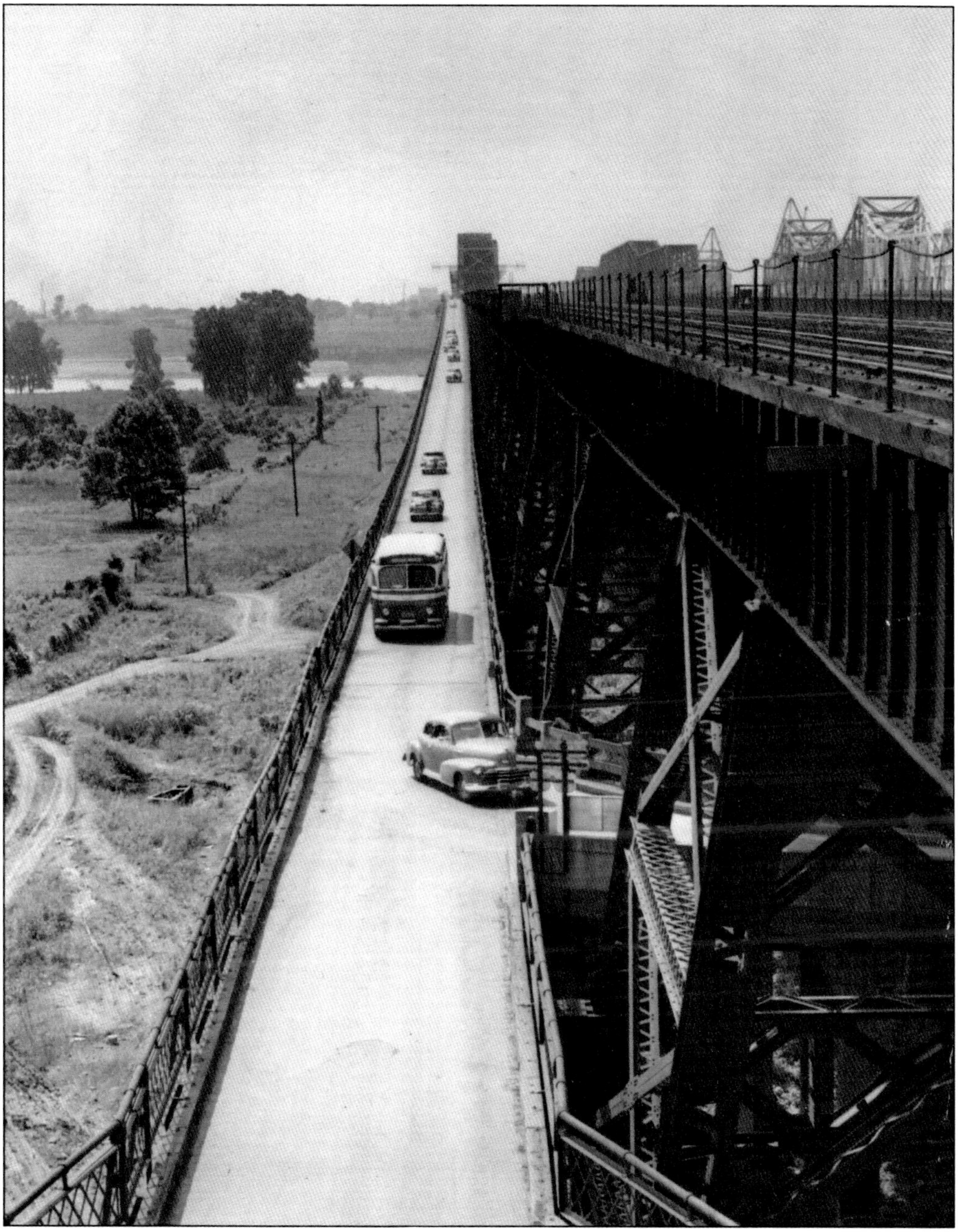

The Harahan Bridge served as the only bridge for automobiles until the completion of the Memphis-Arkansas Bridge in 1949. The Harahan Bridge was used solely for trains after 1949, and the previous approaches and automobile lanes were abandoned. This photograph from 1948 shows the last year automobiles made use of the Harahan Bridge while the Memphis-Arkansas Bridge on the far right was still under construction.

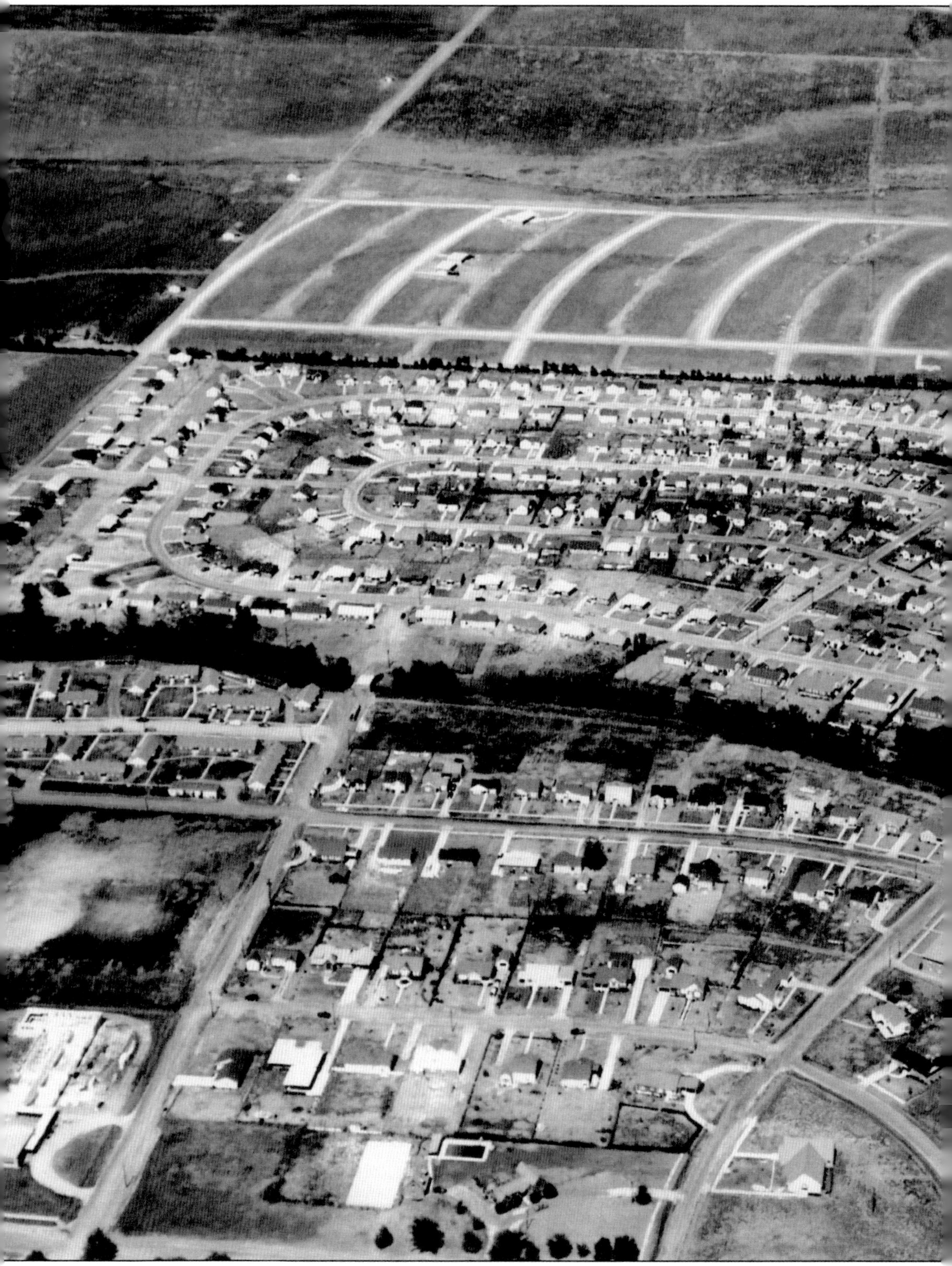

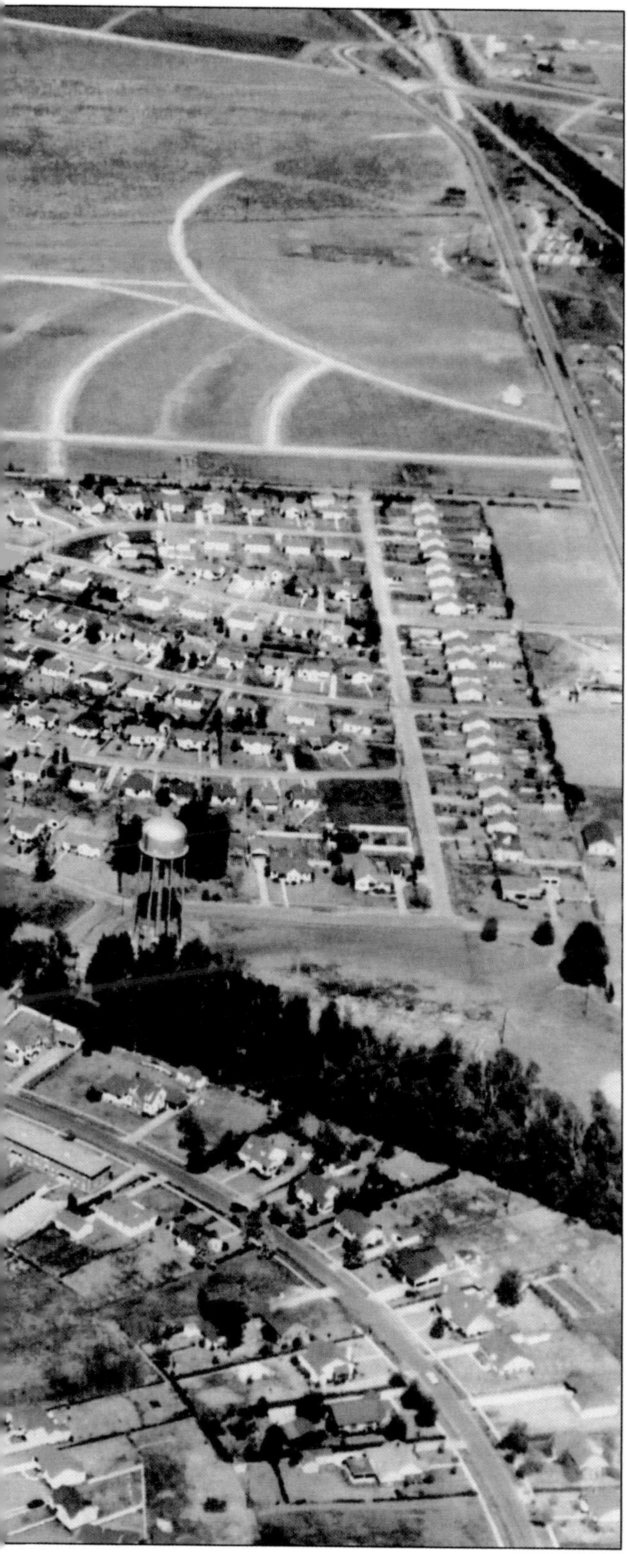

At the center of this aerial view from 1956 is the Worthington neighborhood. These homes were built as part of the postwar construction era in the late 1940s, during a period of exponential growth in West Memphis.

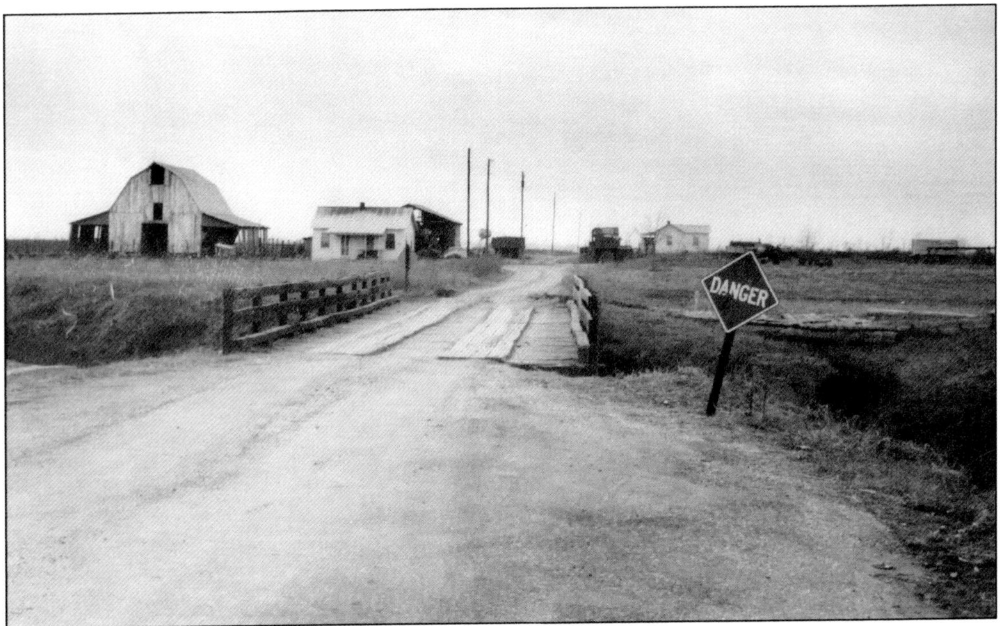

Several new neighborhoods were established during the 1950s and 1960s in the western part of the city. This photograph from 1955 shows West Barton Avenue looking west over 10 Mile Bayou toward the intersection of what is now Rich Road. By the mid-1960s, this entire area would become the Richland subdivision, developed by Jack Rich.

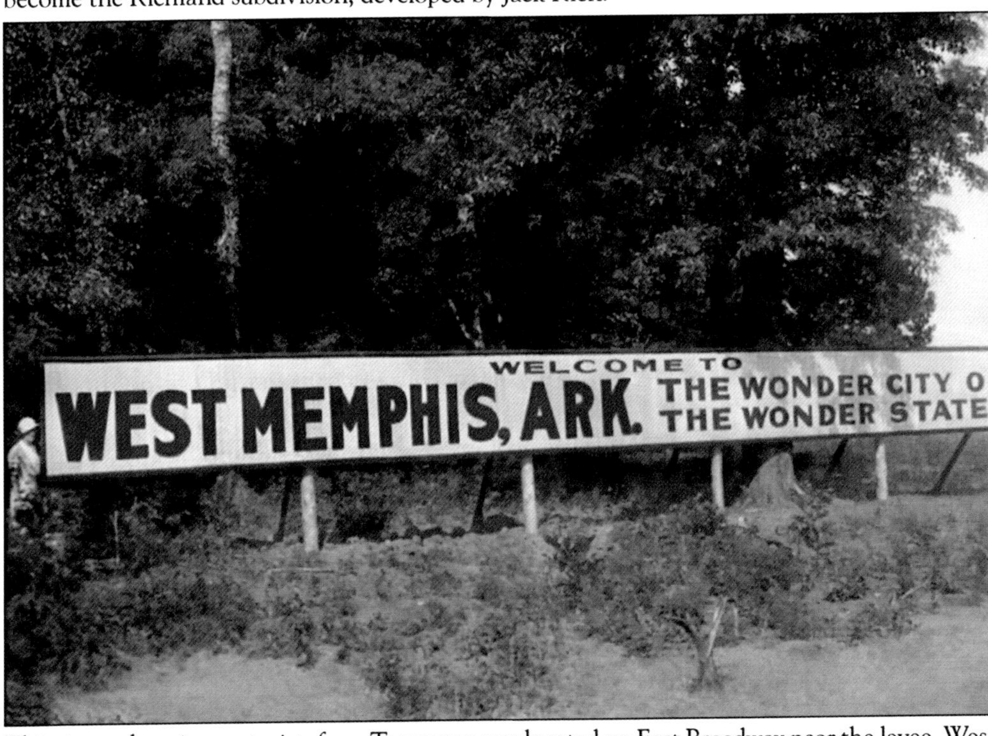

This sign welcoming motorists from Tennessee was located on East Broadway near the levee. West Memphis's population increased from 3,369 in 1940 to 19,374 in 1960, making it the fastest-growing city in the state of Arkansas and thus affirming its position as "the Wonder City."

Two

People

The earliest people to settle in the area of Crittenden County were the American Indians whose platform mounds, such as those found at Mound City, can still be seen in various parts of the region. Archeological and written evidence strongly supports that, in 1541, Hernando de Soto and his expedition crossed the lands of Crittenden County between the Mississippi River and the ancient village of Casqui, where Parkin, Arkansas, is now located. Even though the Spanish and the French had claimed the land in the 16th and 17th centuries, it was not until 1797, when the Spanish created Campo de la Esperanza, that the first permanent European settlement was established in the area.

The majority of those who first settled West Memphis in the early 20th century were not new immigrants but, rather, people who had relocated from various parts of the United States. These early settlers were drawn to West Memphis because it was one of the last undeveloped wildernesses in close proximity to a major city. The affordability of land and the new industries that had been established gave West Memphis an economic advantage, resulting in rapid building and population growth. The foresight and planning of the early leaders, along with the determination of the early residents of West Memphis, is what led to the nickname "the Wonder City."

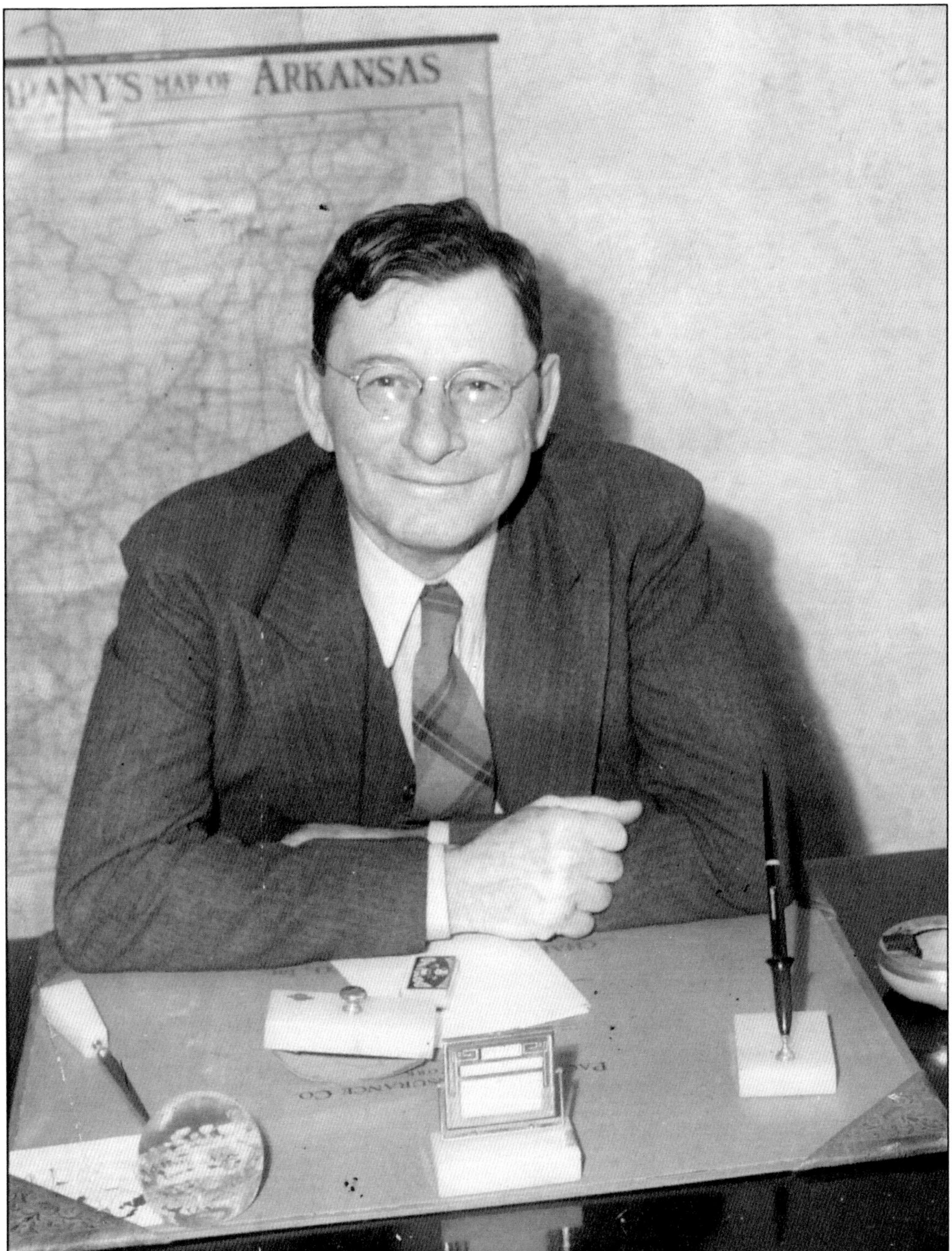

Zack T. Bragg, one of the earliest settlers, rejected the name Bragg for the town he had helped to establish. Bragg founded the first permanent business in the area in March 1914 when he opened his sawmill. In 1927, he became the city's first mayor and continued to involve himself in its political affairs through the 1940s. The first public elementary school in the city, Bragg Elementary School, was named in his honor.

William H. Hundhausen Sr. was elected mayor in 1932 and served for 12 years. One of his greatest contributions was his insistence that, in 1940, the city purchase the existing utility distribution system, which had been privately owned. This acquisition resulted in West Memphis having one of the lowest utility rates in the region, with the profits from the utility company being applied to the city's general revenue.

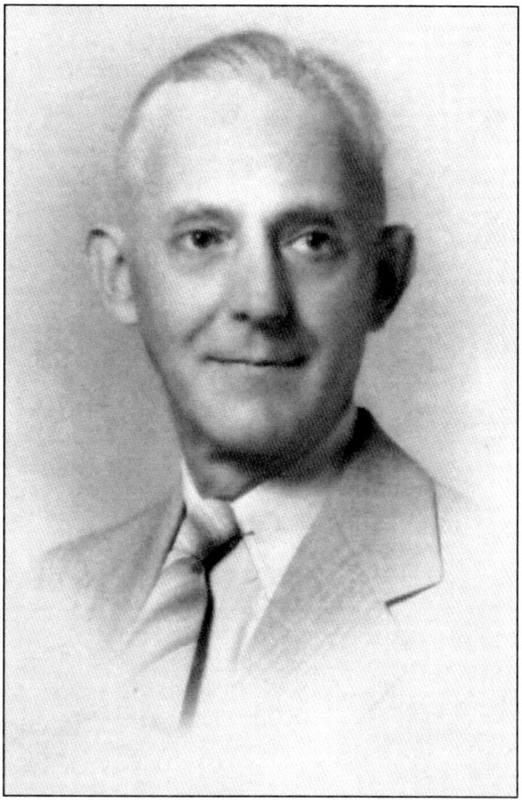

In 1925, after the closure of Bolz Cooperage Company, William H. Hundhausen Sr. opened a grocery store on Missouri Street. During his tenure as mayor and before city hall was built in 1939, Hundhausen was known to conduct official city business in the back of his store. Pictured below in 1936 are, from left to right, William H. Hundhausen Jr., Otis Smith, and William H. Hundhausen Sr. (Courtesy of William H. Hundhausen Jr.)

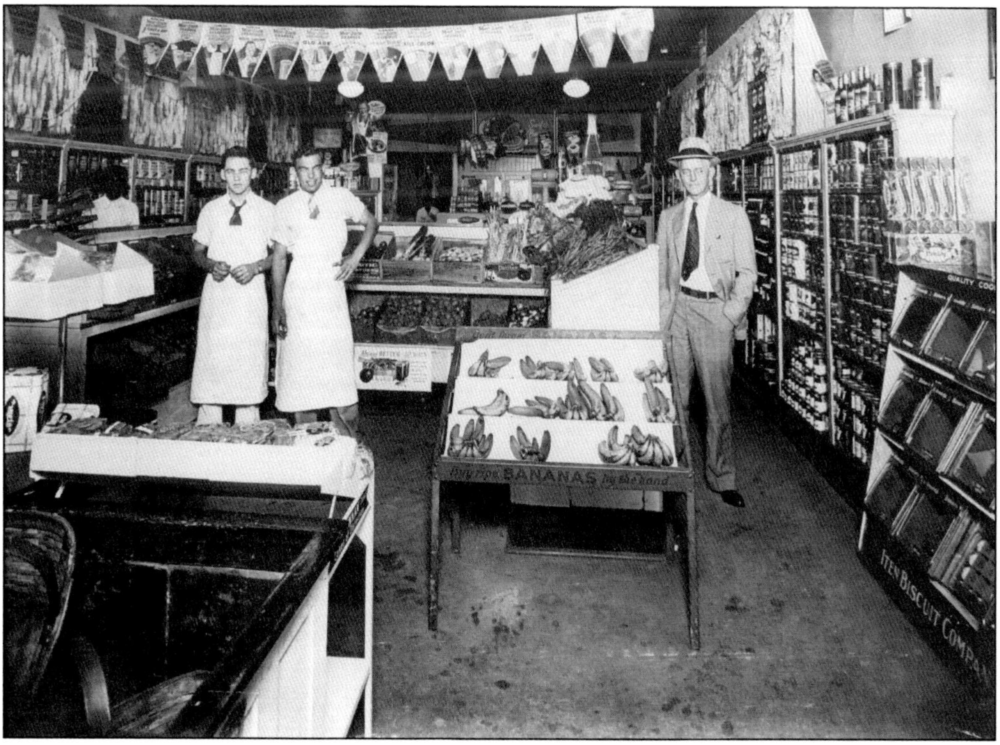

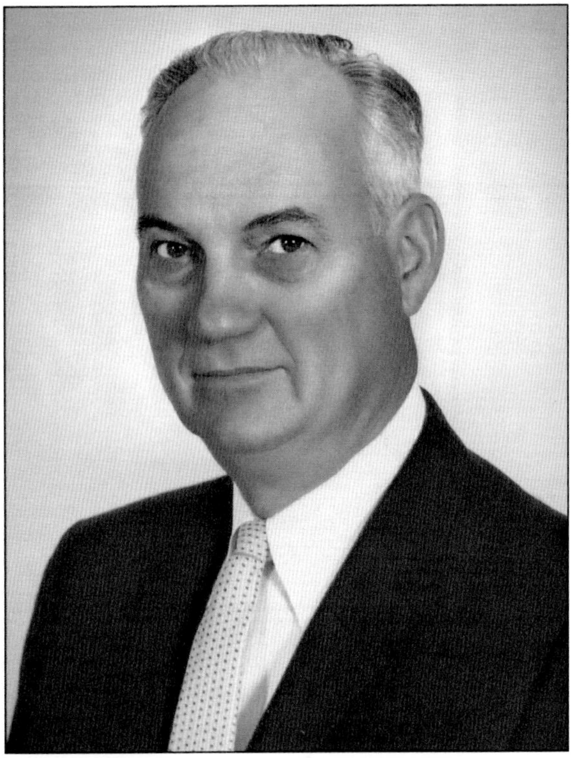

Jack W. Rich came to West Memphis in the mid-1930s and founded Guaranty Loan and Real Estate Company in 1938. While Rich never held political office, he was active in several civic organizations and projects. Beginning in the 1950s, he developed hundreds of acres for housing and businesses in the western part of the city and around Interstate 40. His nephew, country singer Charlie Rich, lived at one of his new houses at 601 Dover Road in the late 1950s.

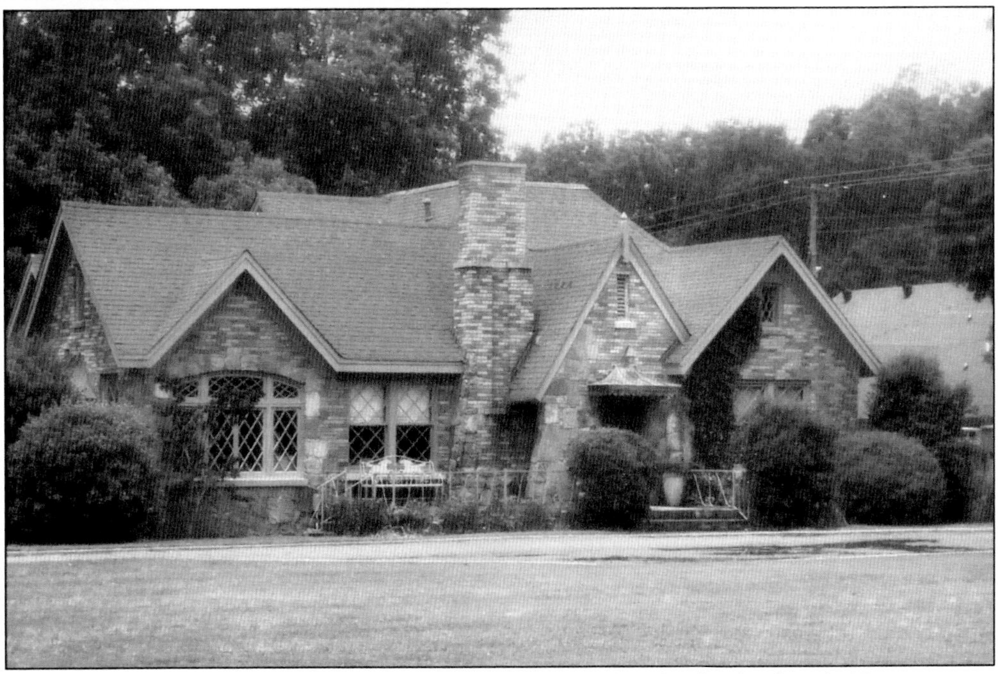

Jack W. Rich built his home at 600 North Avalon Street shortly after he founded his company in West Memphis. He owned hundreds of acres outside the city limits at that time, and by the 1960s, he had developed a majority of the land into residential neighborhoods. The Richland subdivision is named for him as well as the street that bears his name, Rich Road.

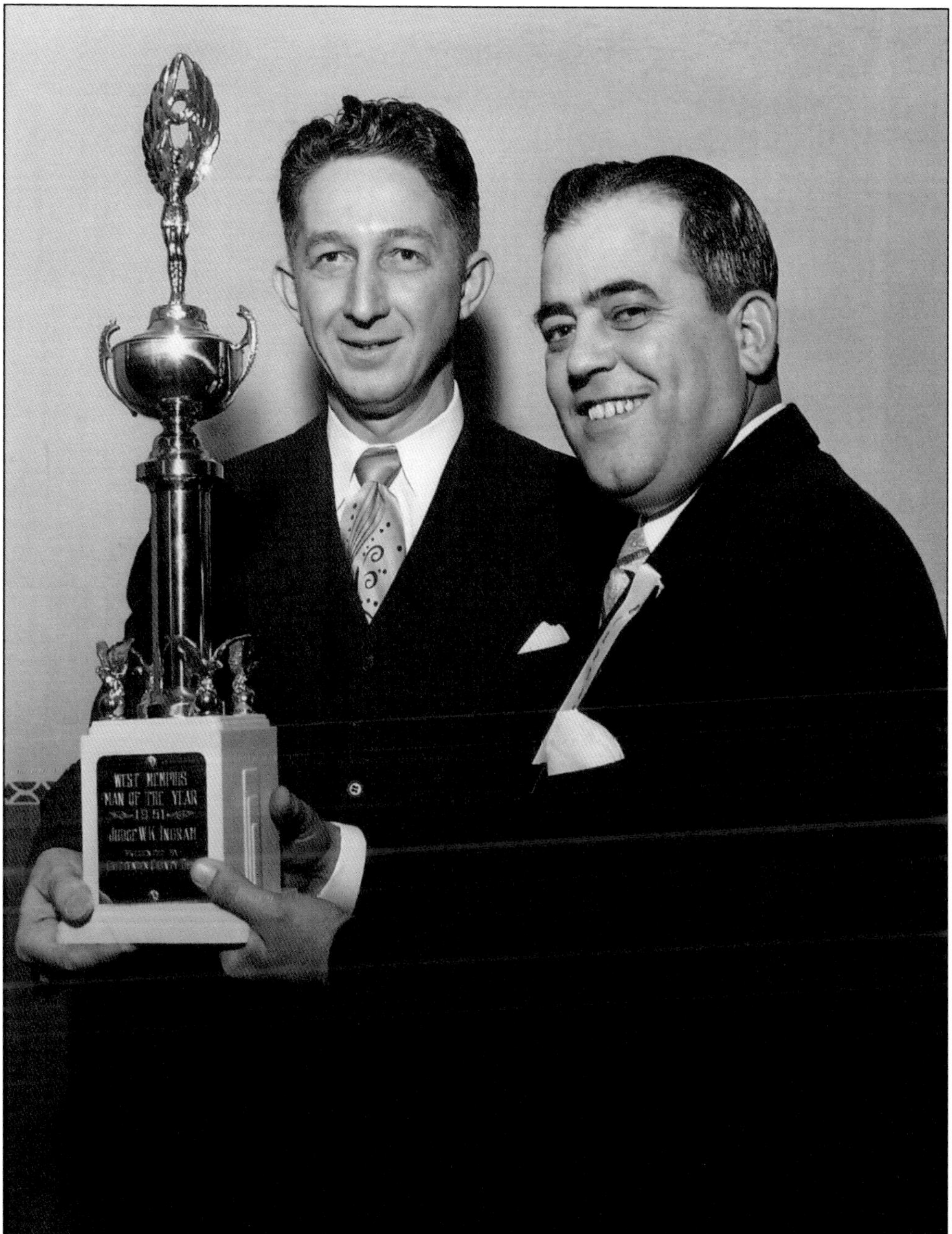

William K. Ingram was a leading politician and civic leader in West Memphis and Crittenden County. Ingram served as Crittenden County judge from 1949 to 1953 and later served on the Arkansas Senate from 1963 until his death in 1981. In 1965, he founded Razorback Concrete, which is still in operation. Ingram (right) is pictured here receiving the Man of the Year award from James C. Hale Sr. in 1951.

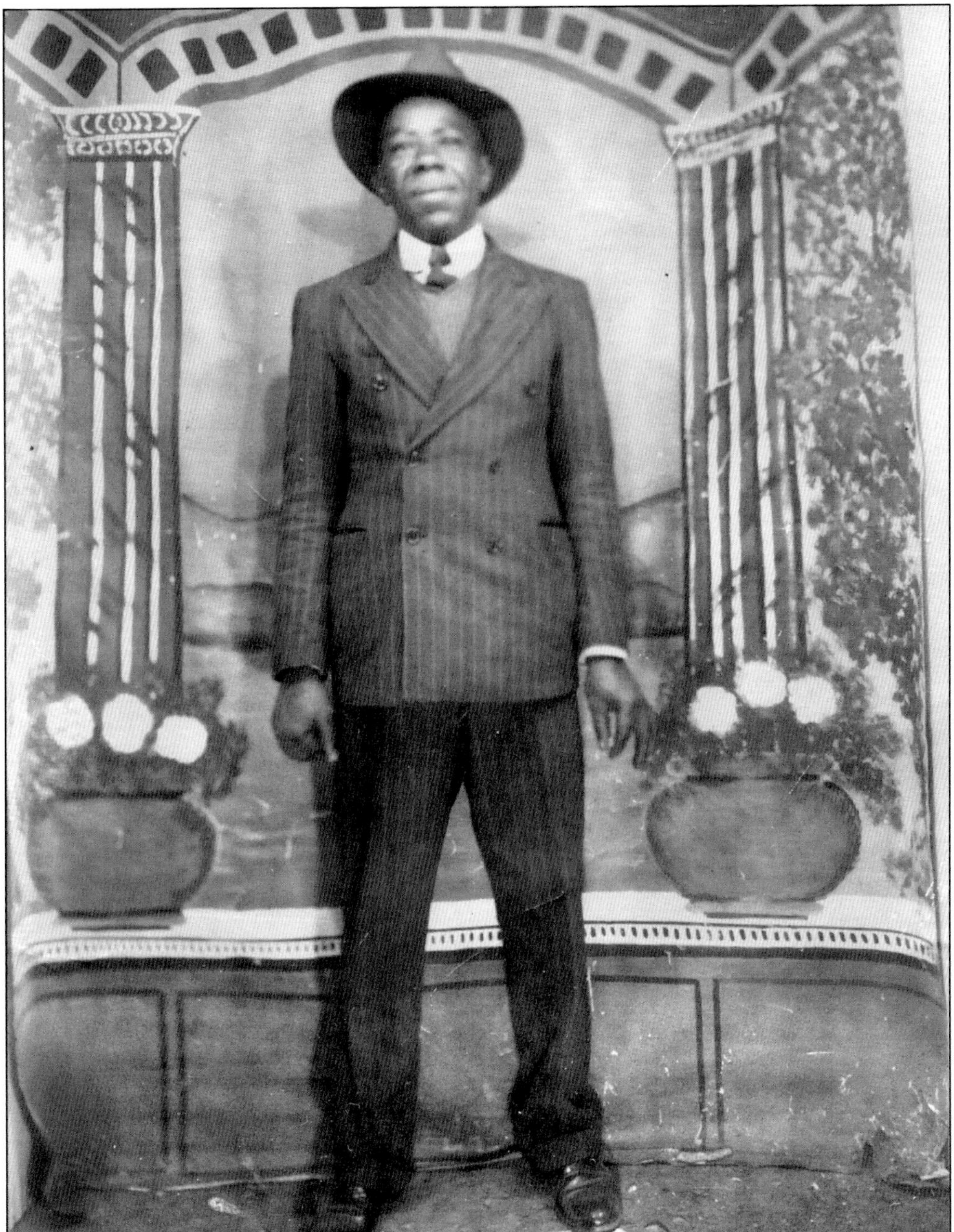

Charles Marcellus Scales, nicknamed "Keiser," was Zack Bragg's right-hand man for many years. Bragg would call upon him during election time to help with campaigning and other voter-outreach programs. His nickname originated when he helped to apprehend a Nazi prisoner of war in West Memphis who had escaped from the Keiser Concentration Camp in Mississippi County. (Courtesy of Dixie Ball Gordon.)

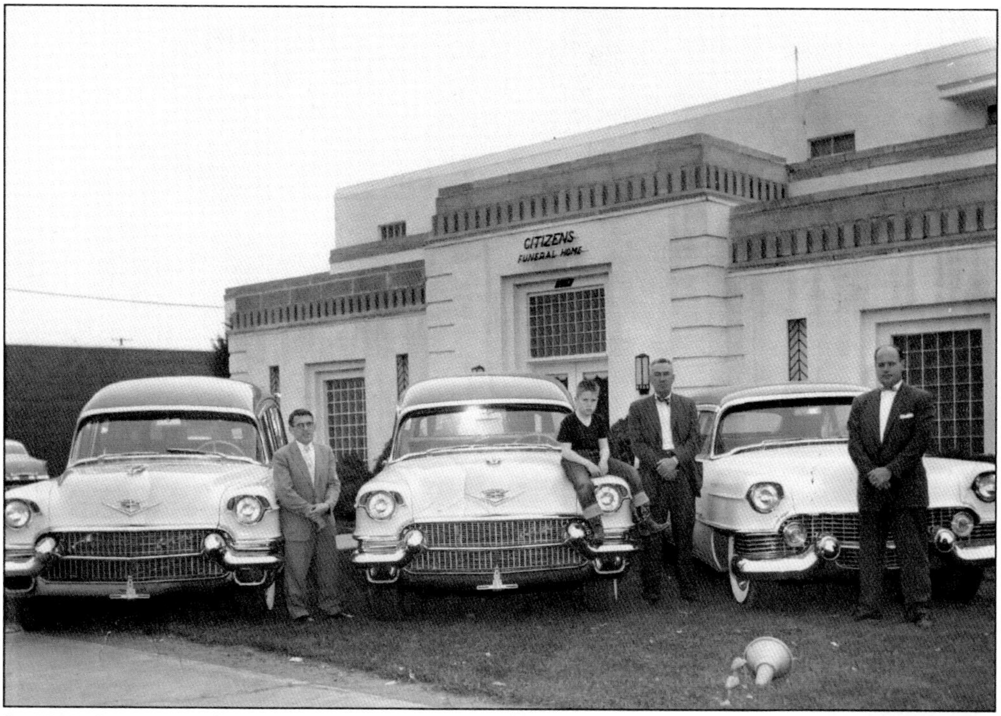

In 1938, James A. Johnson Sr. founded Citizens Funeral Home, which later became Roller-Citizens Funeral Home. Originally located on the southeast corner of Missouri Street and Bond Avenue, the Art Deco–style edifice was torn down in the early 1960s. Pictured here in 1949 are, from left to right, Pat Massengill, James A. Johnson Jr., James A. Johnson Sr., and Marvin Thompson.

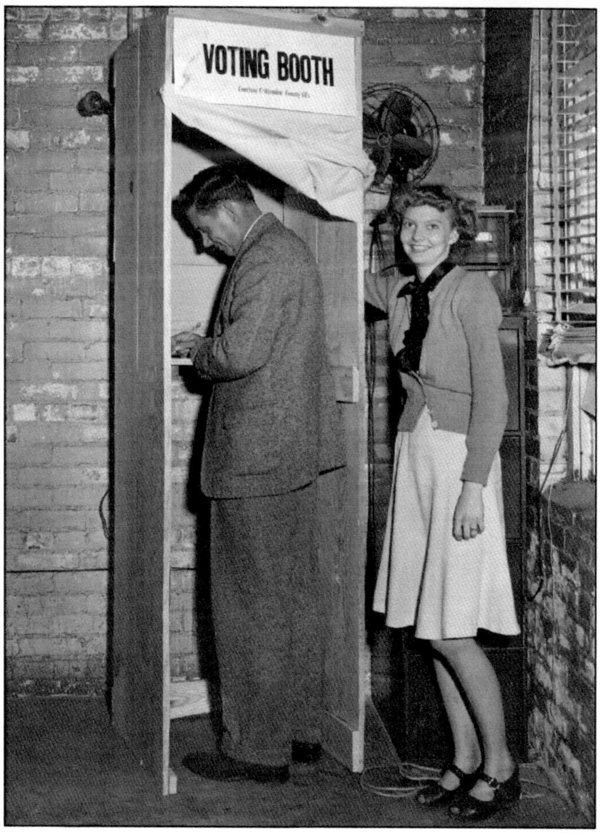

Since the 1930s, West Memphis has been Crittenden County's largest city. While West Memphis never held the county seat, election campaigning in the city has been crucial for county-wide elections. Until the 1970s, all voting polls made use of the traditional handwritten ballot and box.

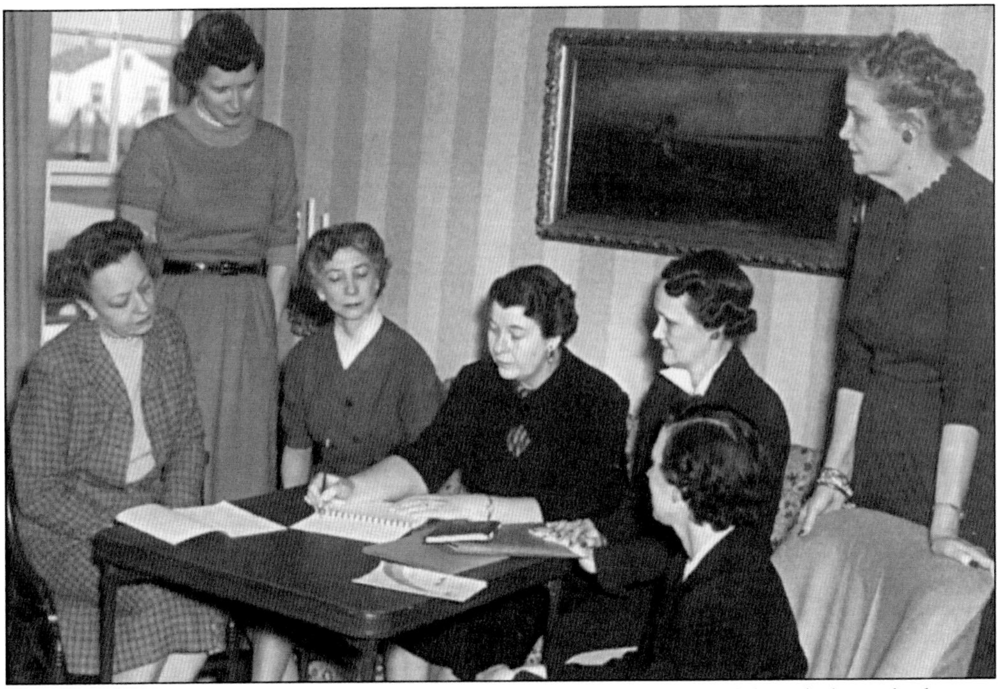

During World War II, a group of West Memphis women formed a club to help with the war effort. After the war ended, the group reorganized to address civic and social work and decided to maintain an active membership of exactly 20 women, thus becoming known as the Twenty Club. Pictured in 1954 are, from left to right, (seated) Ruth Senhousen, Chloe Dacus, Mildred Fall, Octa Norman High, and Evelyn Spear; (standing) Mary Frances Jay and Helen Peters.

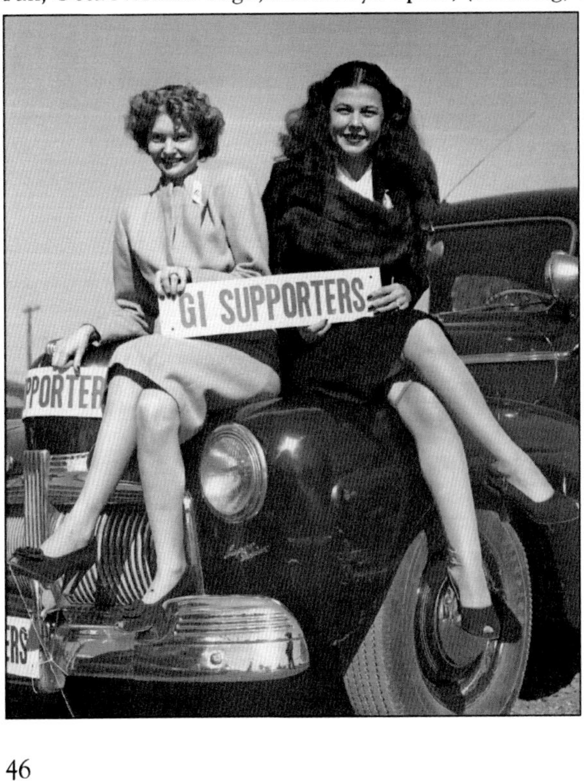

During World War II, West Memphians participated in the war effort on the home front. Pictured here in 1945 are Mary Stevenson (left) and Ruth Murphy, shown supporting the returning troops who served in Europe and the Pacific.

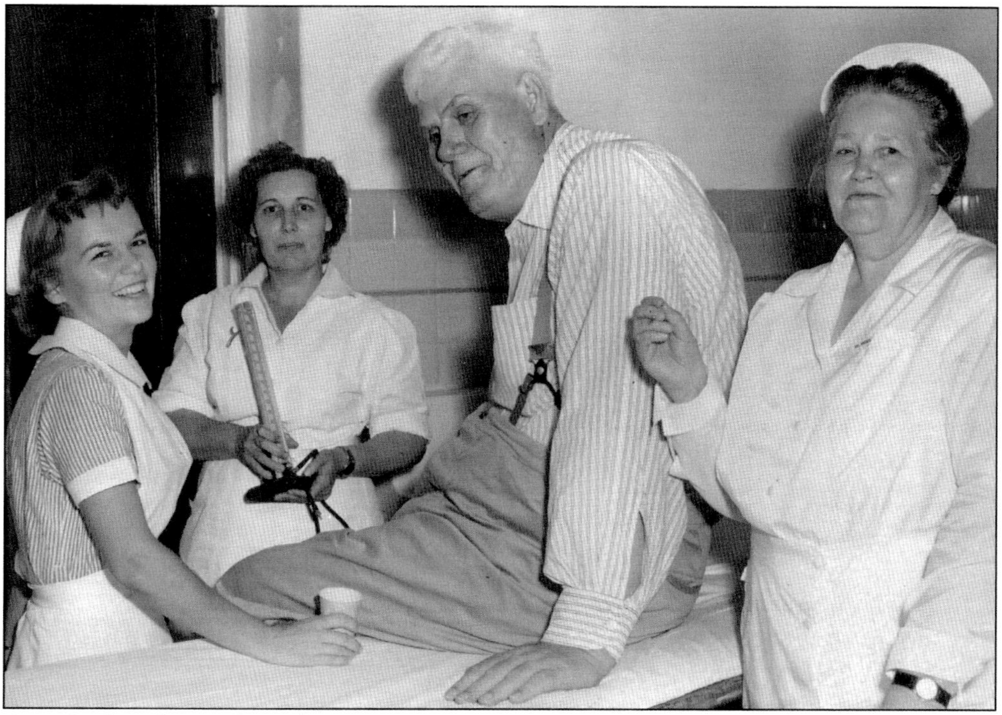

At eight feet, five inches tall, James Grover Tarver of Crittenden County was known as "the Texas Giant" and was billed as the largest man in the world when he worked for various traveling circuses between 1914 and 1940. He retired to a farm near Turrell, Arkansas, and died there in 1958. Tarver is pictured here after a routine checkup with nurses at Crittenden Memorial Hospital in 1956.

Jack (left) and Pete Coughlin became the editors of the *West Memphis News* in the late 1940s after returning home from serving in World War II. The Coughlin brothers fought long and hard to expose the public school system's inadequate facilities for African American students in West Memphis. Their efforts caught the attention of *Life* magazine, which published a feature on the story in March 1949.

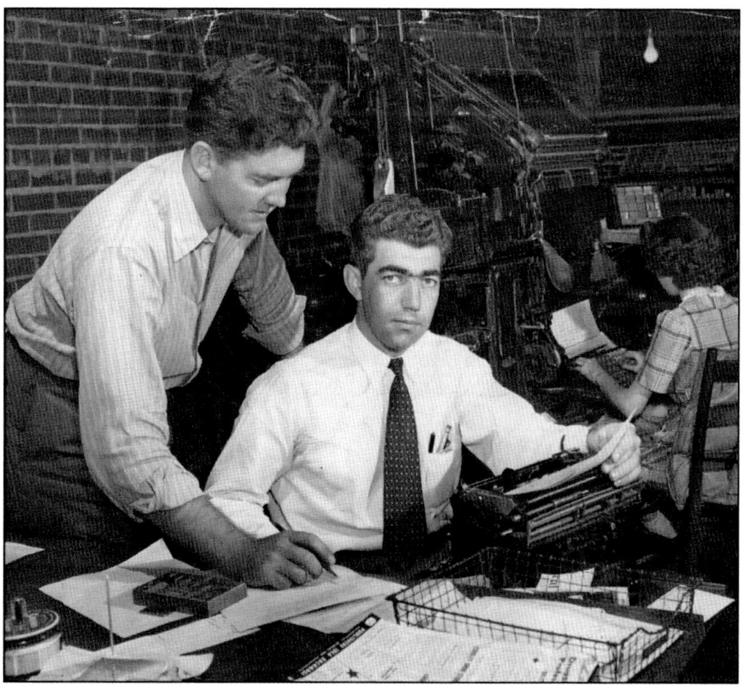

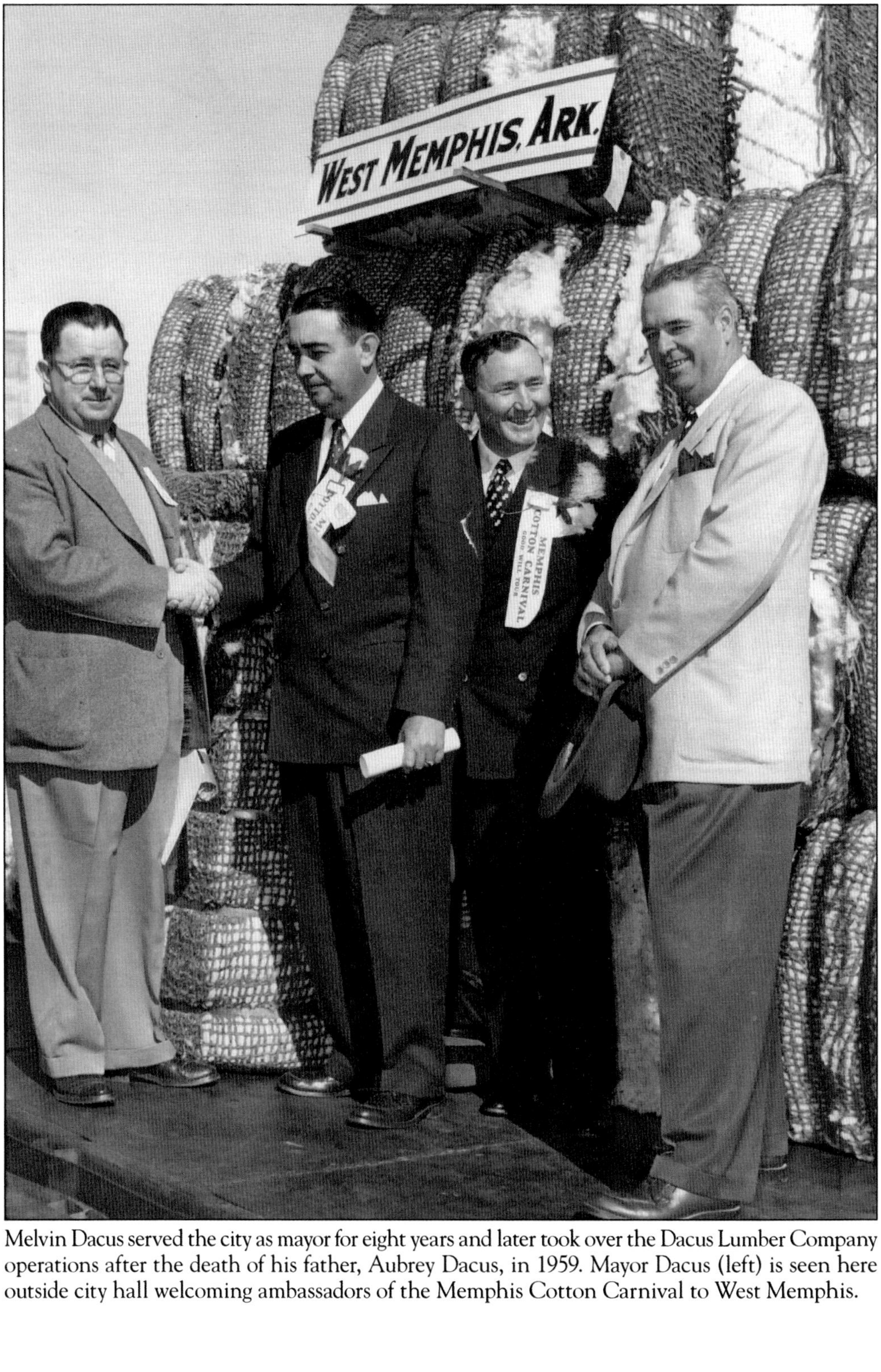

Melvin Dacus served the city as mayor for eight years and later took over the Dacus Lumber Company operations after the death of his father, Aubrey Dacus, in 1959. Mayor Dacus (left) is seen here outside city hall welcoming ambassadors of the Memphis Cotton Carnival to West Memphis.

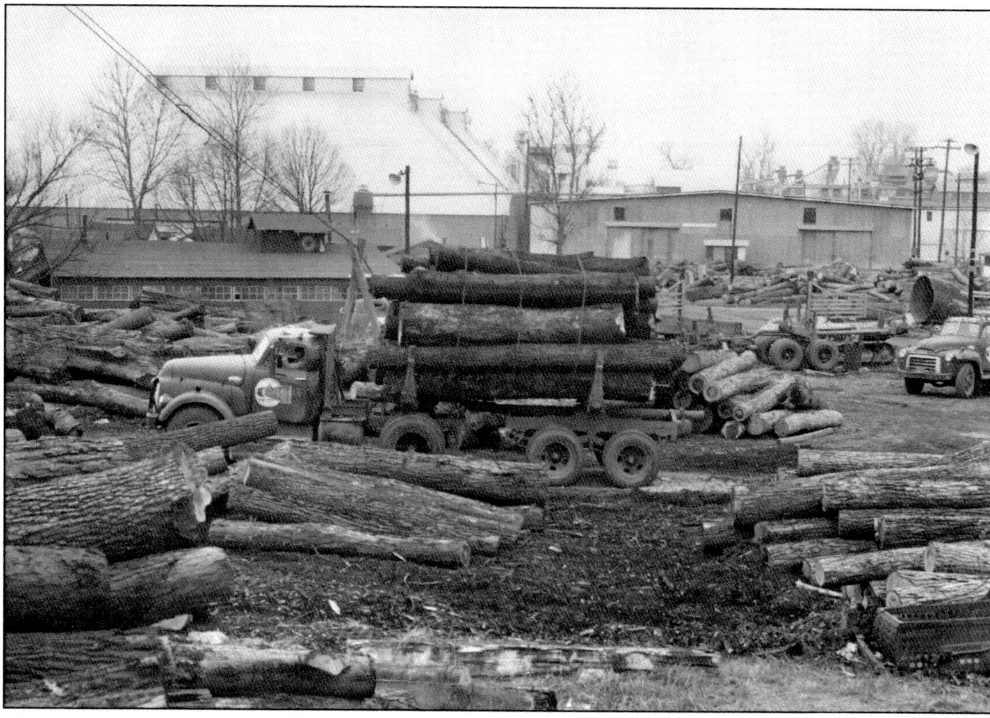

Dacus Lumber Company, which was originally Bragg's sawmill, occupied nearly the entire east side of Missouri Street. The lumber mill closed in 1972, and the land was auctioned in 1976. In 1978, a Kmart and two fast-food restaurants were built on the former site. Today, West Memphis Christian School occupies the former Kmart location.

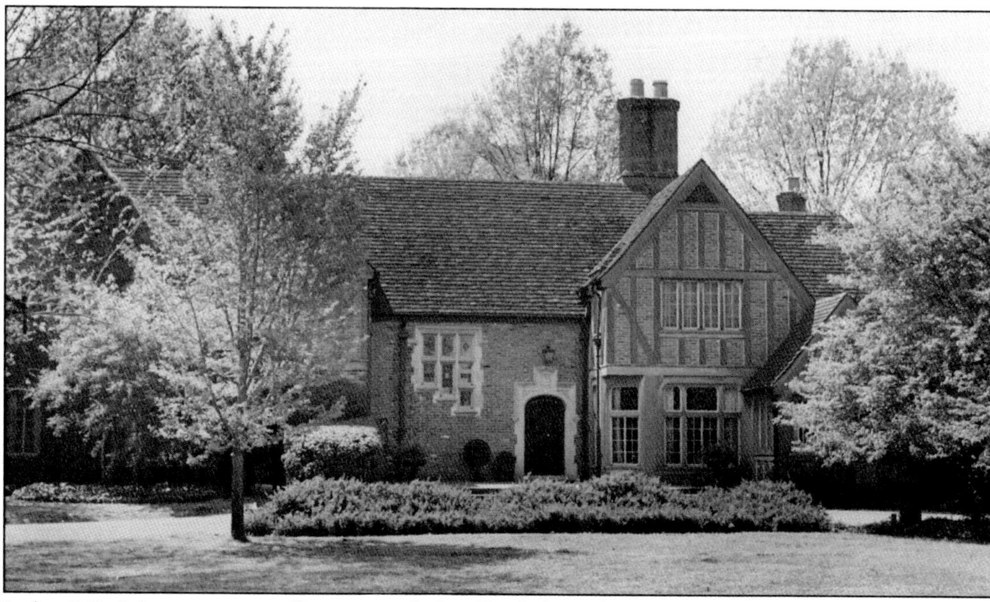

Judge J.C. Johnson originally occupied this English Tudor at 400 North Avalon Street. The custom-built house, known as Hawthorne Place, was completed in 1938 and designed by well-known architect Everett Woods. Later, the house was acquired by Melvin and Chloe Dacus, who resided there until the 1970s.

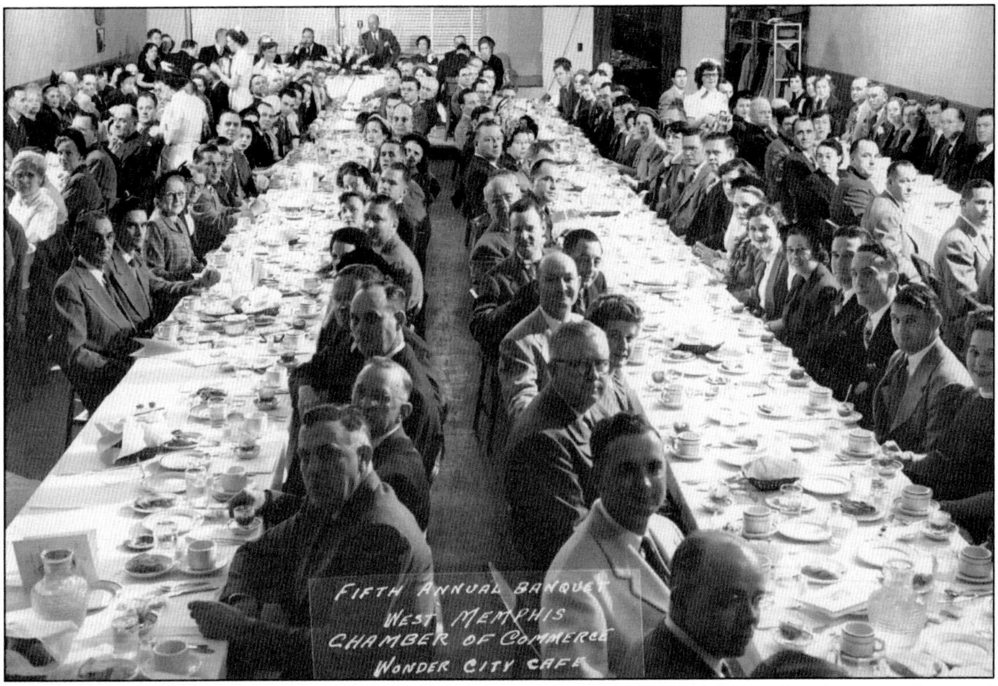

The West Memphis Chamber of Commerce was reorganized in 1945 under the presidency of Jack Rich. Beginning in 1947, annual banquets were first held at the Peabody Hotel in Memphis before being moved locally. Pictured here is the fifth-annual banquet of 1951, held at the Wonder City Café on Broadway.

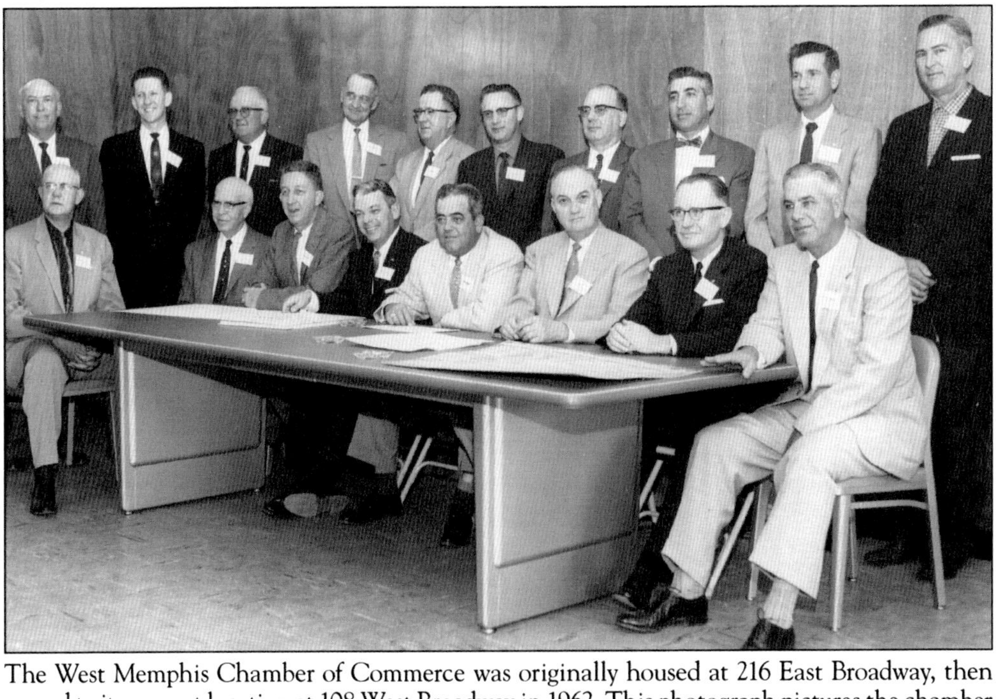

The West Memphis Chamber of Commerce was originally housed at 216 East Broadway, then moved to its current location at 108 West Broadway in 1962. This photograph pictures the chamber directors in 1959. (Courtesy of West Memphis Chamber of Commerce.)

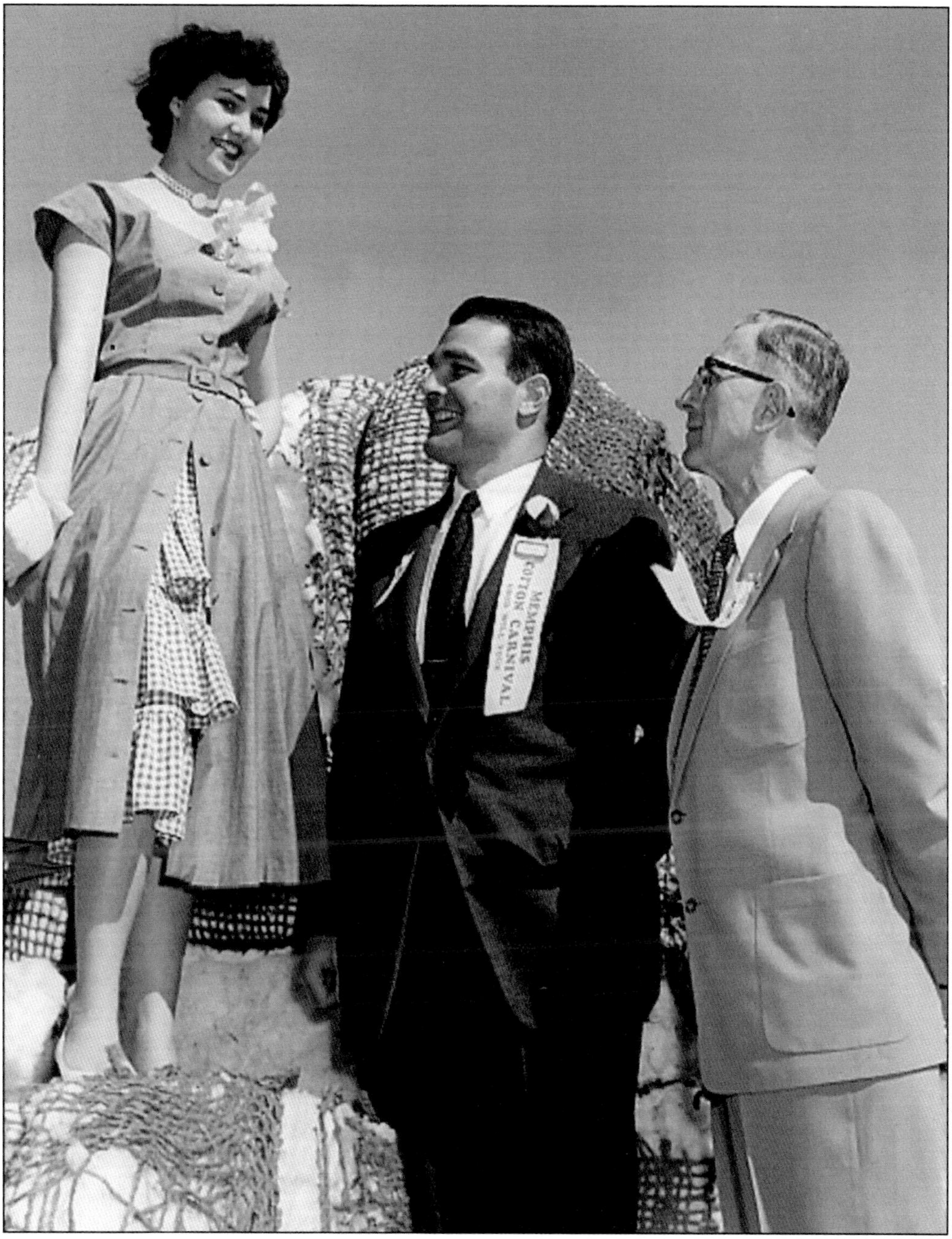

William Fordyce served as mayor of West Memphis for two years, from 1952 to 1954. In this short period, West Memphis witnessed exceptional growth in population and business. Photographed here is Mayor Fordyce (right) with the king and queen of the 1952 Memphis Cotton Carnival.

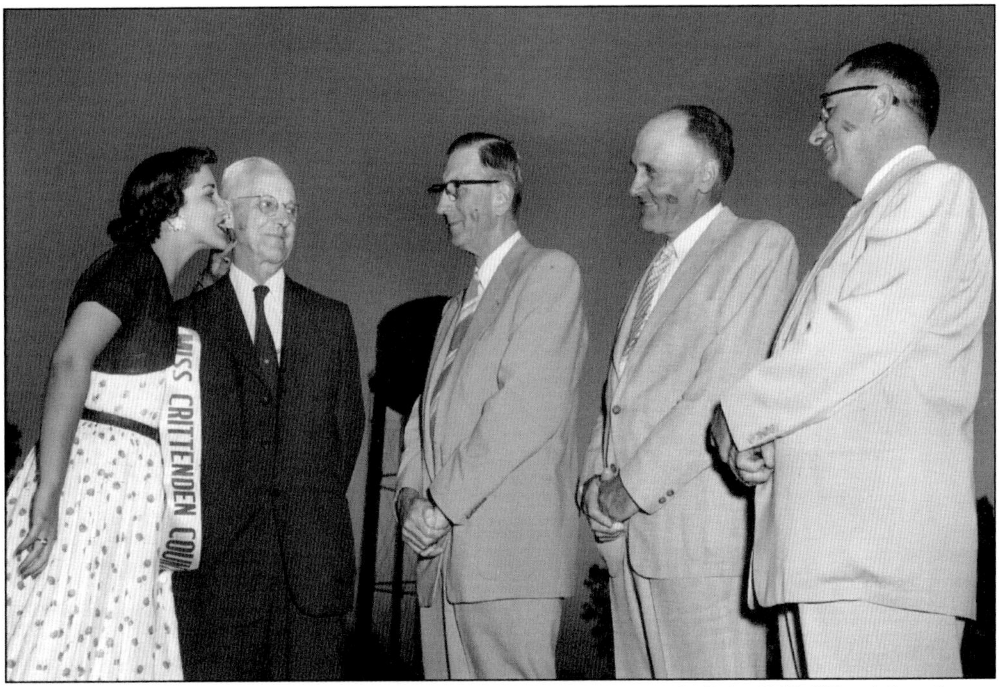

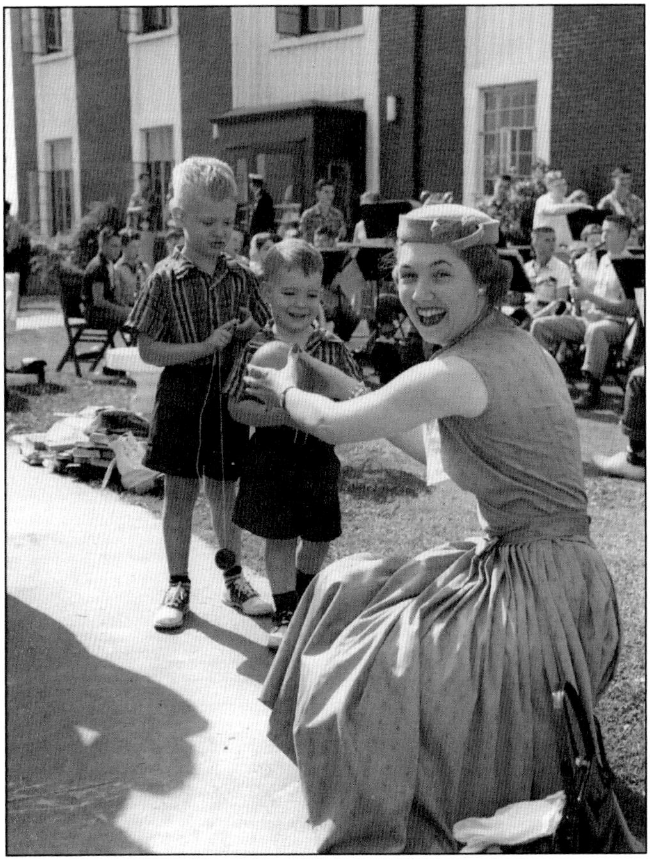

In July 1952, West Memphis celebrated its 25th anniversary of incorporation. The above photograph highlights Miss Crittenden County, Mabel Newton, giving novelty kiss marks to the present and former mayors at Worthington Park. Pictured are, from left to right, Mabel Newton, William H. Hundhausen Sr., William Fordyce, Marshall B. Currie Sr., and Melvin Dacus.

During the 1950s, the city frequently hosted summer picnics and gatherings for West Memphians. Shown here is the 1954 Memphis Cotton Carnival queen, Julia Donelson, visiting West Memphis children outside city hall during one such picnic.

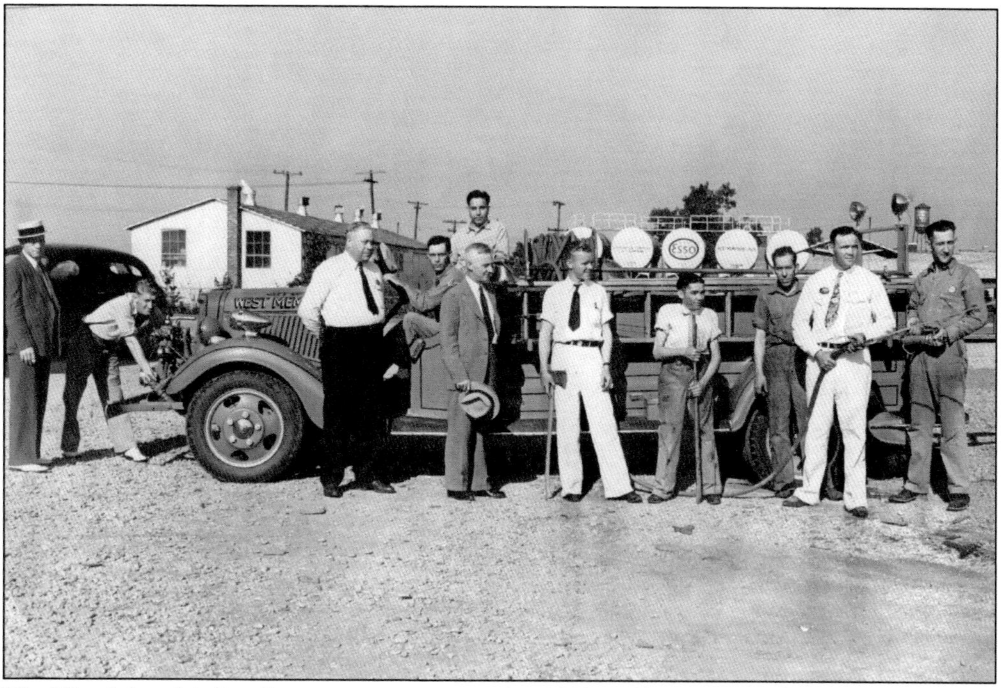

The West Memphis Fire Department was created in 1932 and began as a volunteer unit. In 1936, the fire department purchased a new 500-gallon-per-minute pumper, shown here. Pictured with the new pumper are, from left to right, (standing) Carl Smalley, James G. Moore, C.C. Culp, Mayor William H. Hundhausen Sr., William Collins Jr., Dock White, Tom Warner, Chief Otis Ball, and C.V. Griffin; (seated inside the fire truck) Jimmy Wise and Grady Brown.

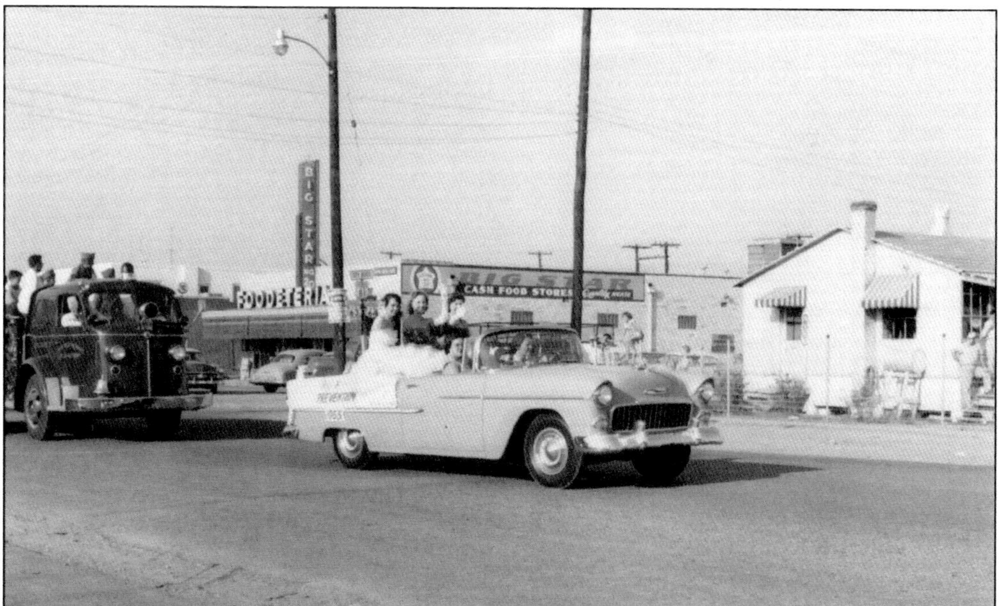

Parades for various events were once commonplace in West Memphis. This photograph shows the lead car in a fire awareness and prevention parade on Missouri Street in 1955. The building in the background is the Big Star Foodeteria, one of the first chain grocery stores in West Memphis.

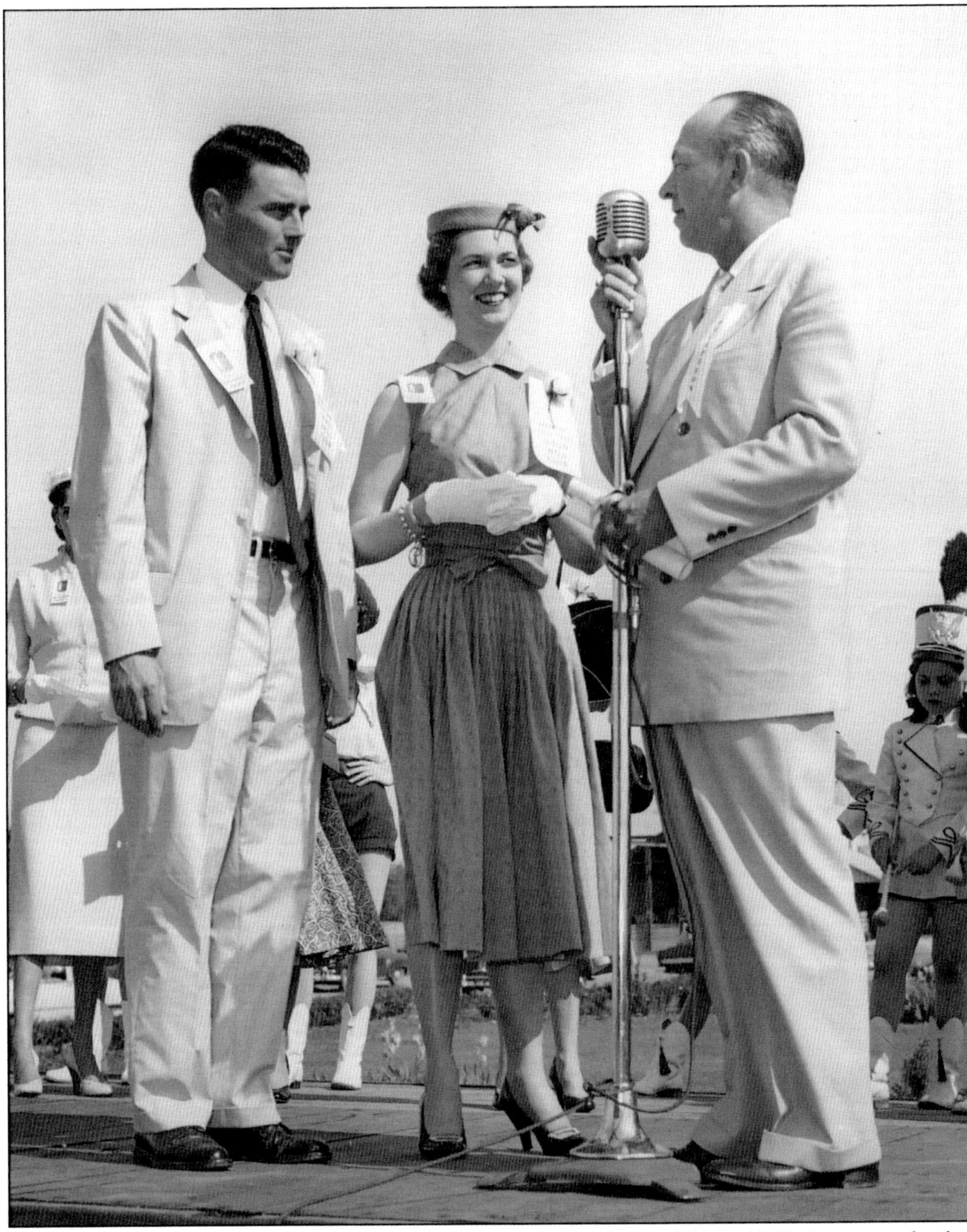

Howell B. Price (right) was the mayor of West Memphis from 1954 to 1963. It was under his administration that most of the streets in the city were paved. Previously, only Broadway, Missouri Street, and a few other main roads had hard surfaces. The funding for street improvements in the 1950s came from the revenue generated by the city's purchase of the utility company in 1940 under the leadership of William H. Hundhausen Sr.

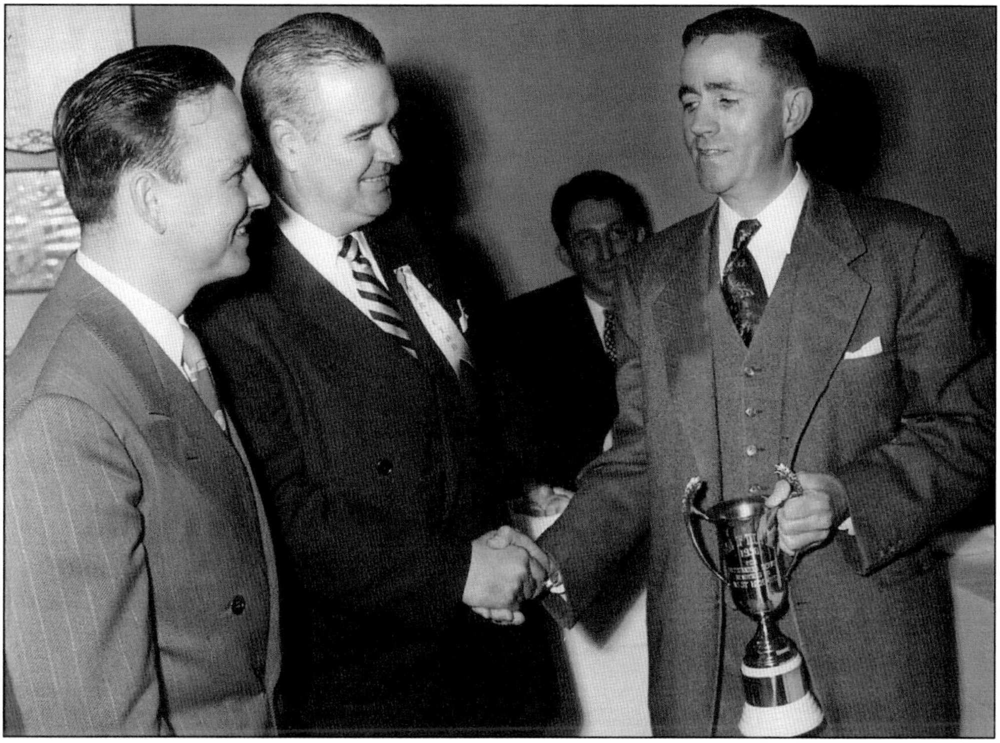

Dr. Ralph Hamilton was a longtime West Memphis physician and a generous contributor to charities and civic organizations around the county. Dr. Hamilton, along with deceased school superintendent O.M. Shultz, was honored in 1976 when Hamilton-Shultz Football Stadium was dedicated. This photograph shows Dr. Hamilton (right) receiving the Man of the Year award in 1950.

Dr. David H. James was the first pediatrician in eastern Arkansas. Since 1957, he and his wife, Ann, have lived in West Memphis, where they raised their 11 children. In 1962, he was the first physician to admit a patient to the newly founded St. Jude Children's Hospital in Memphis. Dr. James has been instrumental in local education and humanitarian efforts and has received numerous awards and honors for his work and dedication.

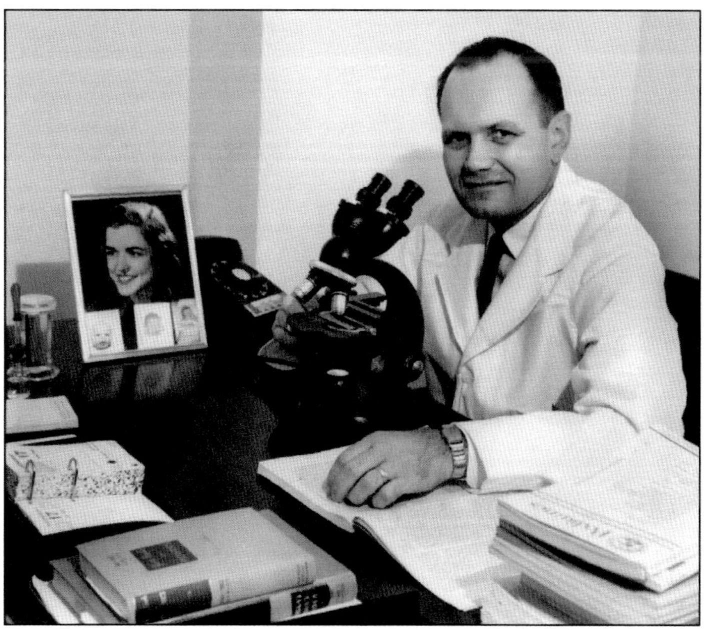

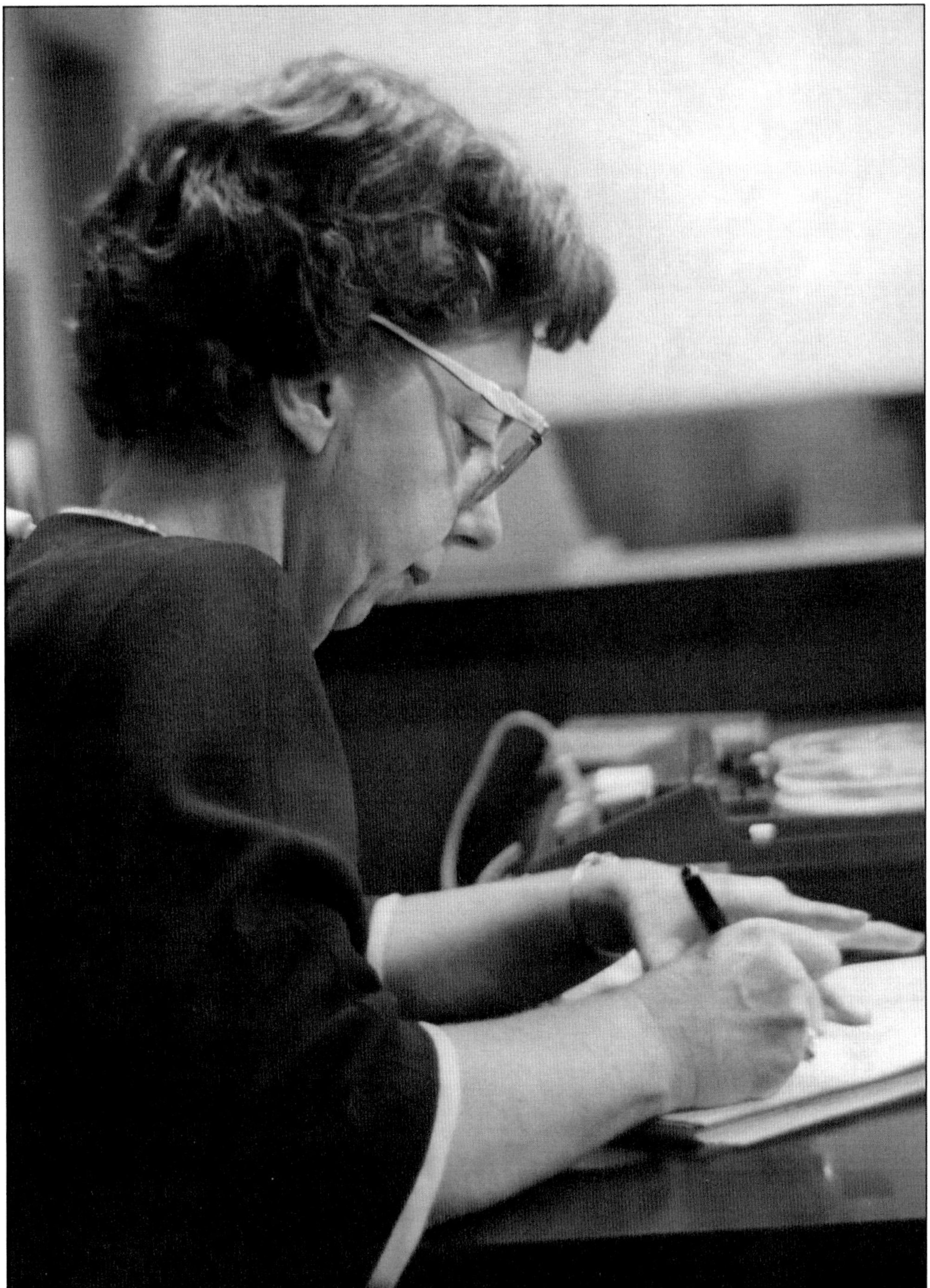

Jean Hillencamp started work for the City of West Memphis in 1939 as the secretary to Mayor Hundhausen. One of the only city employees at that time, she fulfilled many other roles, including issuing permits, collecting bills and taxes, maintaining the city ledgers, and answering the police station's telephone. In 1942, she was appointed as the municipal court clerk, a position in which she remained for 40 years.

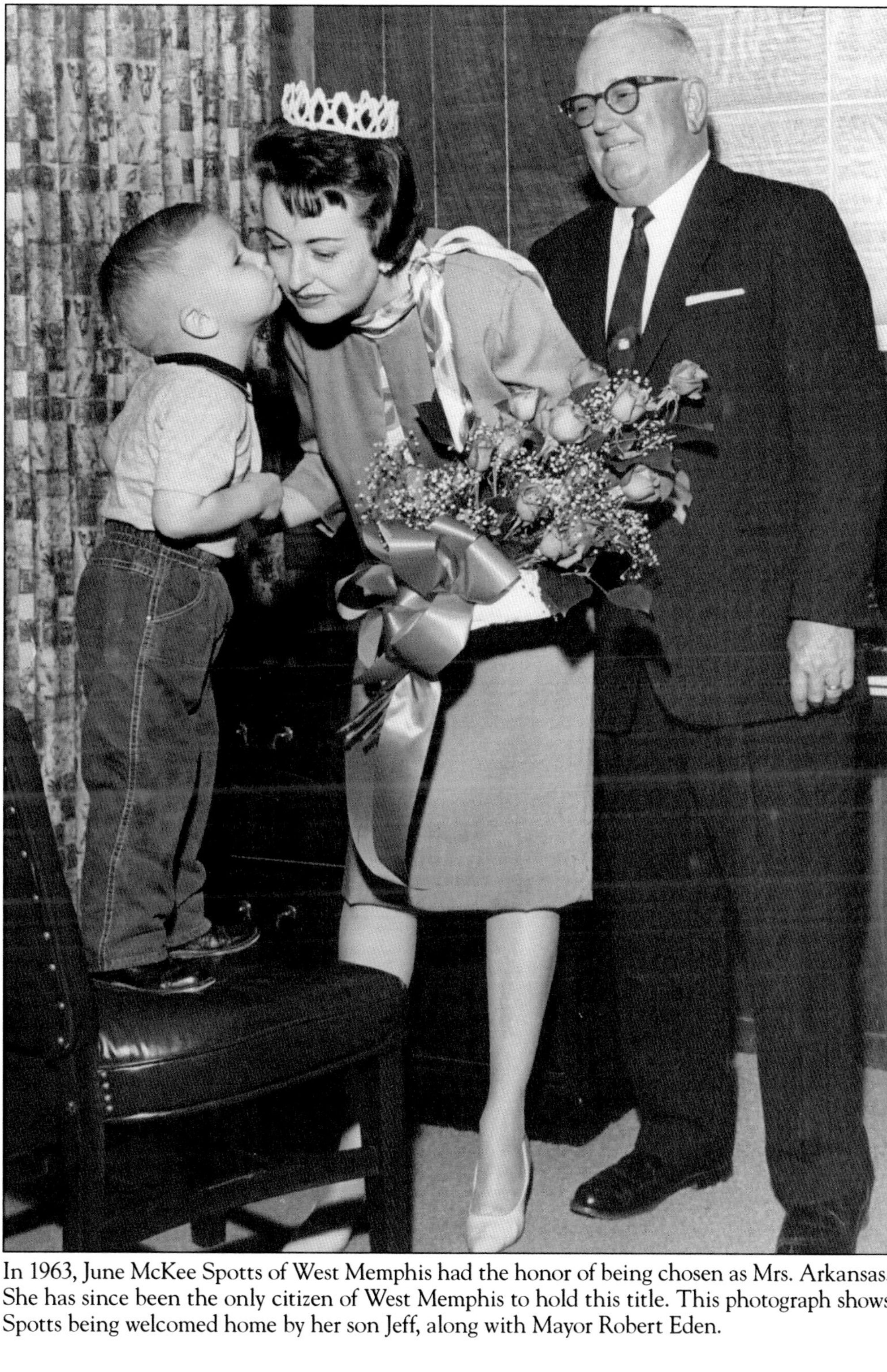

In 1963, June McKee Spotts of West Memphis had the honor of being chosen as Mrs. Arkansas. She has since been the only citizen of West Memphis to hold this title. This photograph shows Spotts being welcomed home by her son Jeff, along with Mayor Robert Eden.

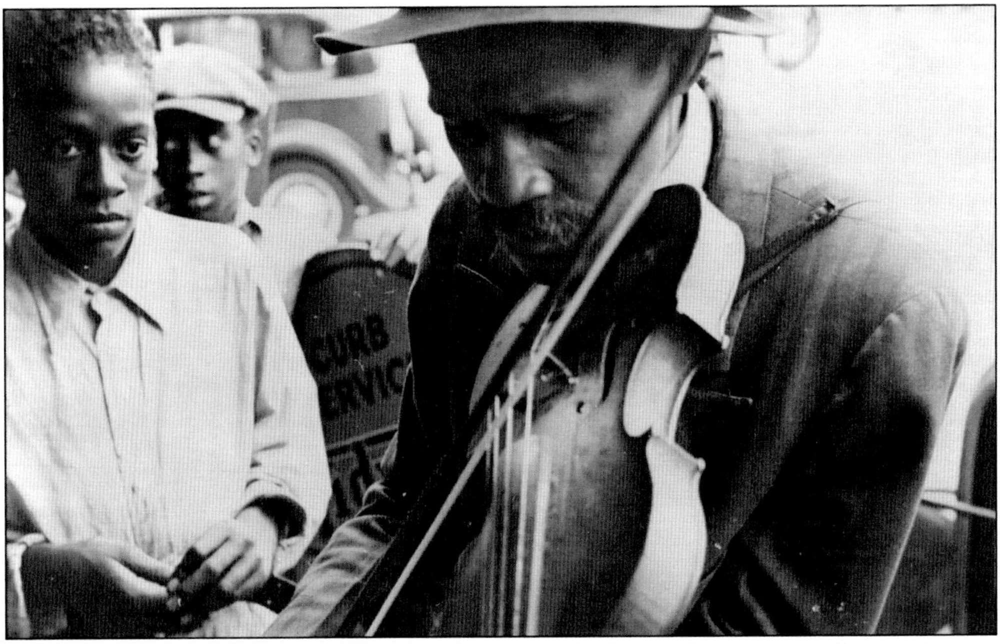

The area around Eighth Street and Broadway became widely known for its music and entertainment from the late 1930s through the 1950s. Many well-known musicians, including Riley B. King ("B.B. King") and Chester Arthur Burnett ("Howlin' Wolf"), lived in West Memphis, where they started their professional careers playing at different venues along Eighth Street. Pictured above is a blind musician playing on the corner of Broadway and Ninth Street in 1935.

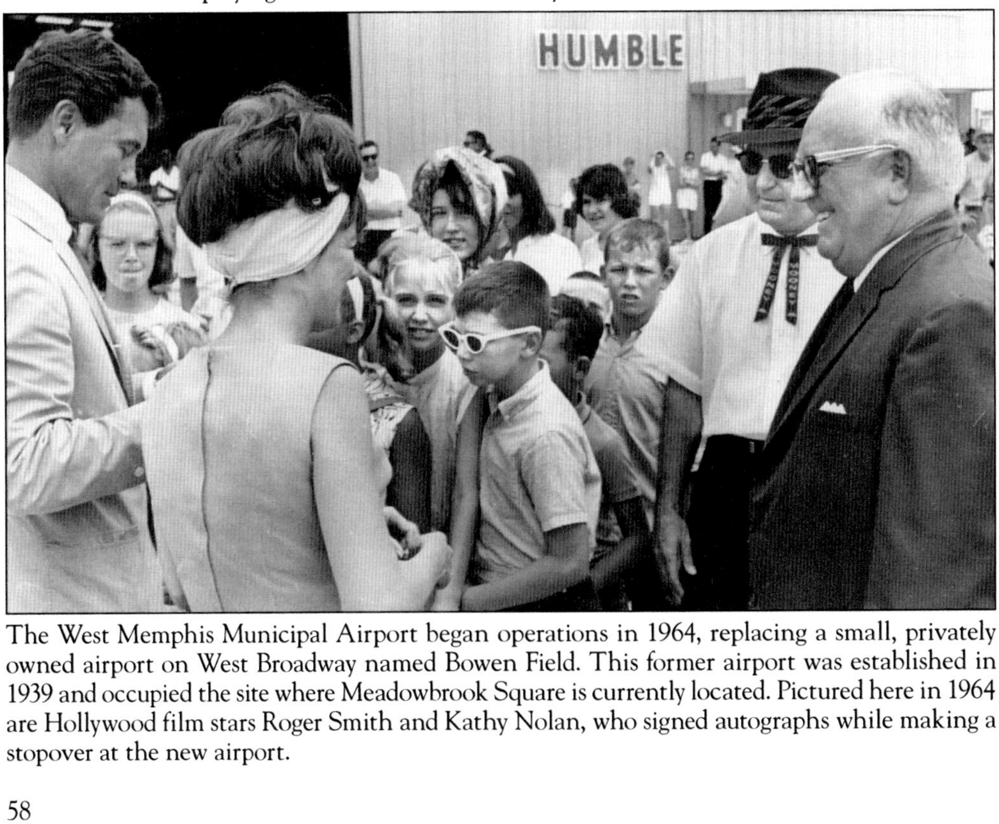

The West Memphis Municipal Airport began operations in 1964, replacing a small, privately owned airport on West Broadway named Bowen Field. This former airport was established in 1939 and occupied the site where Meadowbrook Square is currently located. Pictured here in 1964 are Hollywood film stars Roger Smith and Kathy Nolan, who signed autographs while making a stopover at the new airport.

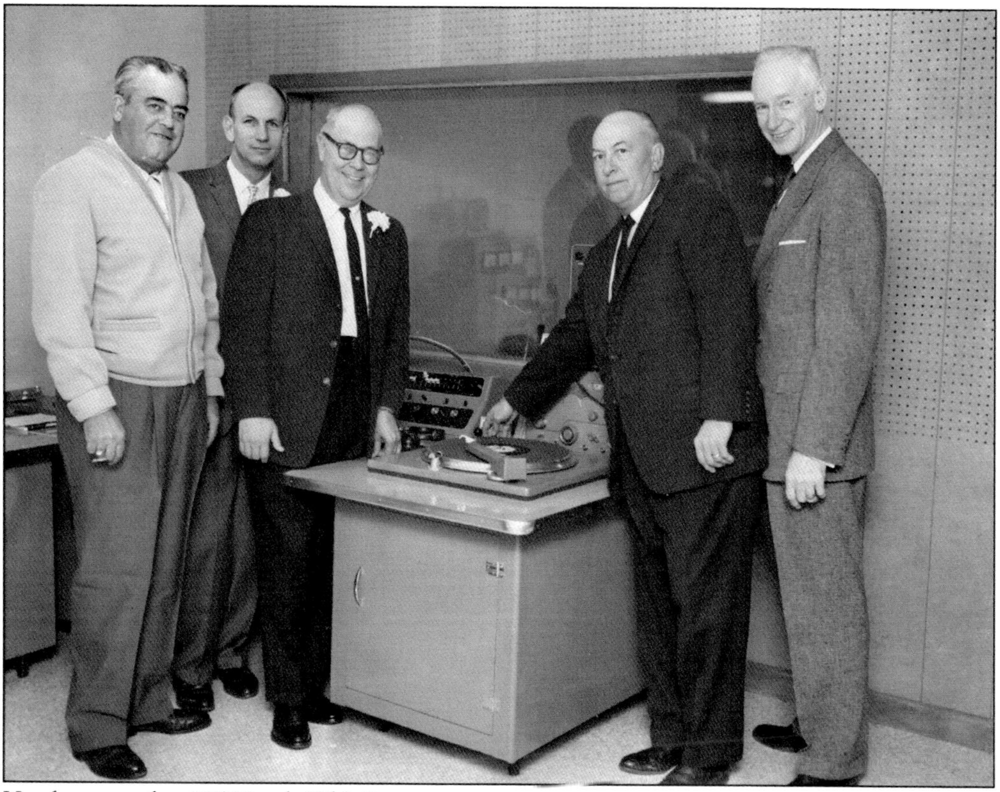

Headquartered at 105 North Fifth Street, the KSUD radio station first went on the air in 1961. An earlier radio station with the call letters KWEM, located at 231 East Broadway, helped to launch the careers of Elvis Presley, Howlin' Wolf, and many others. Photographed here at KSUD are, from left to right, William Ingram, Carlton Garner, Harold Sadbury, Mayor Howell B. Price, and Took Gathings.

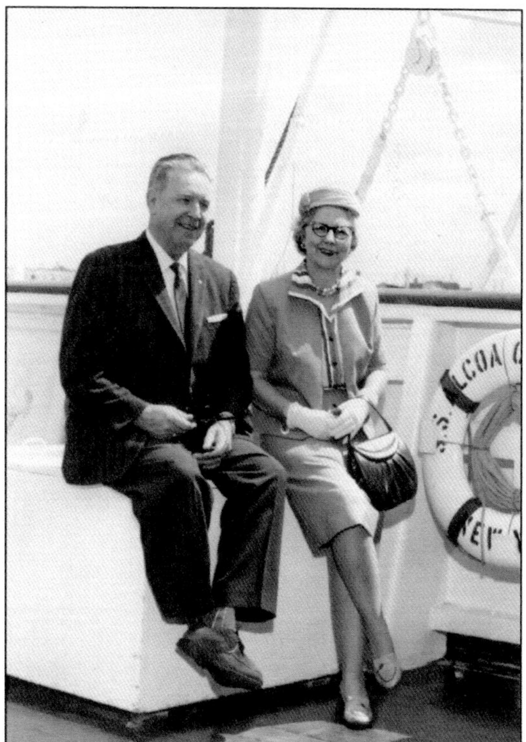

John Spotts and his wife, Helen, were longtime residents of West Memphis. In 1940, he opened Spotts drugstore on Broadway, which would serve three generations of West Memphians at its nostalgic soda fountain before closing in the early 1980s. Spotts also served in various civic positions, including city clerk and city recorder during the 1930s.

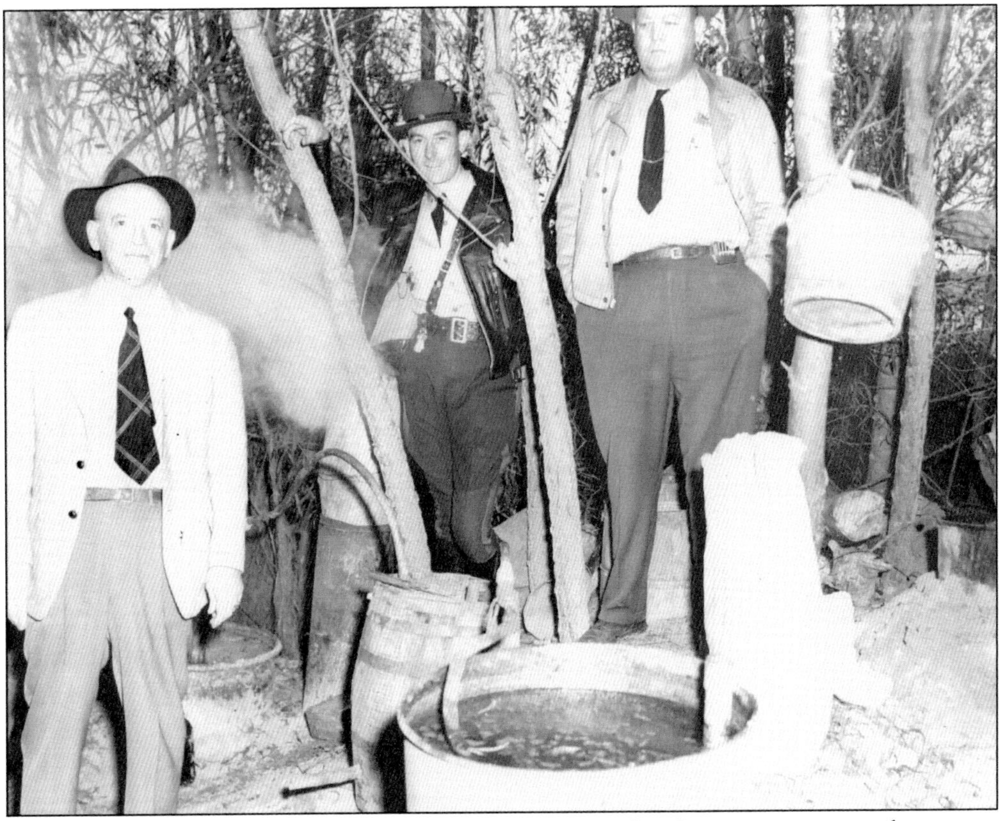

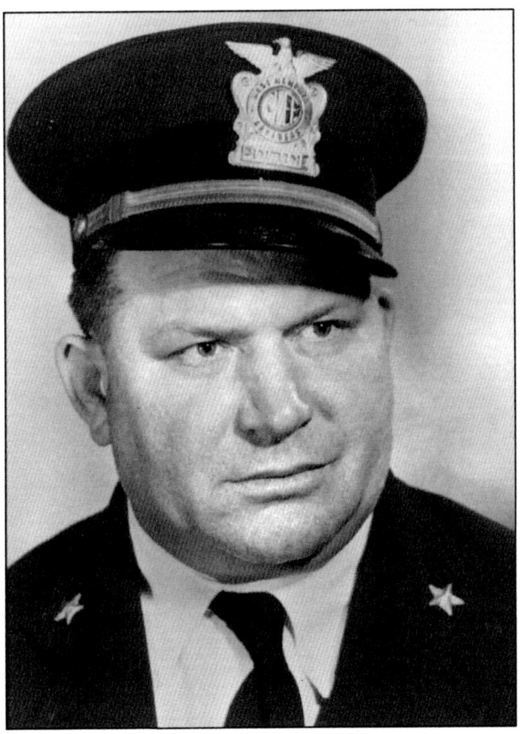

Crittenden County was never a dry county except during Prohibition. However, the production and sale of moonshine has always been illegal. This photograph shows law enforcement officers confiscating an illegal moonshine still just outside West Memphis in 1948. From left to right are Sheriff Cecil Goodwin, State Trooper John Roberts, and Deputy Sheriff James Burrow.

Harold D. Holland served as the West Memphis chief of police from 1942 until his retirement in 1966, holding this position longer than any other police chief in the city. Holland had previously been a patrol officer with the city since 1935. Before West Memphis's incorporation in 1927, the Crittenden County Sheriff's Office provided police protection.

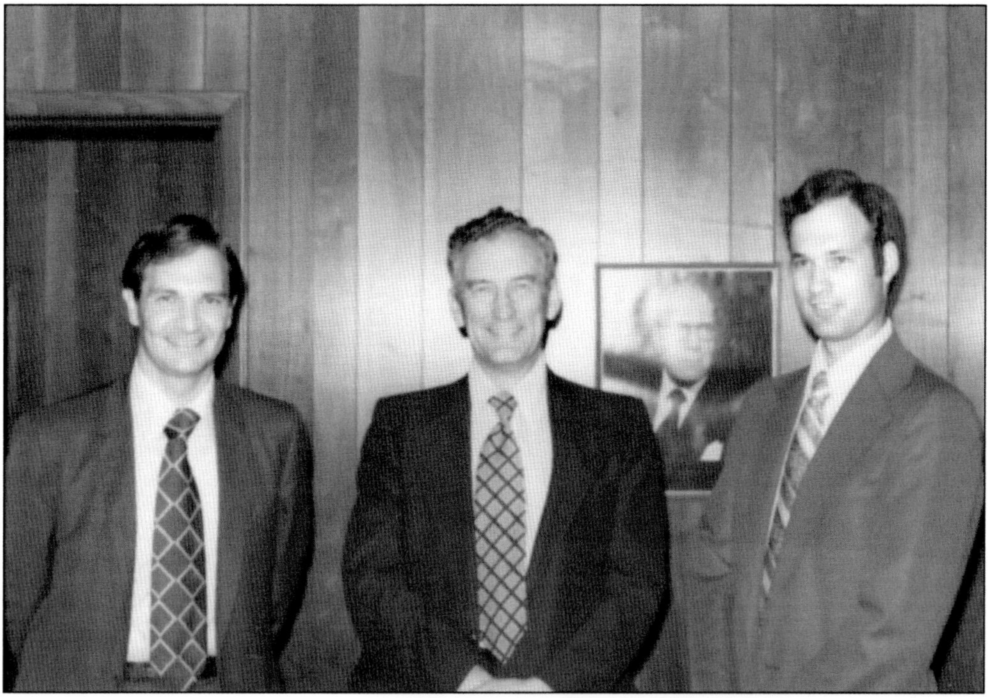

The Federal Bureau of Investigation established a resident agency in West Memphis in 1962, during the tenure of FBI director J. Edgar Hoover. The agency in West Memphis was in charge of Crittenden, Cross, St. Francis, Monroe, Phillips, and Lee Counties. Pictured here at the West Memphis office in the early 1970s are, from left to right, Special Agents John Beauregard, James Skelley, and Roy Long.

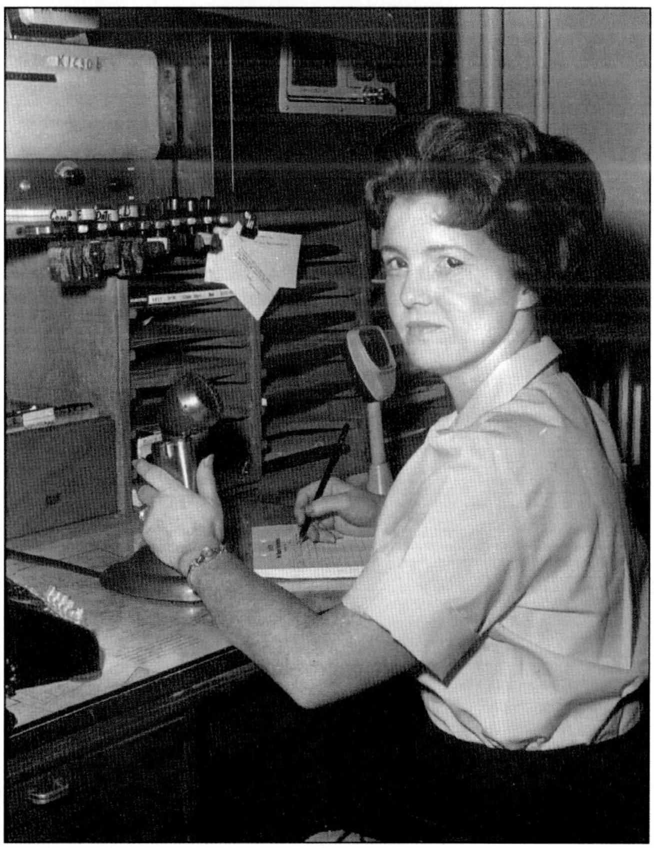

Pearl Lyons became the first female police officer in West Memphis when she began as a dispatcher in 1963. Lyons continued with the West Memphis Police Department for over 25 years and was promoted to captain before her retirement.

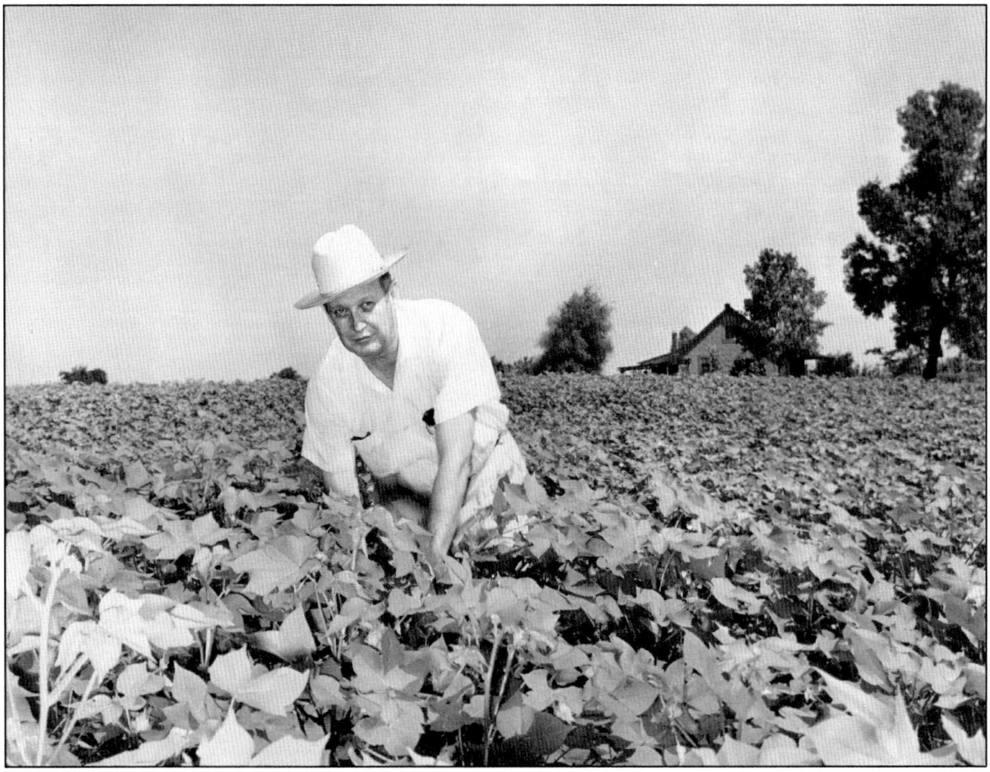

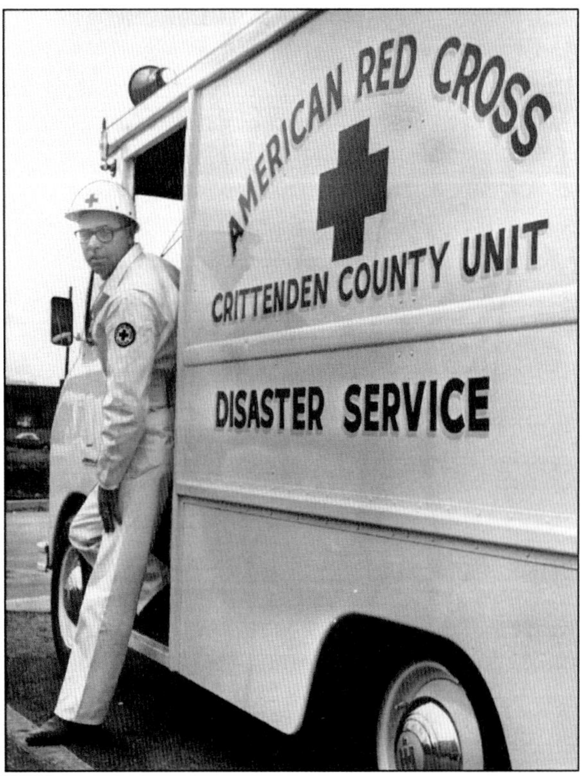

Cecil Goodwin was the Crittenden County sheriff from 1943 until his death in 1963. During his tenure as sheriff, the courthouse in Marion was renovated, the jail was remodeled, and a new county office building was constructed to house the sheriff's department. In addition to Goodwin's law enforcement career, he also had extensive farming interests around Marion.

West Memphis has been fortunate to avoid many natural disasters since the Great Flood of 1912. The most severe and deadliest weather event occurred on December 14, 1987, when an F3-rated tornado ravaged the eastern part of the city, killing 6 people and injuring over 100. This tornado destroyed hundreds of homes and businesses, including Maddux Elementary School.

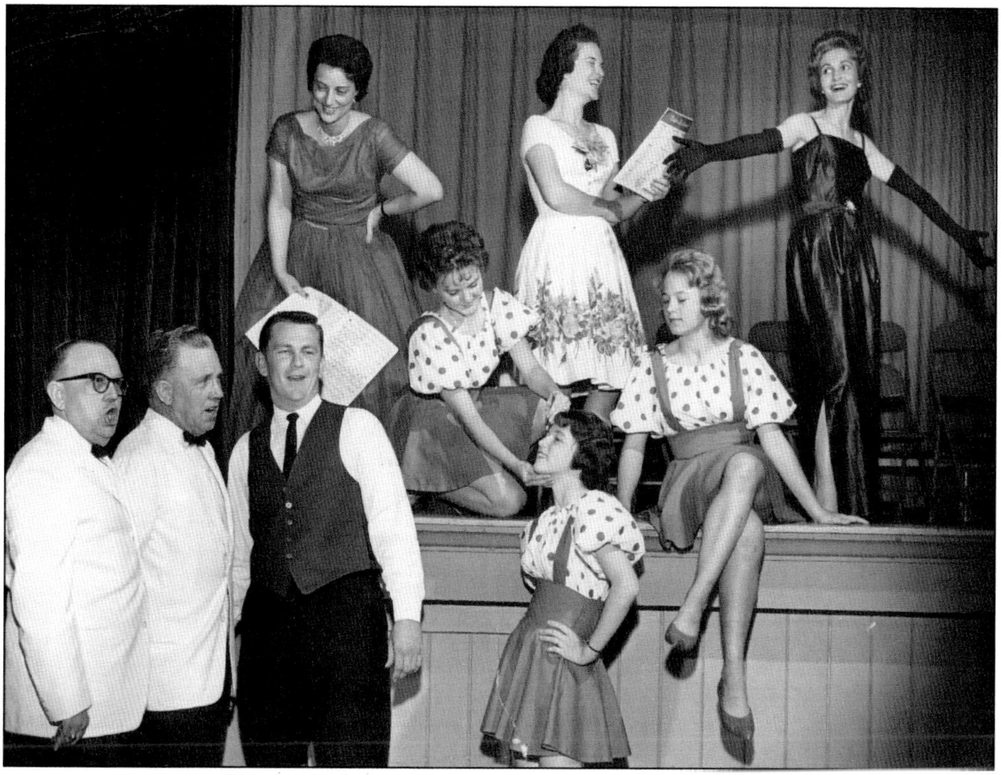

The West Memphis Kiwanis Club sponsored the Kiwanis Kut-Ups, shown here in 1963, to provide entertainment at various venues to raise money for charitable organizations. Over the years, several clubs and fraternal organizations have been active in West Memphis to assist with community and charitable needs.

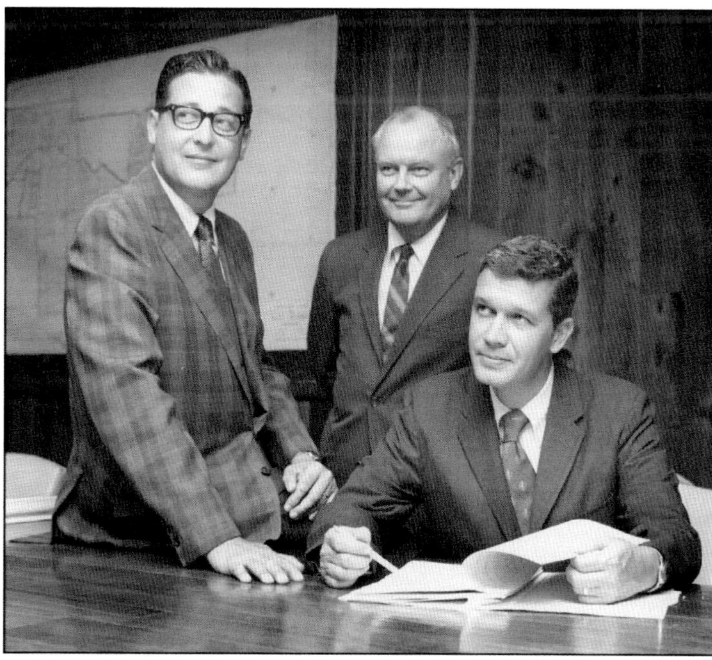

The West Memphis Community Chest was a charitable fundraising organization that collected money from local businesses and individuals, then distributed it to community projects. Photographed here are, from left to right, the 1969 officers: Jack Hogan, Richard Scruggs, and Patrick Kelly Magruder Sr.

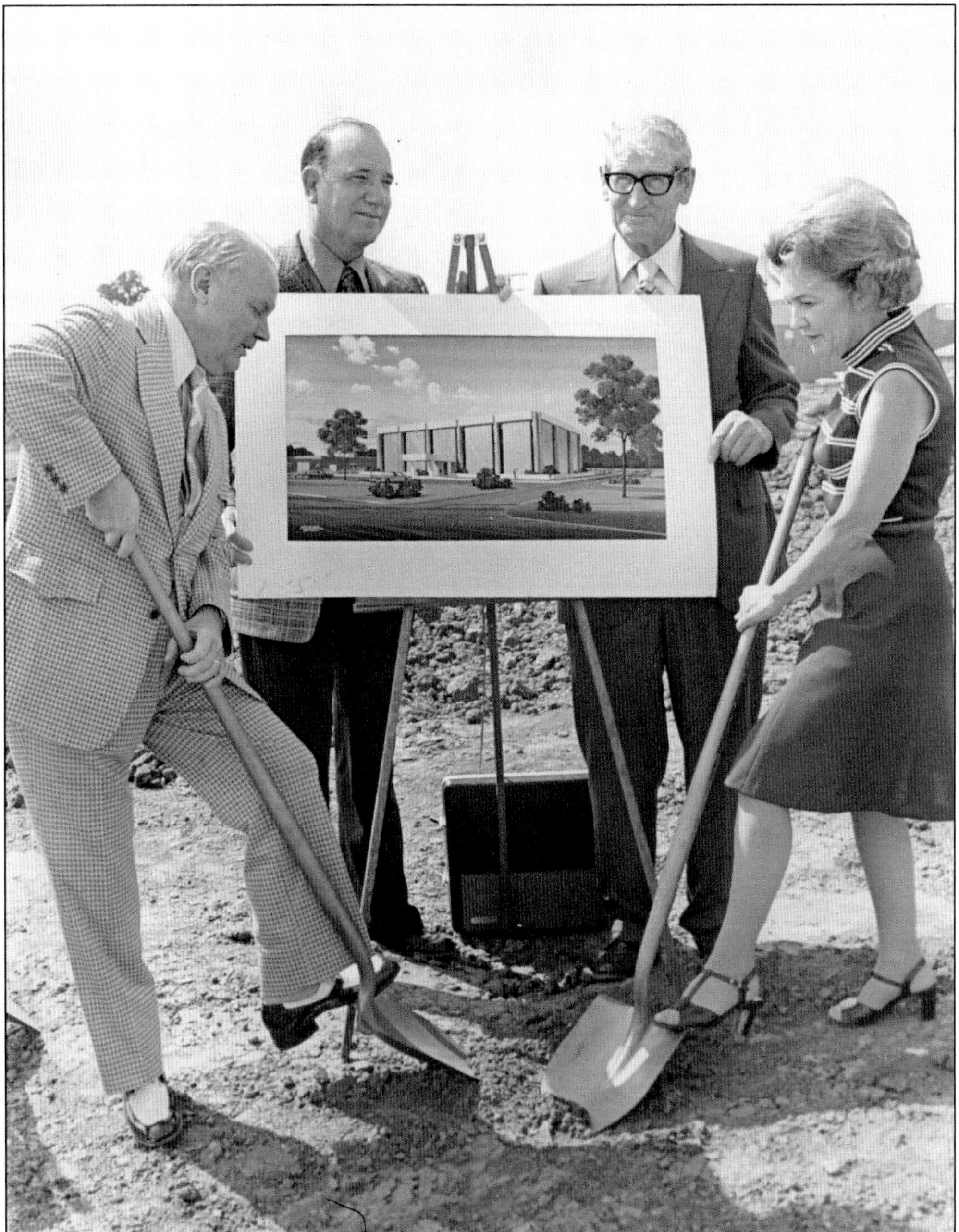

In 1974, the citizens of West Memphis elected Joyce Ferguson as the first female mayor. Ferguson, who also had the distinction of being the first female mayor of a first-class city in the state of Arkansas, held this position for two terms, from 1975 to 1982. This 1975 photograph was taken at the ground breaking for the R.F. Scruggs Building near Crittenden Memorial Hospital. Pictured are, from left to right, Richard Scruggs, Judge Jack Brawley, L.H. Polk, and Mayor Joyce Ferguson.

Three

City and Community

Logging was the first permanent industry in West Memphis, as established by Zack Bragg when he opened his sawmill in 1914. The following year, the Bolz Cooperage Plant began operations on South Eighth Street. In 1923, the Federal Compress and Warehouse Company built a large facility that occupied the south side of Broadway, between the Burlington Railroad and Seventh Street. These three early businesses ushered the beginning of the city of West Memphis and formed its earliest core.

In 1922, Highways 61 and 70, both initially cleared in 1917, were paved from the levee to Marion, and Highway 70 was completely paved to Lehi, Arkansas, by 1926. The names Broadway and Missouri Street were officially adopted in 1936. The completion of these two major segments brought a surge of automobile traffic through areas that had previously been impossible to transverse. Future businesses in West Memphis developed along these two routes, not only because of the heavy automobile traffic, but also because these were the only two paved streets in West Memphis for several years. At one point during the 1930s, there were 28 cafés and service stations within a two-mile stretch along Broadway and Missouri Street, which primarily catered to travelers.

In 1951, a bypass was completed between the levee and Highway 61 to divert northbound traffic away from the center of West Memphis. Interstate 55, which later extended and improved this bypass route, was completed between the Memphis-Arkansas Bridge and Turrell, Arkansas, in 1958. In December 1962, Interstate 40 opened between Missouri Street and Lehi, and for the first time, neither eastbound nor westbound motorists were forced to travel through the center of West Memphis along Broadway. With this traffic shift came a greatly diminished demand by motorists for many of the previously well-established businesses. As a consequence, West Memphis's downtown area began to decline as more businesses closed or migrated near the new interstate system.

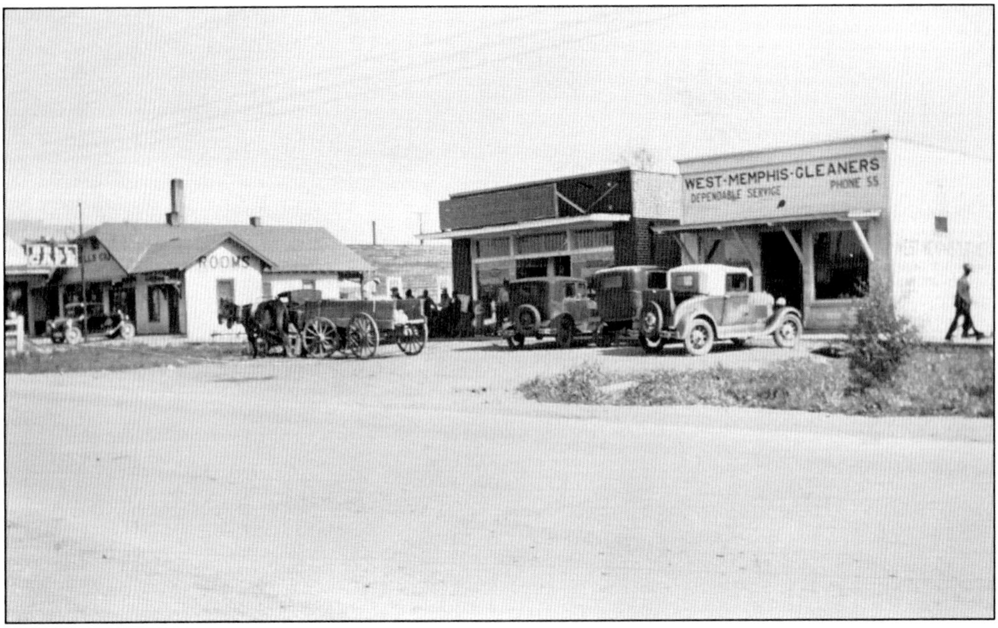

This 1932 photograph shows the south side of the 300 block of East Broadway. Bell Café is visible on the left, and West Memphis Cleaners is located on the right. The center business is J.G. Fields Grocery.

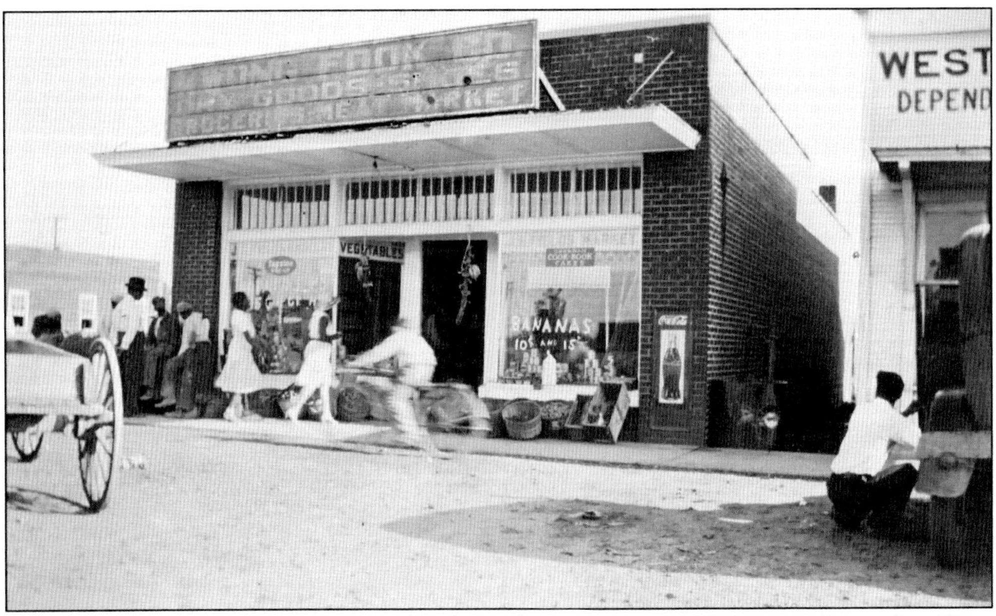

J.G. Fields Grocery was one of several independent grocery establishments located in West Memphis during the 1930s. In addition to small grocery stores, shops dedicated to the sale of meat, fish, fruits, and vegetables, respectively, were also located along Broadway and Missouri Street. (Courtesy of Michael Finger.)

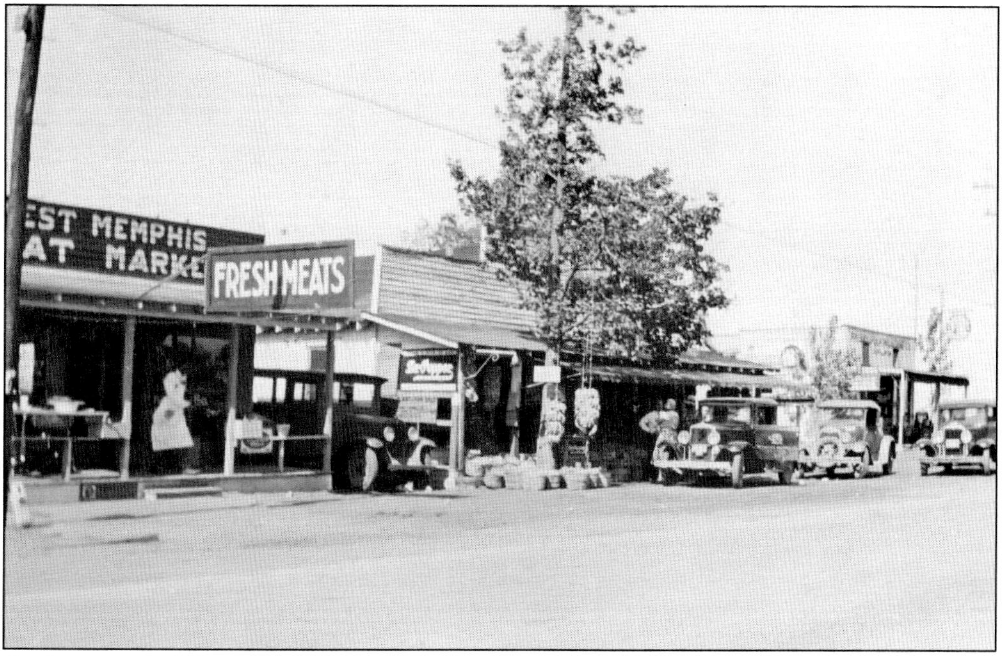

At the center of this 1932 photograph is the West Memphis Fruit Store, located at 720 East Broadway. Later that same year, the West Memphis Meat Market, shown on the left, was torn down and replaced with the Little Building by Dan Little that still stands at 716 East Broadway.

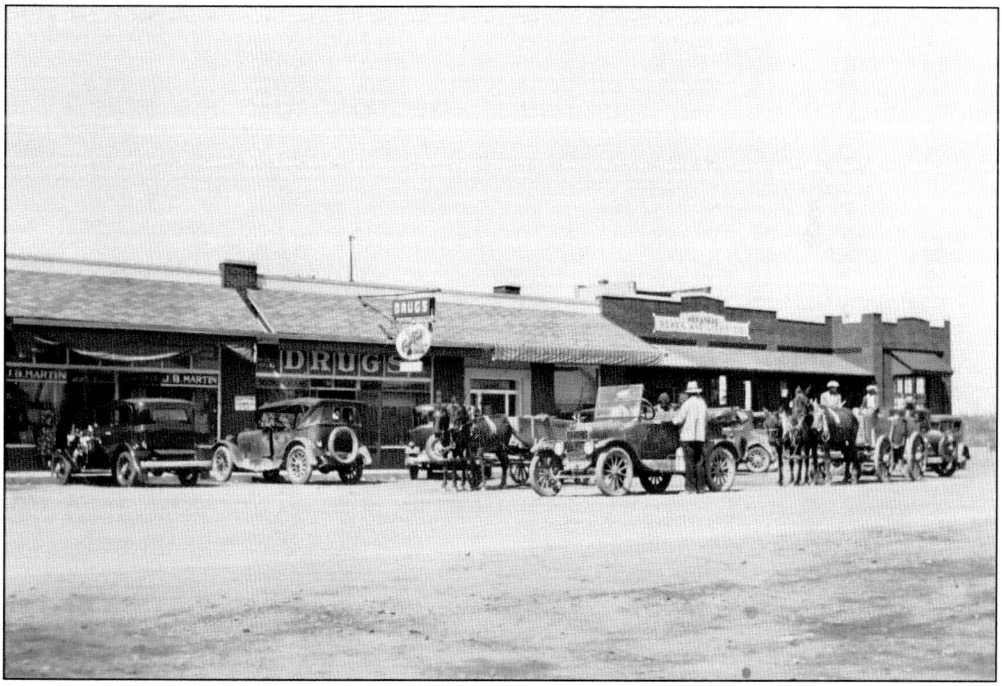

The building on the left originally housed the Bank of West Memphis as well as other retail shops. In 1940, this building became Spotts drugstore. The building on the right, originally the Arkansas Power and Light facility, has been home to the Delta Ice Company since 1942. (Courtesy of Michael Finger.)

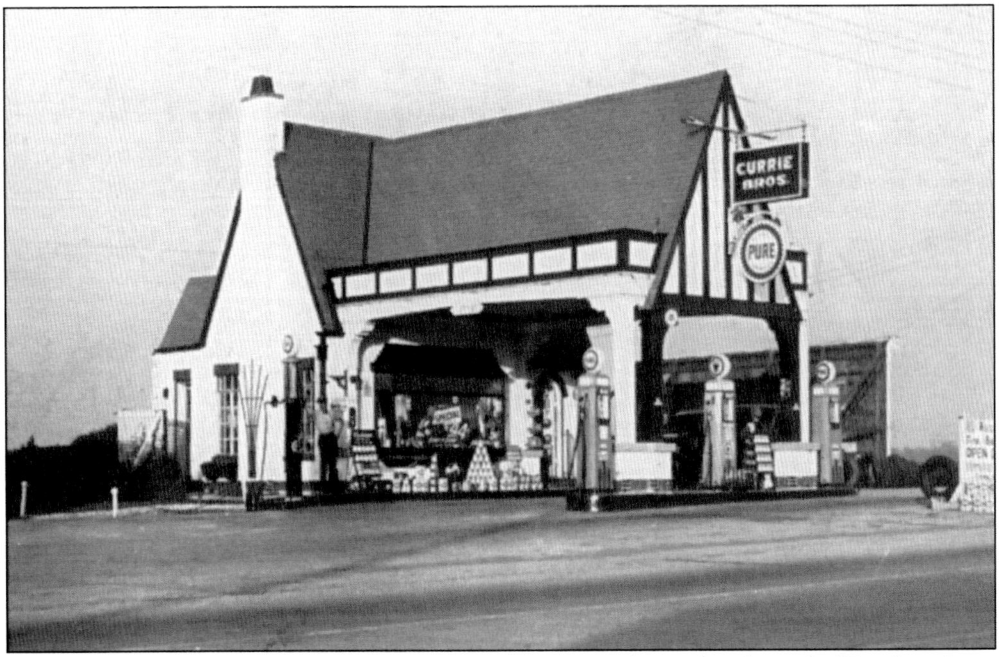

This 1939 photograph depicts Currie Brothers service station located at the end of East Broadway, near the levee. Before the construction of the interstate system, both westbound and eastbound motorists were forced to travel on Highway 70 through West Memphis along Broadway.

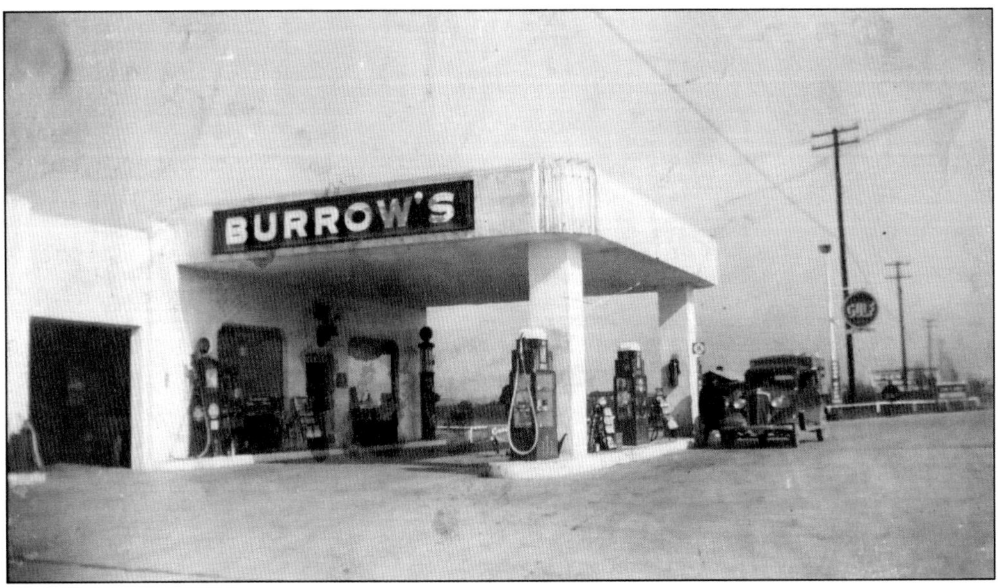

Burrow's service station, located on East Broadway, was owned and operated by Jim Burrow, who was also a deputy sheriff for Crittenden County. The station, photographed here in 1941, was located near the current location of Pancho's Restaurant. (Courtesy of Dixie Ball Gordon.)

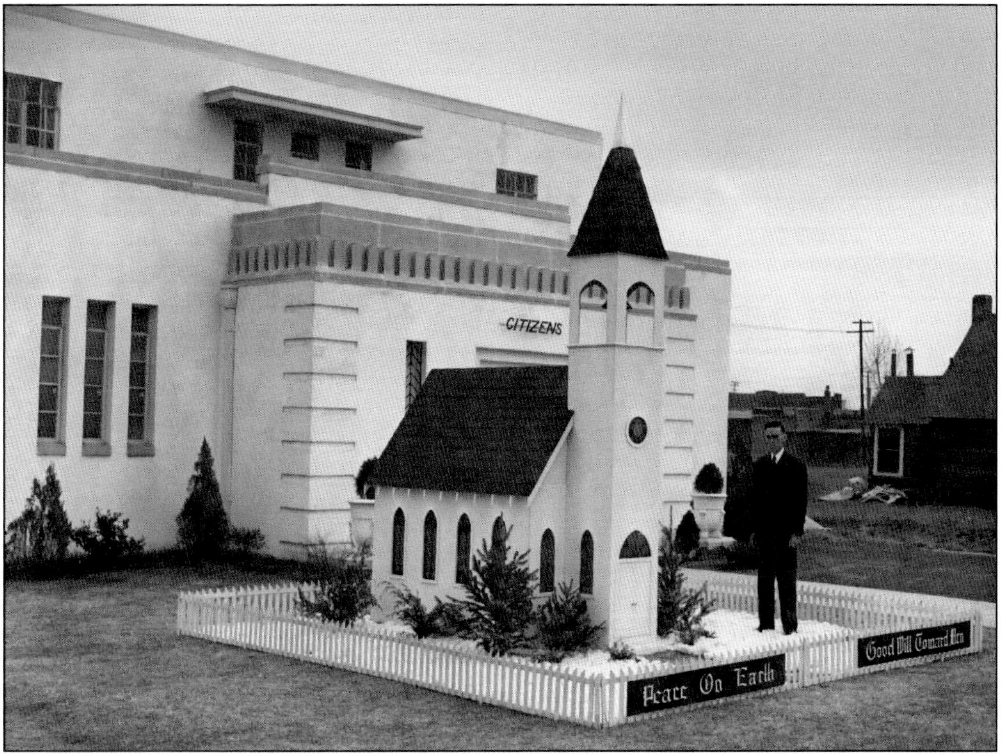

Established in 1938 by James A. Johnson Sr., Citizens Funeral Home was West Memphis's first funeral parlor, the original location of which was on the southeast corner of Missouri Street and Bond Avenue before moving to Pine Street in 1962. This photograph shows Johnson standing beside a Christmas display in 1938.

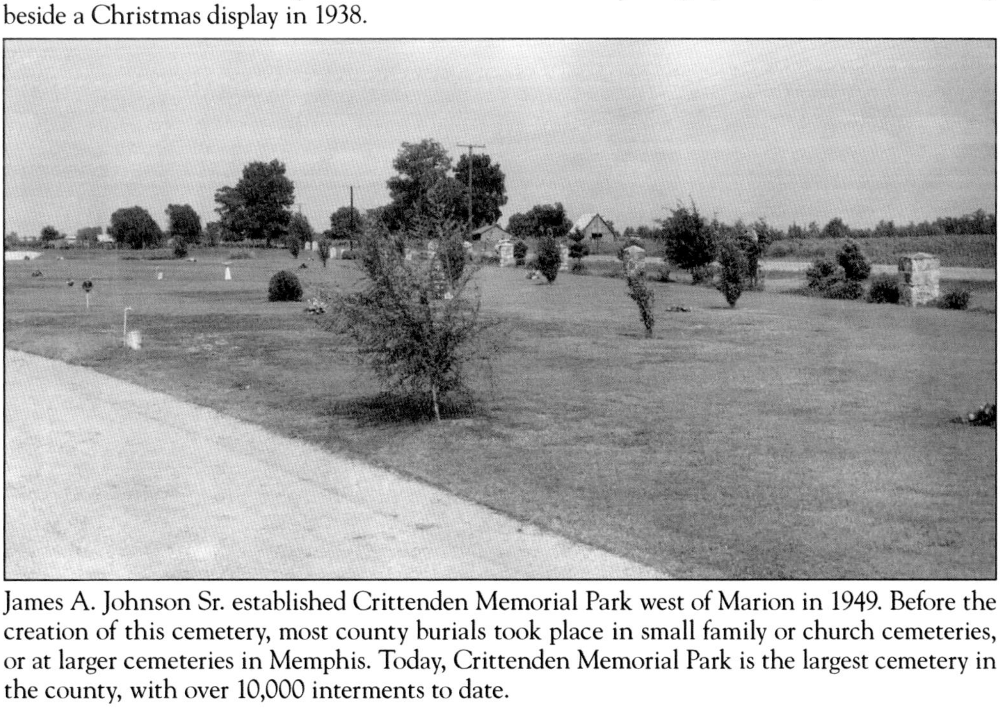

James A. Johnson Sr. established Crittenden Memorial Park west of Marion in 1949. Before the creation of this cemetery, most county burials took place in small family or church cemeteries, or at larger cemeteries in Memphis. Today, Crittenden Memorial Park is the largest cemetery in the county, with over 10,000 interments to date.

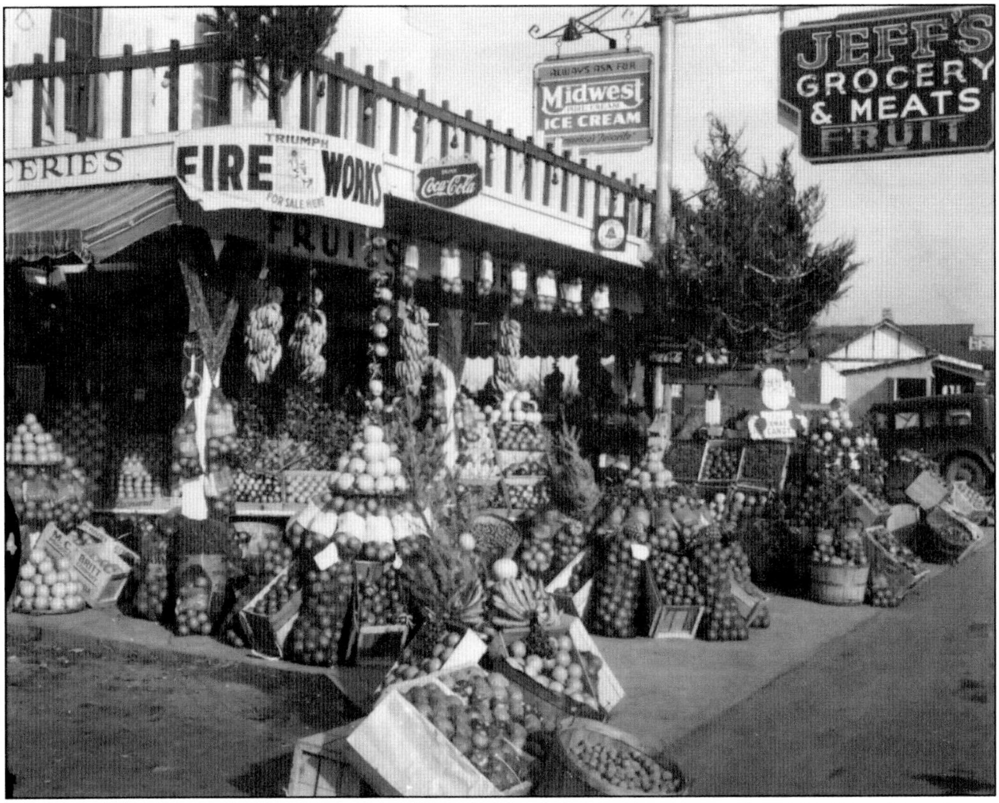

Jeff's Grocery & Meats, housed within the Jeffords Building, was located at 1204 East Broadway. This photograph from 1939 shows the lavish displays of fruits and vegetables outside the store, the proprietor of which was A.W. Jeffords.

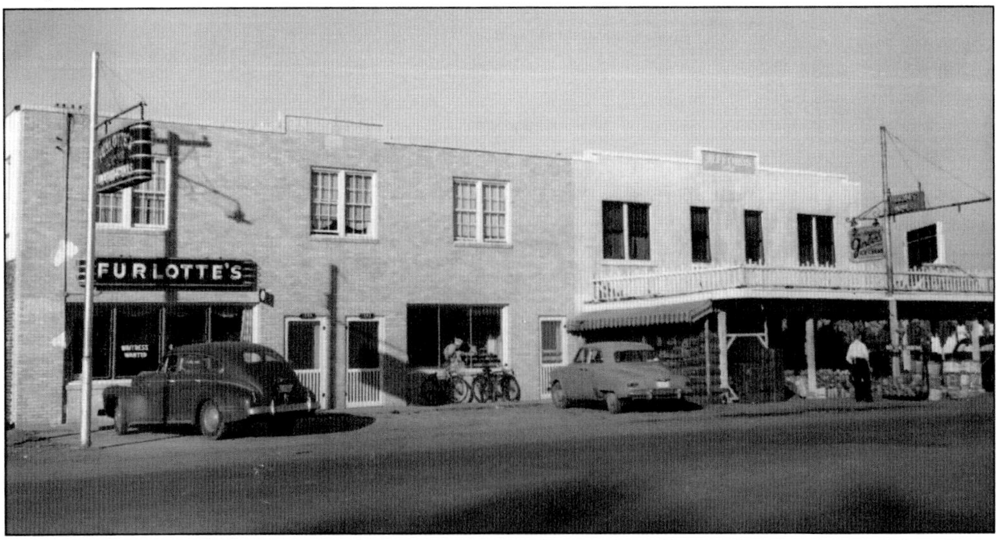

The Jeffords Building, consisting of two sections, was located on the northeast corner of Broadway and Twelfth Street. The first section was built in 1937 and housed Jeff's Grocery. In 1946, a new section was constructed on the left and was home to Furlotte's restaurant for several years. Both sections of the building burned in 1978.

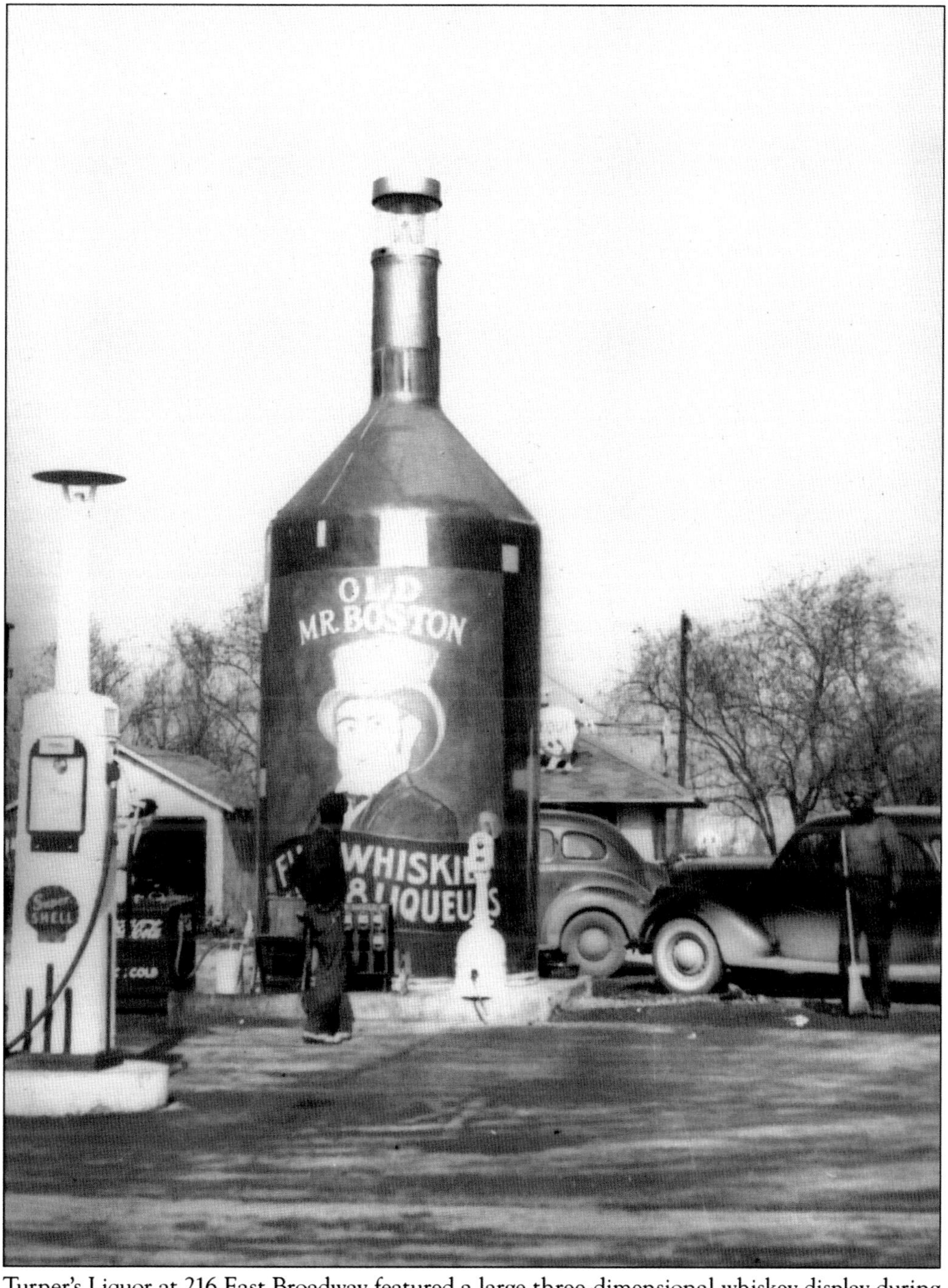

Turner's Liquor at 216 East Broadway featured a large three-dimensional whiskey display during the 1930s, demonstrating the typical roadside advertisement of the era. Next door was Broadway's first hotel, originally named the West Memphis Inn, then later, in 1934, the Turner Hotel. Both the liquor store and hotel were torn down in 1941 to make room for a new building that housed Watkins Café for many years.

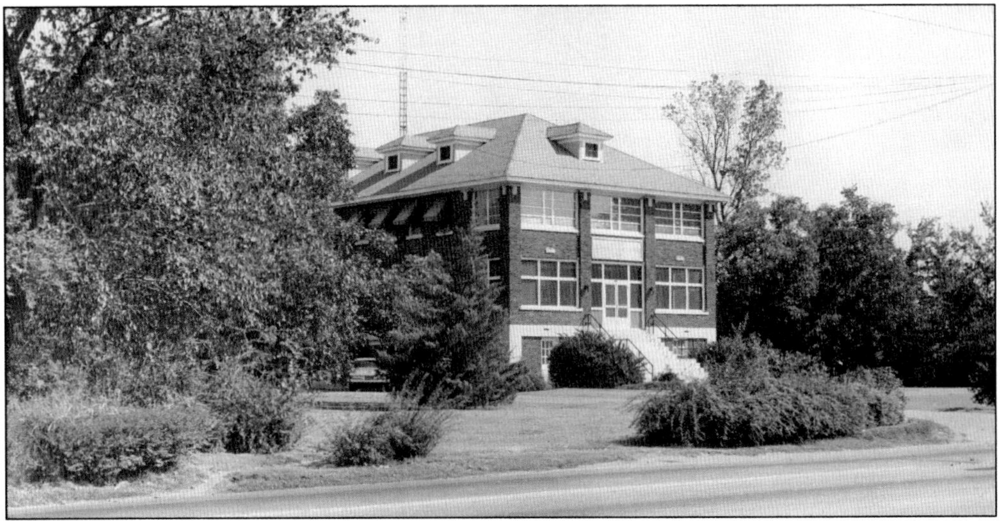

The St. Francis Levee District built its second headquarters at the northeast corner of East Broadway and Ingram Boulevard in 1929. Contrary to popular belief, the building was not elevated to ensure against a levee breach, but rather, it was raised to save money by placing garage space below the first floor of the structure. In 1970, the levee district moved to a new building on Interstate 40 at Ingram Boulevard.

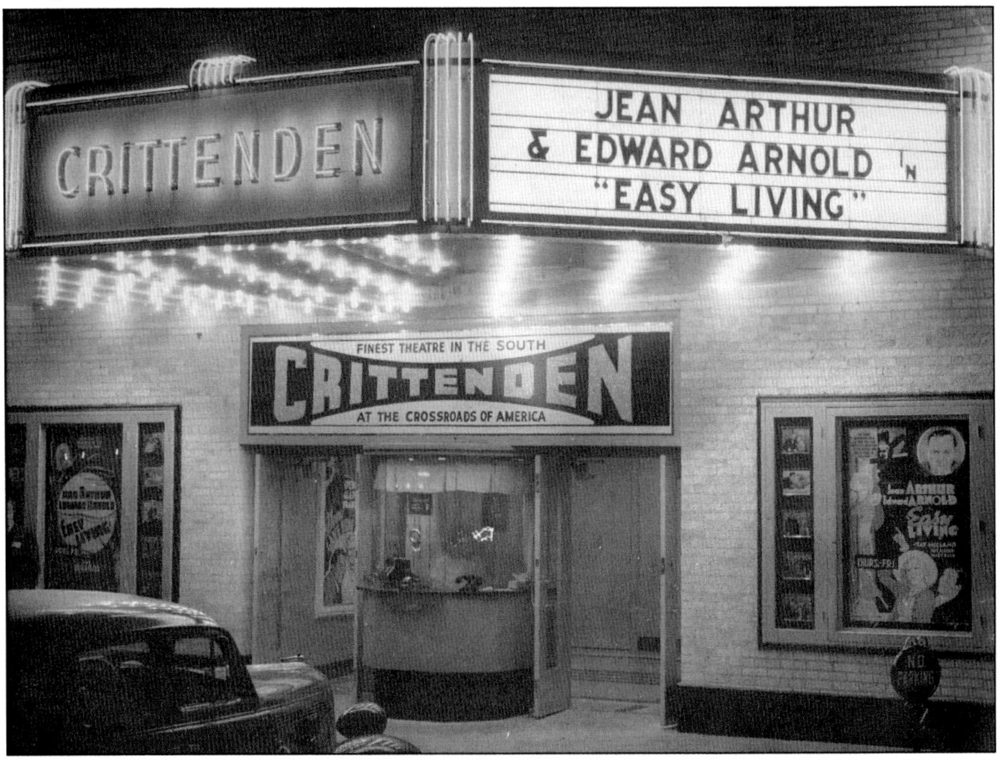

The Crittenden Theatre opened in 1937 and was located at 104 Missouri Street, beside Hundhausen's Grocery. At the time, it was considered East Arkansas's finest theater. The 750-seat theater closed in 1954, and the building was converted to a short-lived bowling alley in the late 1950s. The structure was razed in 2007 after serving various capacities.

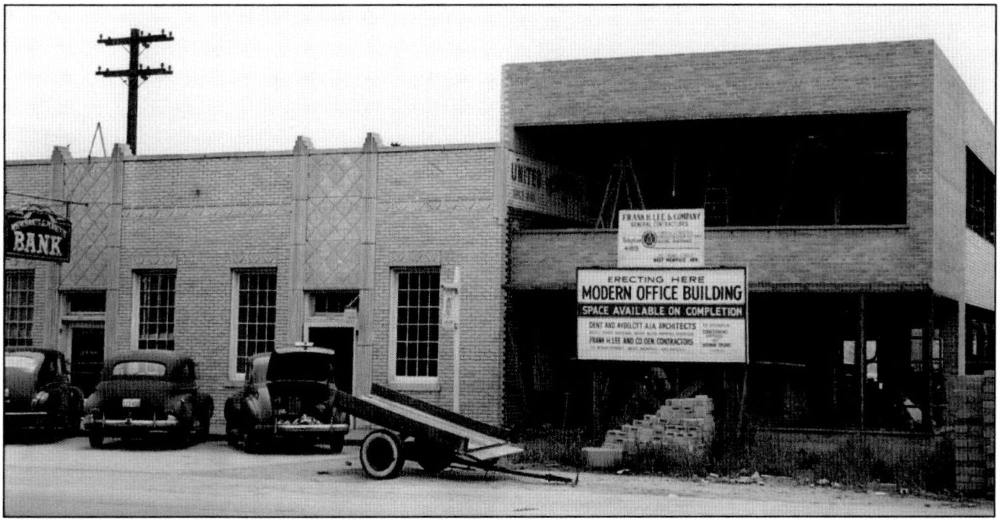

Merchants and Planters Bank, shown on the left, was established in 1940. In 1946, a new addition was built adjacent to the bank at 231 East Broadway to house the KWEM radio station. The station helped develop the early careers of musicians such as B.B. King, Howlin' Wolf, Johnny Cash, and Elvis Presley, who played live over the airwaves. Several great artists had their first opportunity to be broadcast through KWEM's offer of 15 minutes of airtime for a $25 fee.

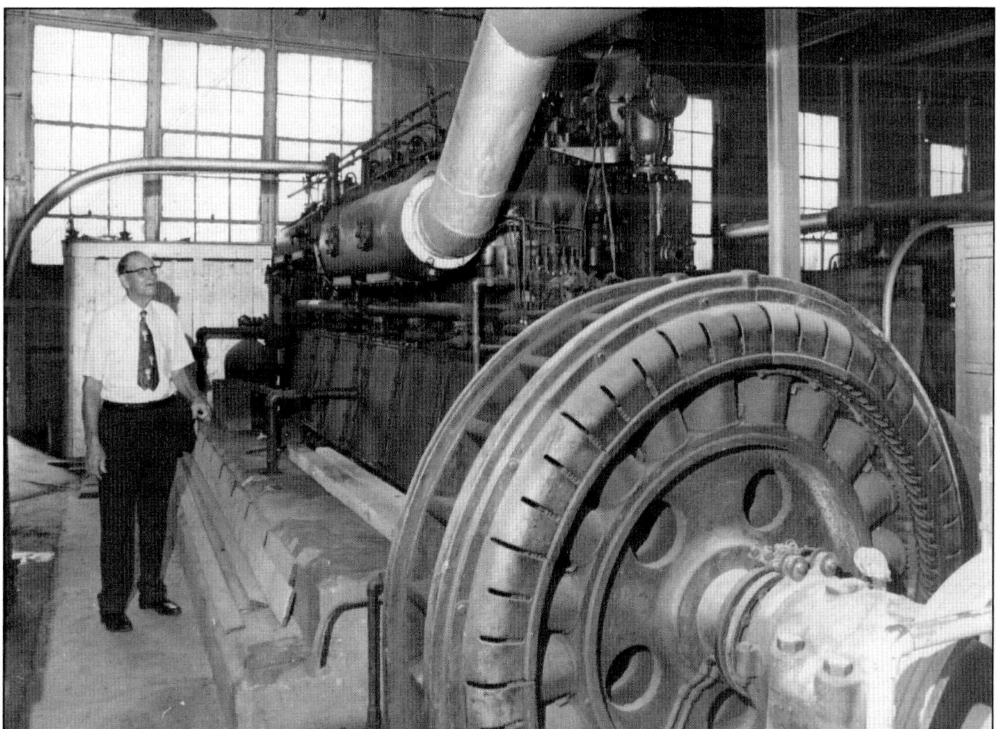
In 1935, power for the water plant on South Second Street was produced using two World War I submarine engines. The City of West Memphis's ownership of the utility company has resulted in low utility rates for businesses and residents since 1940. The engines in this photograph remained in operation until the 1980s.

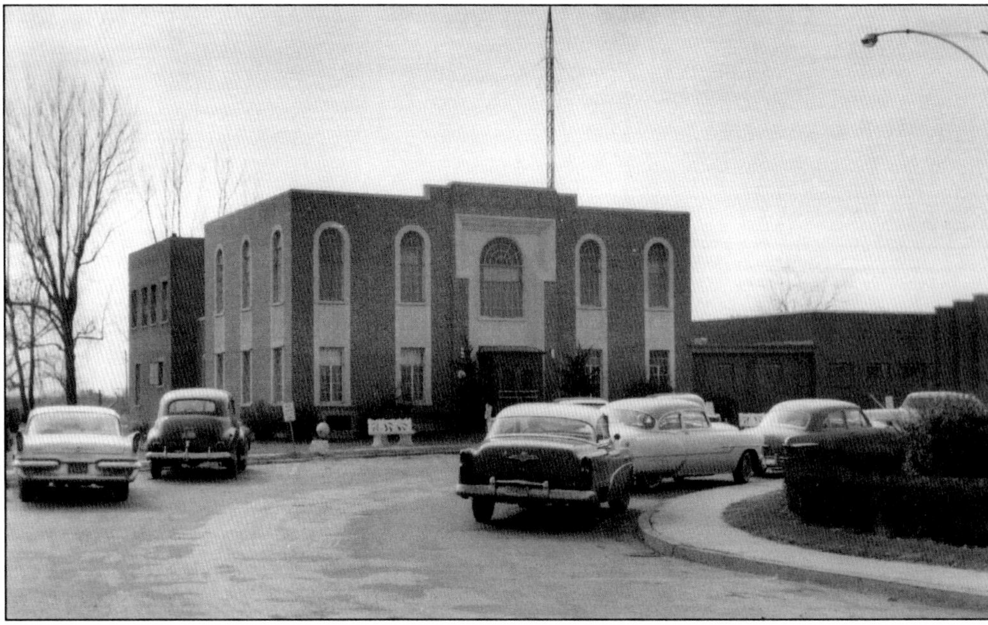

The first city hall in West Memphis was constructed in 1939 with funds from the Works Progress Administration, which was part of Pres. Franklin D. Roosevelt's New Deal program. This building was used as the city hall until a new structure was built in 1975 on South Redding Street. Presently, the former city hall building is used by the West Memphis Municipal Court.

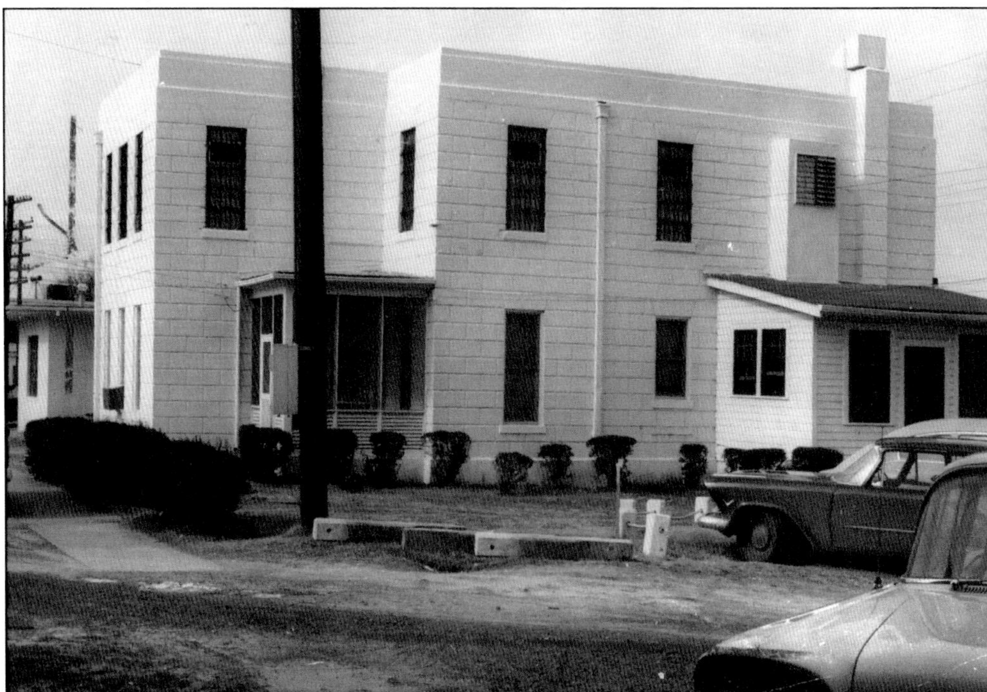

The original city hall building also served as the headquarters of the police department and the municipal court. Additions were made for a new courtroom in 1955 as well as a city jail, shown here, in 1961.

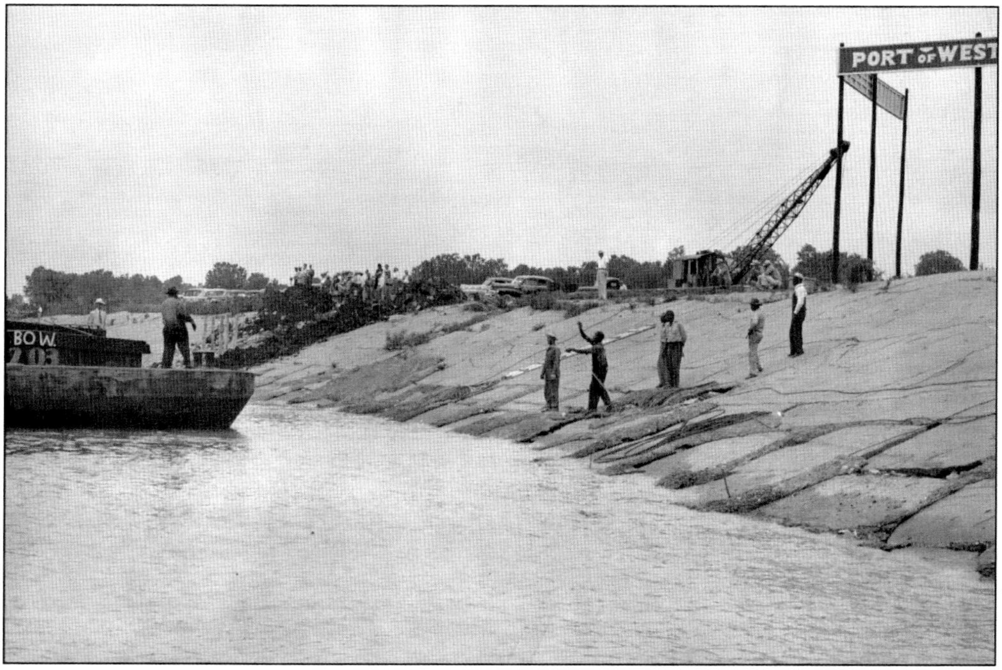

The West Memphis River Port, located at the south end of Eighth Street, opened in 1948. This facility continues to allow barge freight on the Mississippi River to be loaded and unloaded at West Memphis.

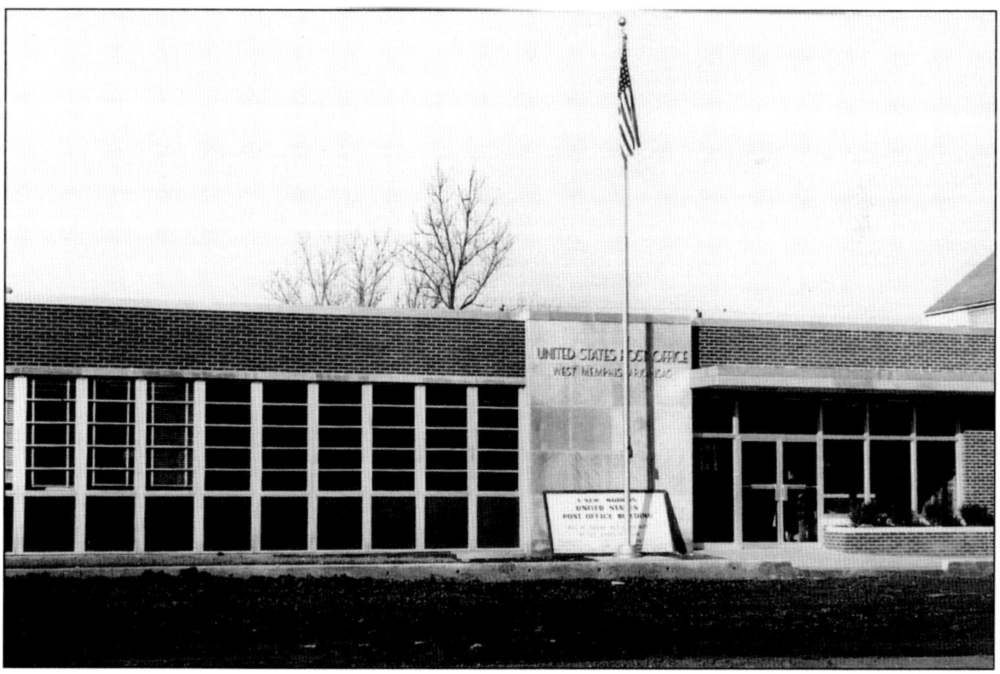

Although West Memphis has had a post office since 1920, the first structure constructed solely for that purpose opened in 1957 and was located on the southwest corner of Missouri Street and Bond Avenue. This facility remained in use until a new post office was constructed on East Cooper Avenue in 1978.

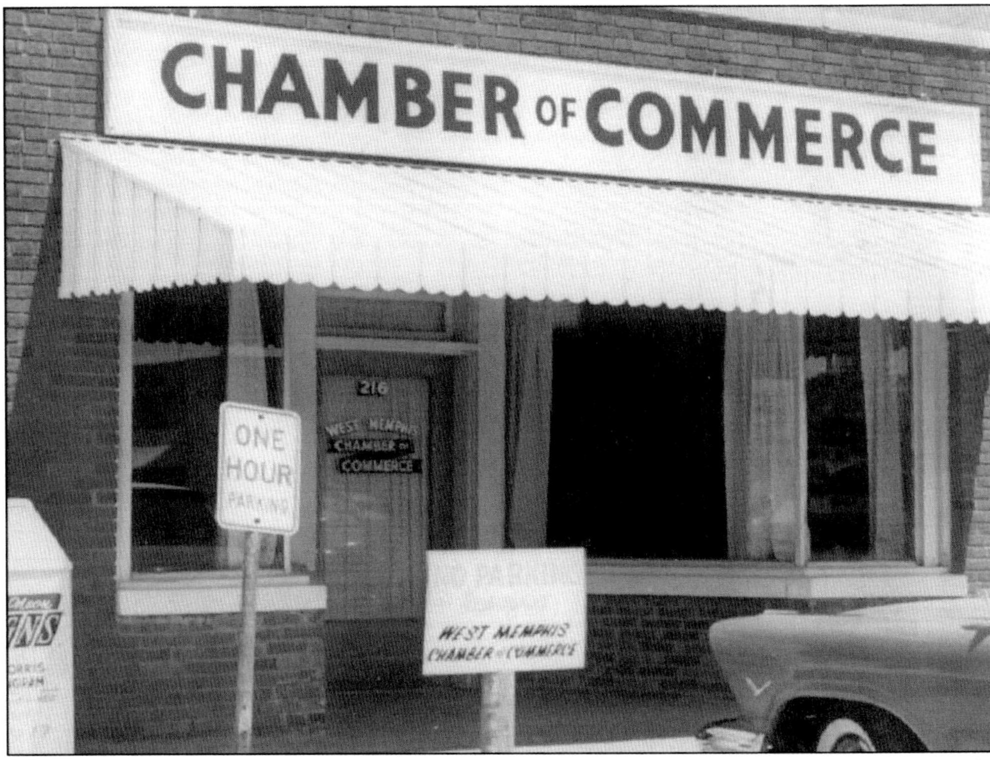

The West Memphis Chamber of Commerce has been in continuous operation since 1945. The chamber was initially located at 216 East Broadway before moving to its present location at 108 West Broadway in 1962. (Courtesy of West Memphis Chamber of Commerce.)

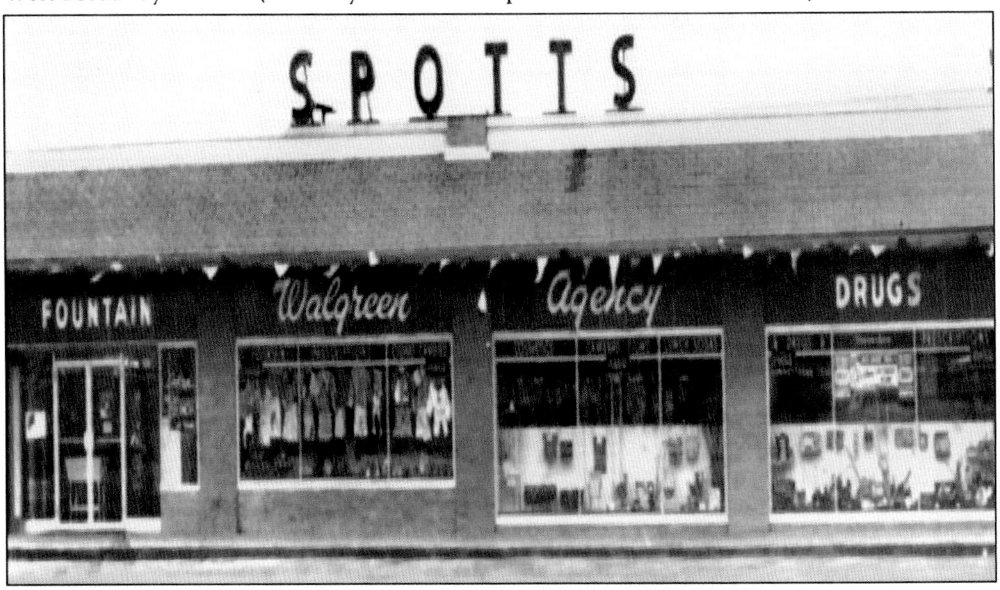

Spotts drugstore opened in 1940 at 108 East Broadway and occupied a building that was constructed in 1928 to house the Bank of West Memphis. For over 40 years, the drugstore was also the location of a soda fountain that served three generations of West Memphians before its closure in the early 1980s.

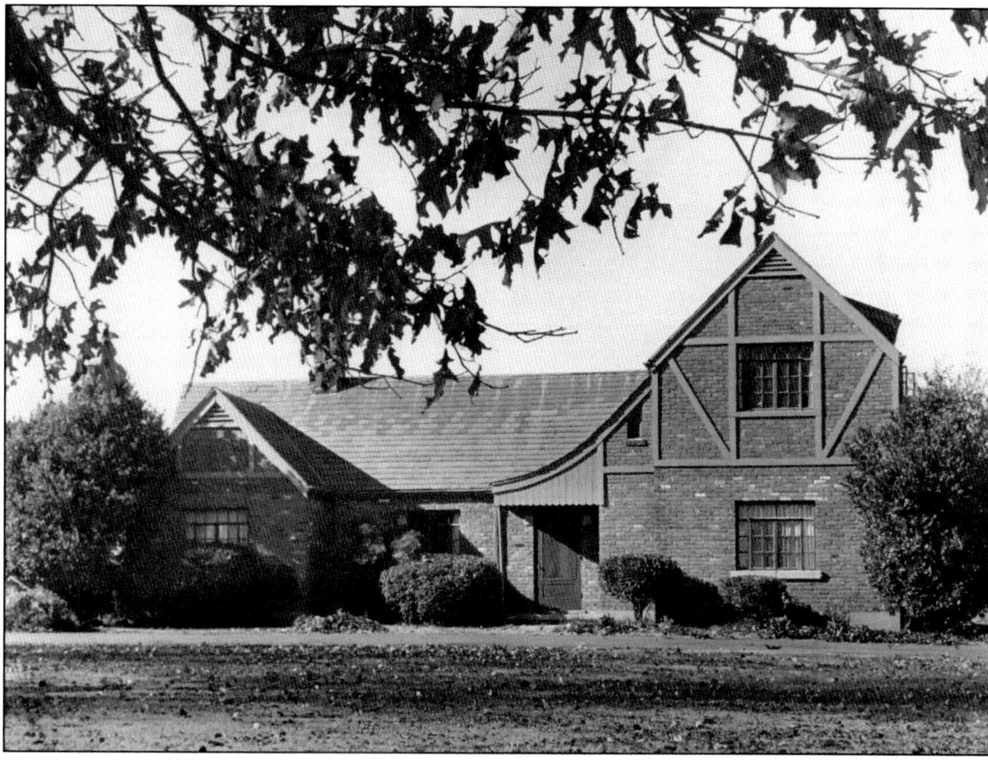

This house at 213 West Barton Avenue was constructed in 1933 and was the home of Sydnor Hall, the president of the then privately owned utility company. In 1946, the property was converted for use by the West Memphis Athletic Club and between 1949 and 1959 was the site of the West Memphis Country Club. The property was purchased by Holy Cross Episcopal Church in 1967 to serve as a rectory.

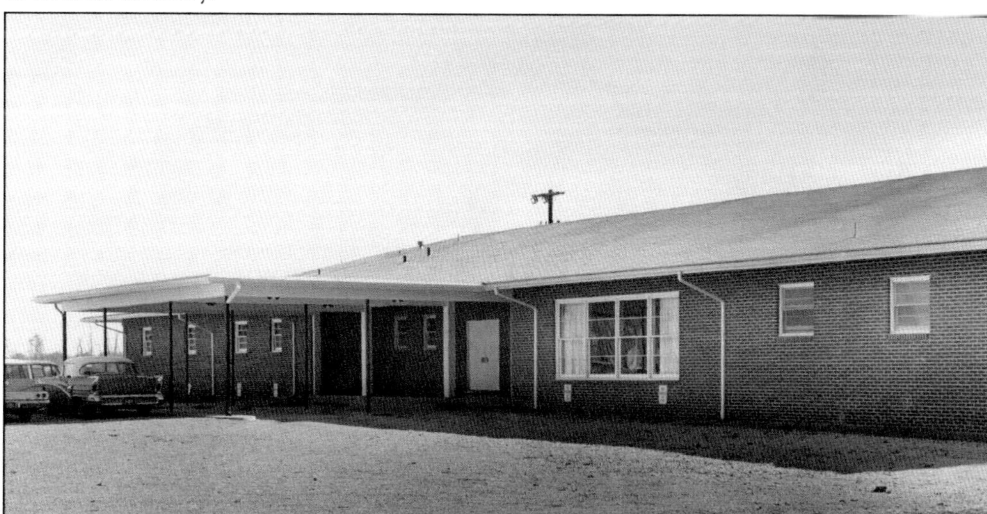

Meadowbrook Country Club was an outgrowth of the original West Memphis Country Club on West Barton Avenue. In 1959, Meadowbrook Country Club and its golf course were developed within an area where an original hardwood forest had survived removal by logging or clear-cutting earlier in the 20th century.

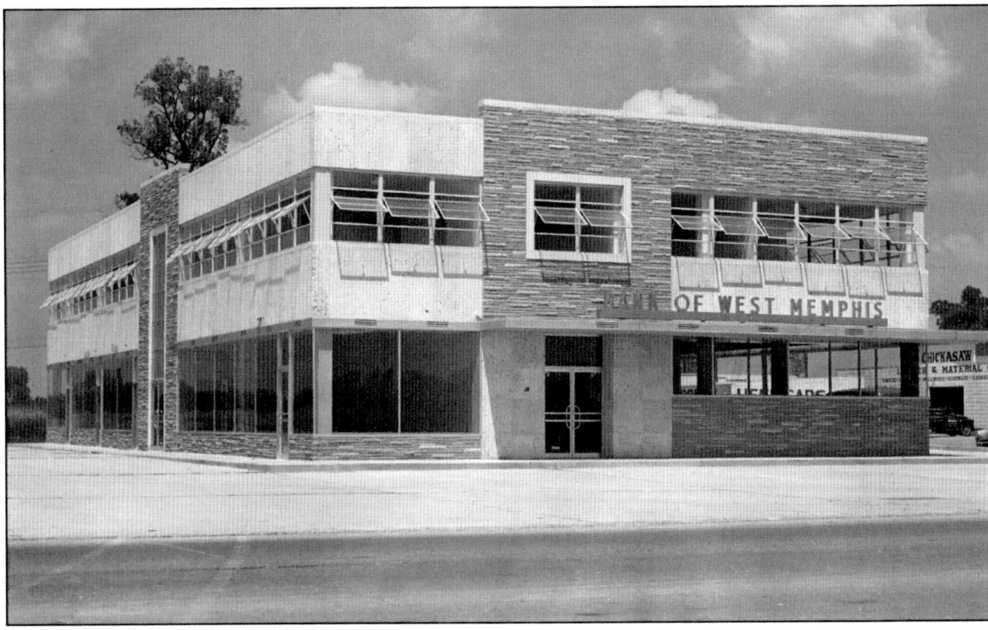

The Bank of West Memphis first opened in 1928 at 114 East Broadway, then moved to a new building at 626 East Broadway, shown here, in 1952. At the time, it was considered the most modern office building in the county. In the late 1970s, the exterior of the structure was significantly altered and updated. Since 2000, the building has been the headquarters of the West Memphis Police Department.

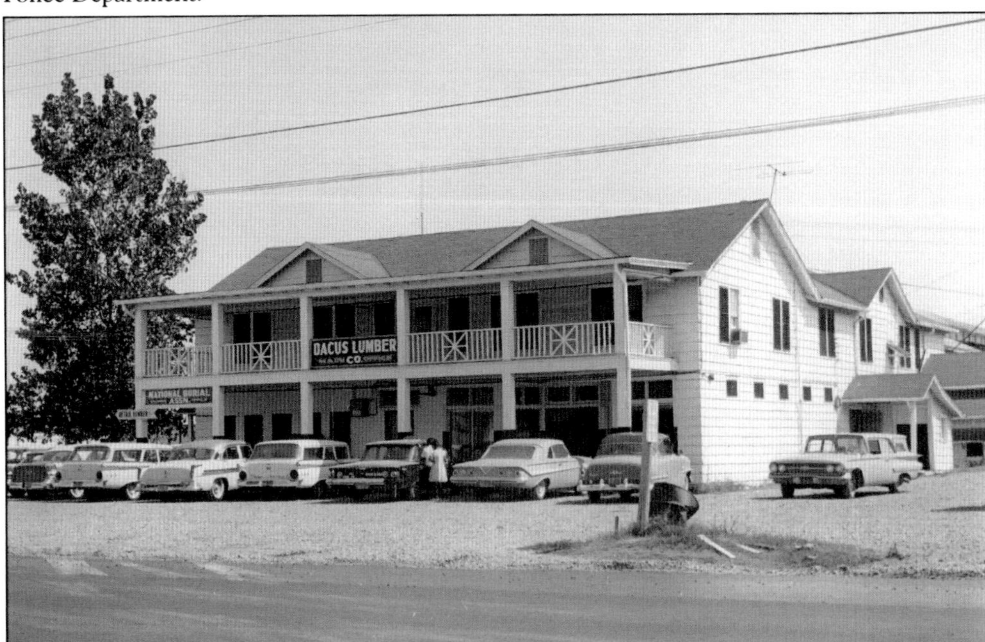

Aubrey Dacus purchased Zack Bragg's sawmill on Missouri Street in 1935 and renamed it Dacus Lumber Company. It originally occupied the eastern side of Missouri Street between the West Memphis Oil Mill and 15 Mile Bayou. Dacus Lumber Company ceased its lumber operations in 1972, and the property was sold four years later to various commercial establishments.

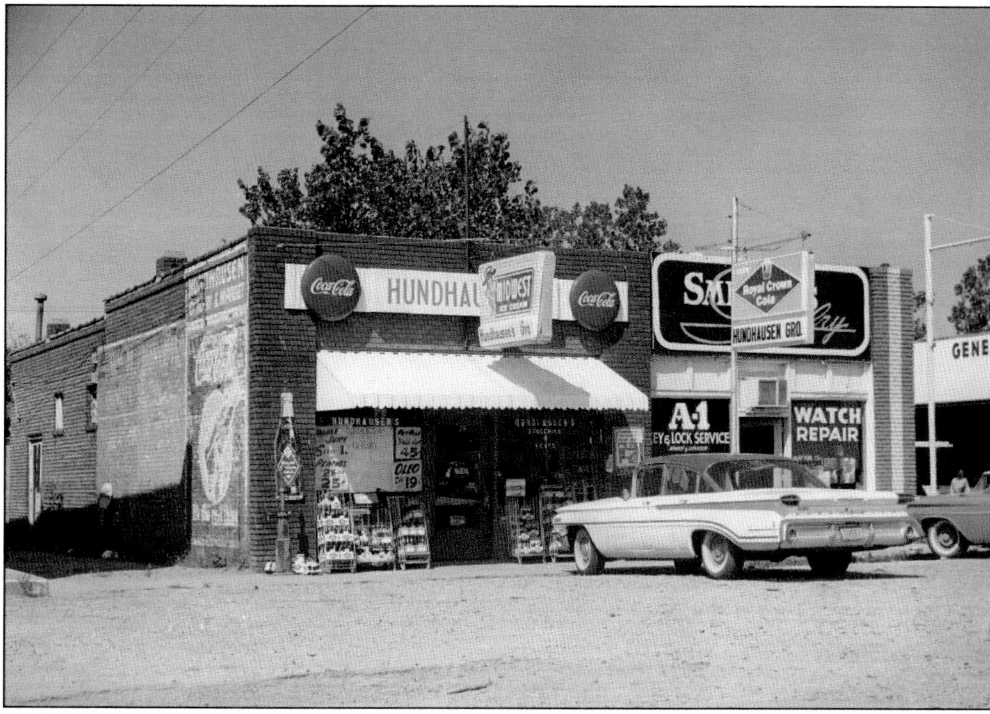

William H. Hundhausen Sr., one of West Memphis's founding fathers, operated Hundhausen's Grocery, pictured here in 1961, at its original location for nearly 40 years.

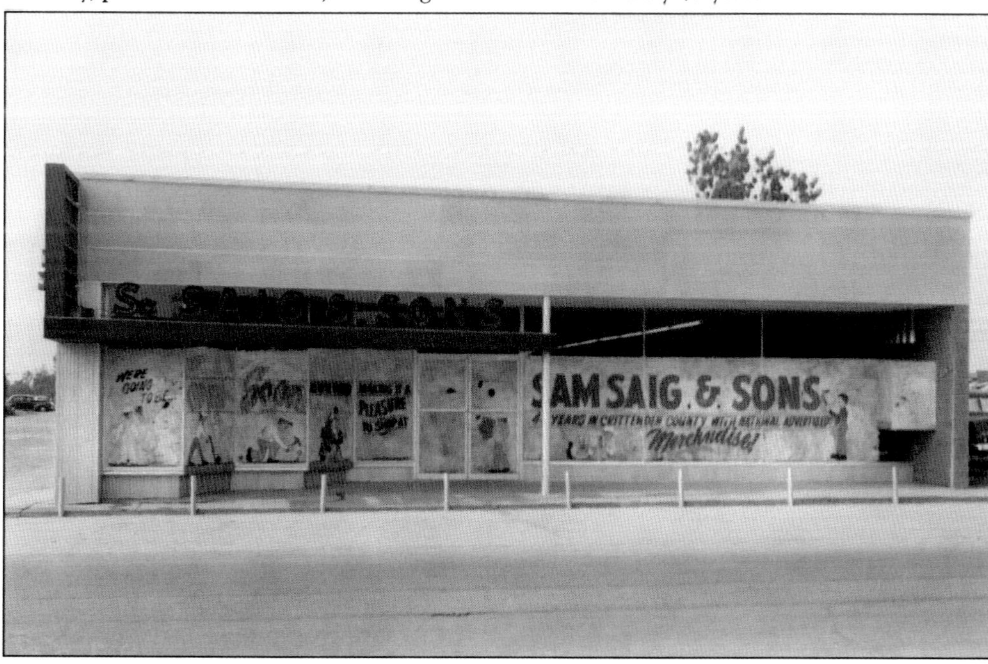

Sam Saig, an independent merchant, arrived in Crittenden County from Lebanon in 1914. Originally located in Earle, his store was later moved to West Memphis. Photographed here is the West Memphis location the week prior to its grand opening in 1955. Saig's haberdashery is the oldest-operating retail establishment in the county, marking 100 years in 2014.

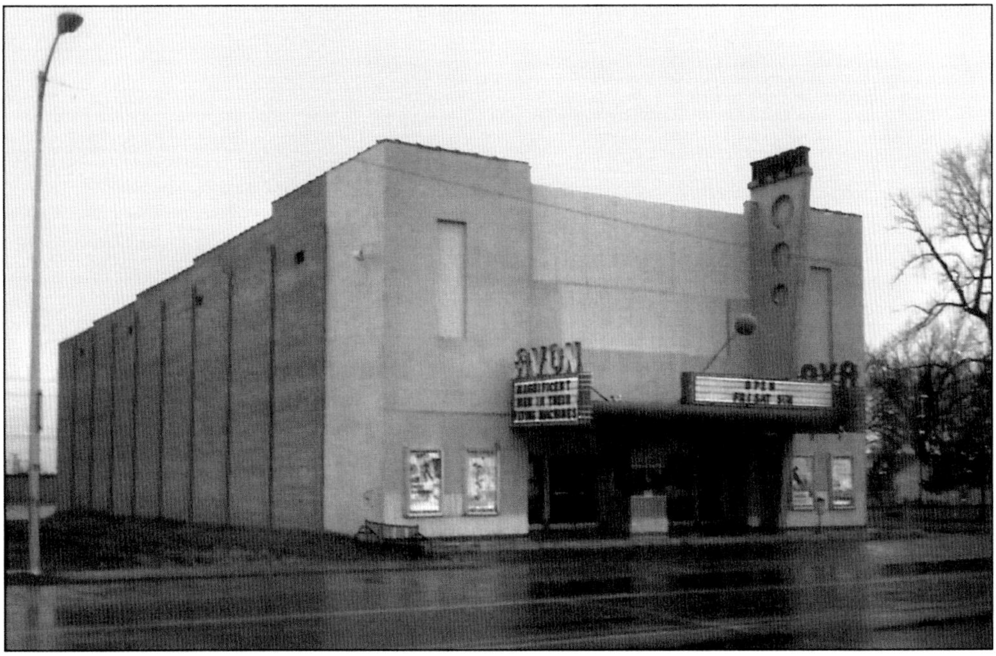

The Joy Theatre was built in 1949 on the southeast corner of Broadway and Rhodes Street. It was renamed the Avon Theatre in 1953 after being leased by Malco Theatres. The building operated as a theater until 1969 and later had multiple uses before being torn down in 1995. (Courtesy of Malco Theatres, Inc.)

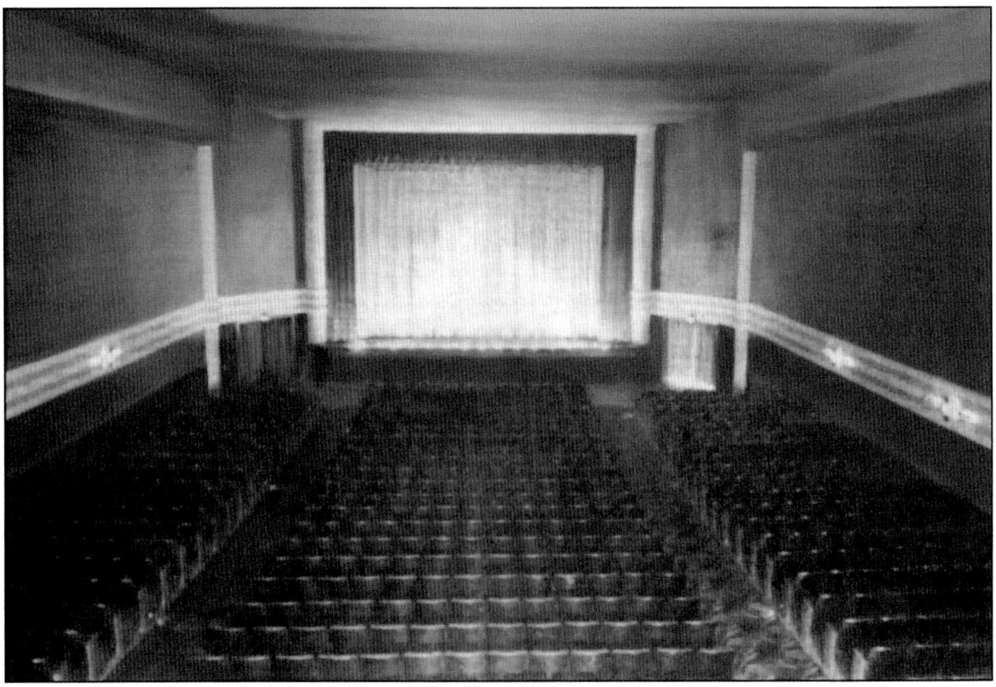

The 1,025-seat Avon Theatre remained racially segregated throughout its entire existence, even after the Civil Rights Act of 1964. In addition to being used as a movie theater, the Avon hosted live performances, including live KWEM radio broadcasts.

Perhaps the most famous person to grace the Avon's stage was Elvis Presley, who rented the theater for private performances. Elvis also had strong connections to KWEM Radio, where he made his first radio debut in 1953 as well as subsequent guest appearances. (Courtesy of Elvis Presley Enterprises, Inc.)

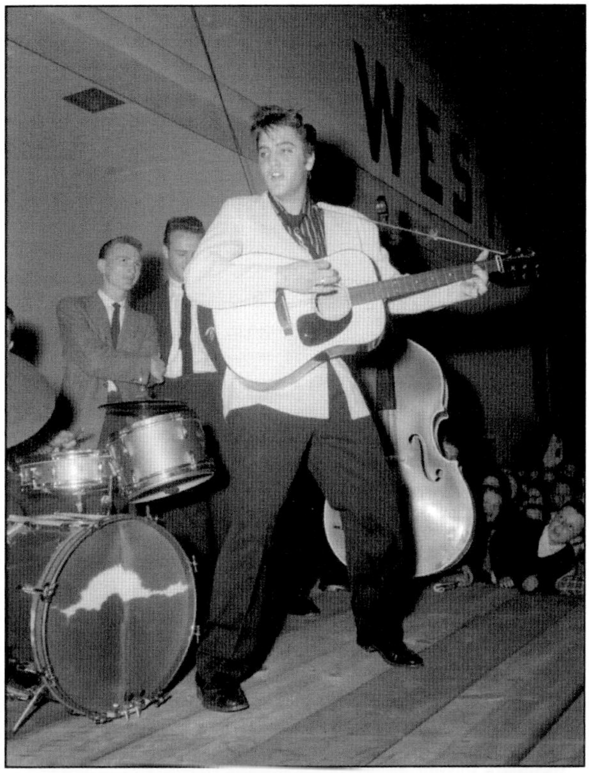

During the 1950s, several local musicians performed at the Avon Theatre for live KWEM radio broadcasts. Delta Dan and the Swamp Riders, photographed here with Dan Craft standing at right, had a loyal following in the Mid-South and performed weekly on KWEM Radio between 1948 and 1955.

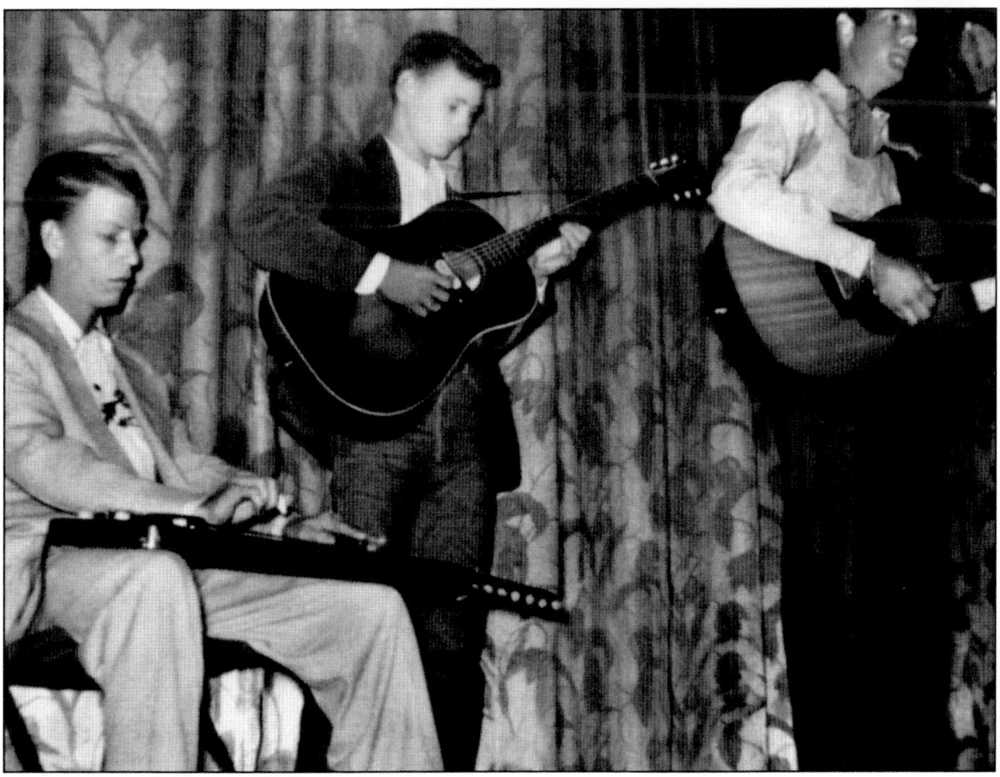

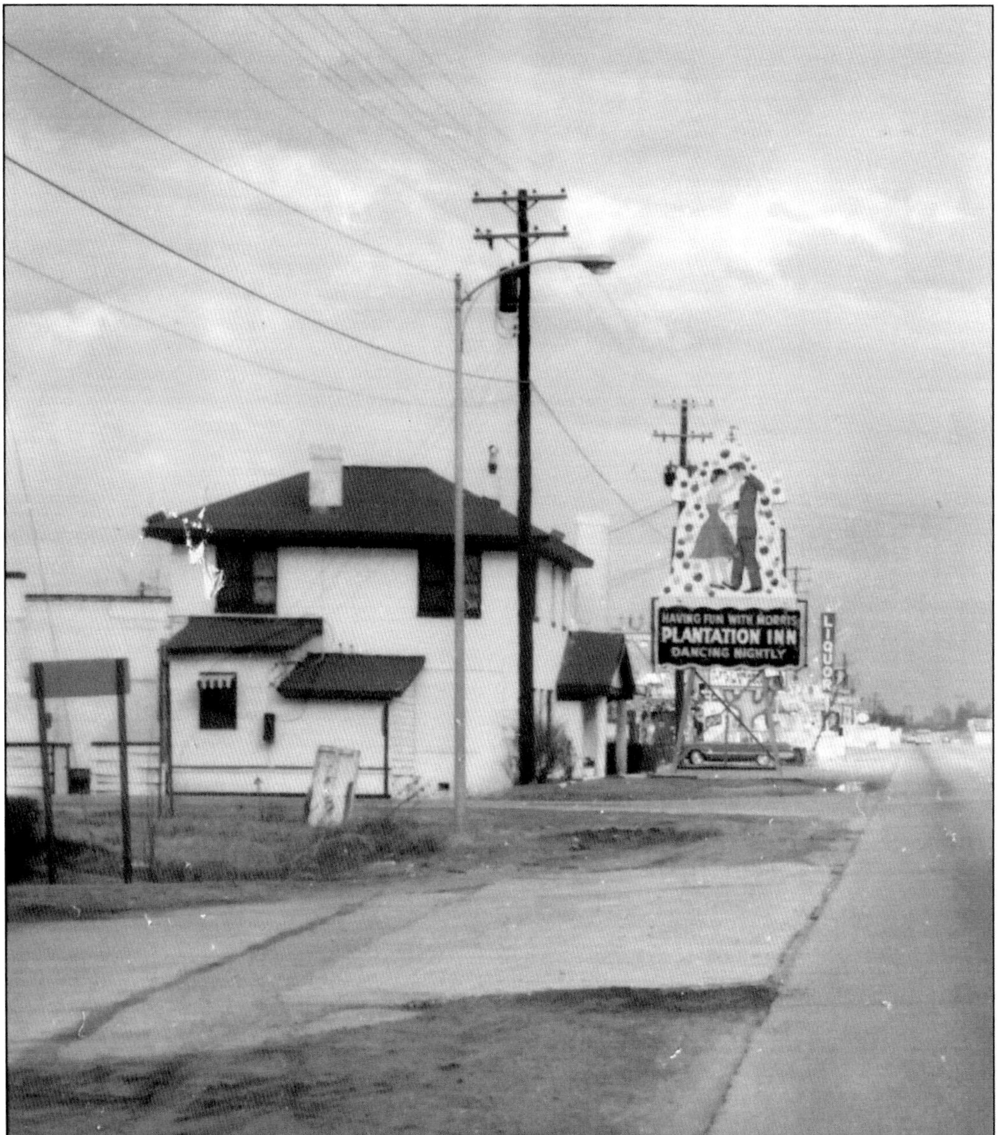

A dancing club with a well-known second-floor gambling operation, the Plantation Inn opened in 1925 on East Broadway. In 1942, the facility was purchased by Morris Berger, who later established Pancho's Mexican restaurant in 1956 and continued the Plantation Inn as a nightclub. The inn was instrumental in the early careers of musicians such as Phineas and Calvin Newbern, Willie Mitchell, and Isaac Hayes, all of whom frequently played at the Plantation Inn during the 1950s. The establishment closed in 1965, and the building was demolished the following year. Currently, the Plantation Inn's former site is a parking lot for Pancho's restaurant.

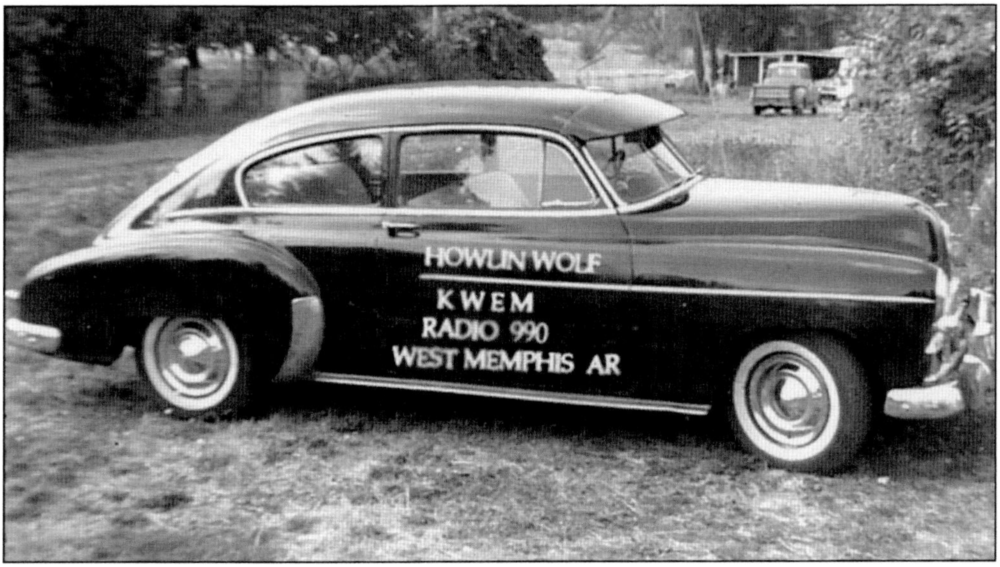

Chester A. Burnett, better known as "Howlin' Wolf," lived on South Eleventh Street in the late 1940s and early 1950s. Between 1949 and 1952, Burnett had a daily radio show on KWEM Radio. He later recorded with Sun Studio in Memphis and with Chess Records in Chicago. Burnett's recordings have been inducted into both the Grammy and the Rock and Roll Hall of Fames. (Courtesy of Dale Franklin.)

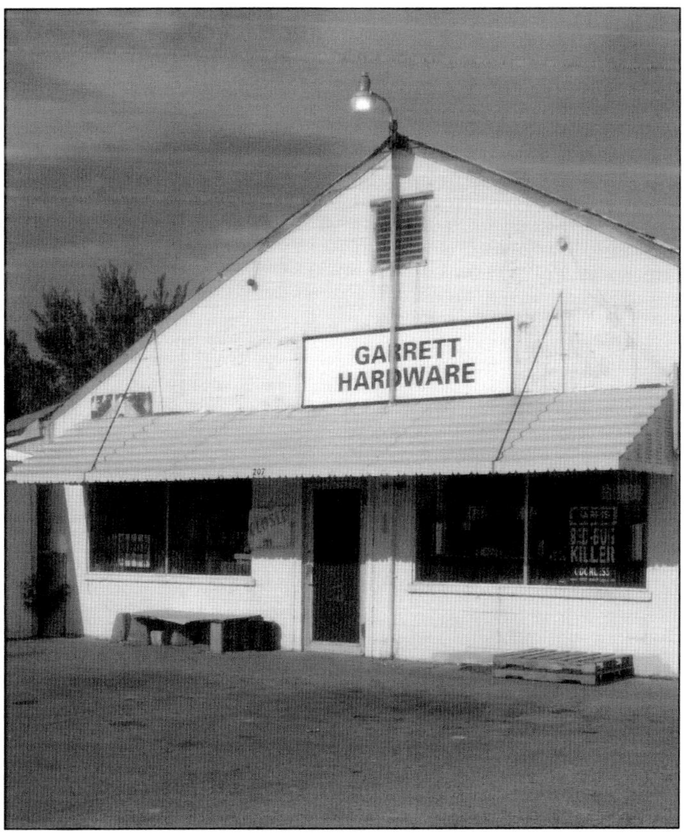

Garrett Hardware first opened in 1953 on Seventh Street and was relocated to a nearby building the following year. Established by W.E. Garrett, it is the last independently owned hardware store in Crittenden County and has been operated by the original family since its opening.

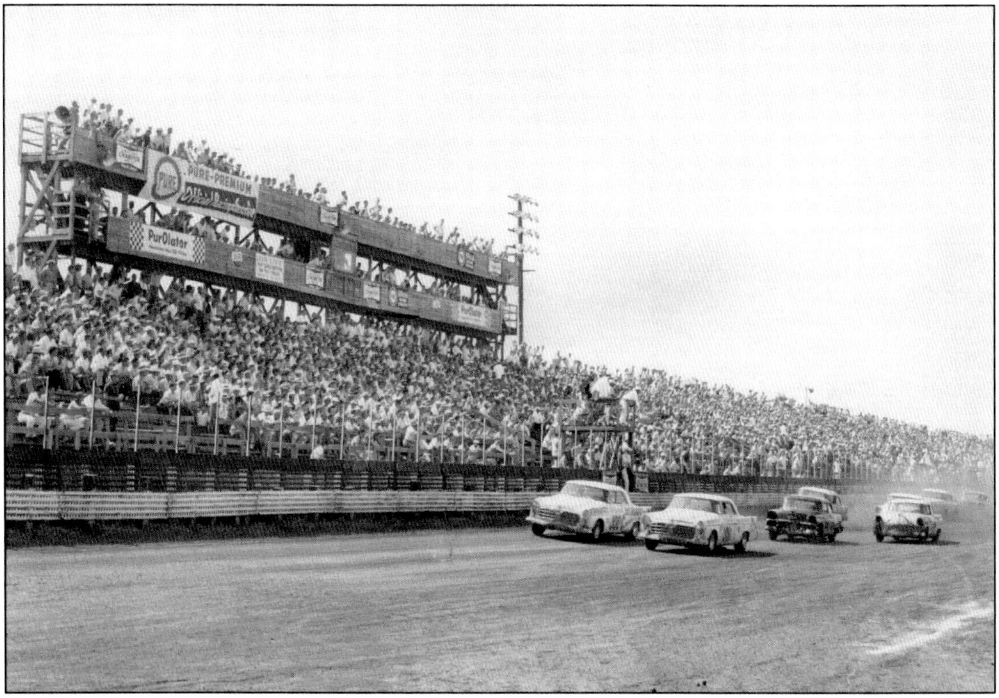

The Memphis-Arkansas Speedway, pictured here, operated briefly from 1954 to 1957 and was located seven miles west of West Memphis, near Lehi, Arkansas. Riverside International Speedway in West Memphis was completed in 1950 and is the oldest continually operated dirt track in the state of Arkansas as well as one of the oldest race tracks in the country.

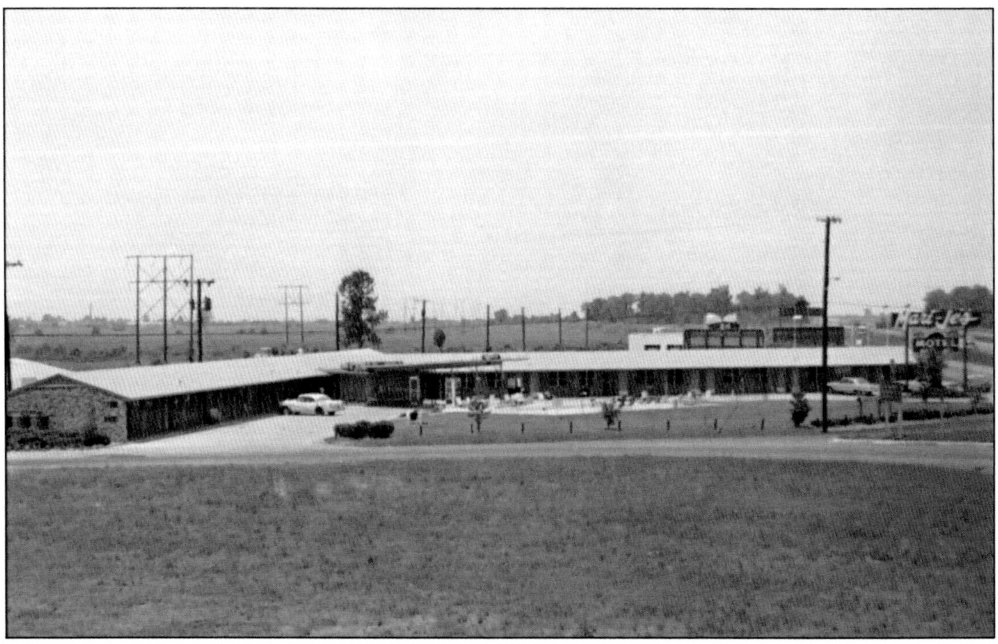

The Mari-Jes Motel was one of the first businesses erected along the newly completed Interstate 55 in the late 1950s. The motel's location at Interstate 55 and Ingram Boulevard was also advantageous to the recently established Southland Greyhound Park, just across the interstate.

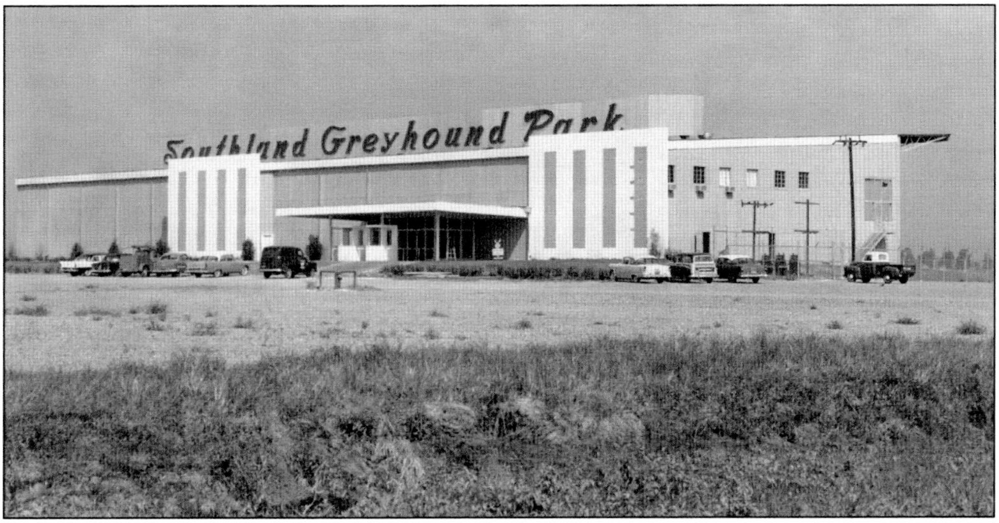

Legal greyhound racing began in Crittenden County in 1935 with the opening of Riverside Kennel Club, near the Harahan Bridge. Riverside closed in 1943 and was later succeeded by the opening of Southland Greyhound Park, photographed above, in 1956.

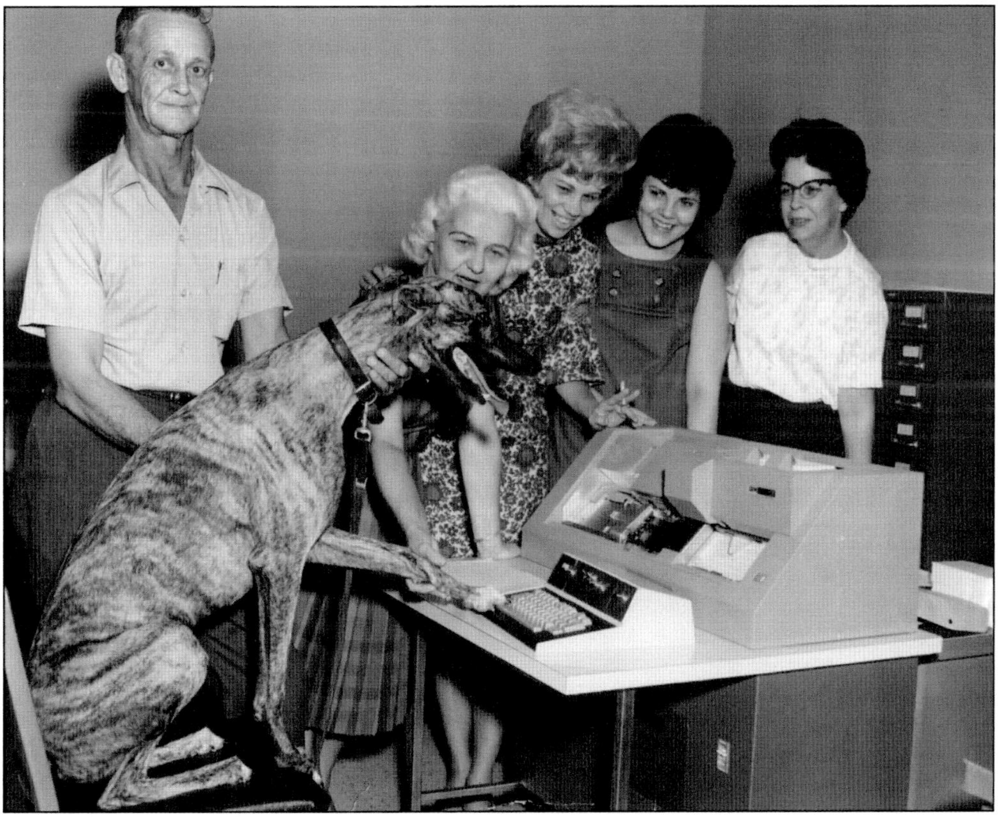

Following its opening, Southland was the only gambling site in the Mid-South for several decades. In addition to its pari-mutuel system of greyhound wagering, it has offered games of skill since 2008. This photograph from 1966 shows employees, along with one of the greyhounds, gathered around an early computerized system for calculating and displaying odds and payouts.

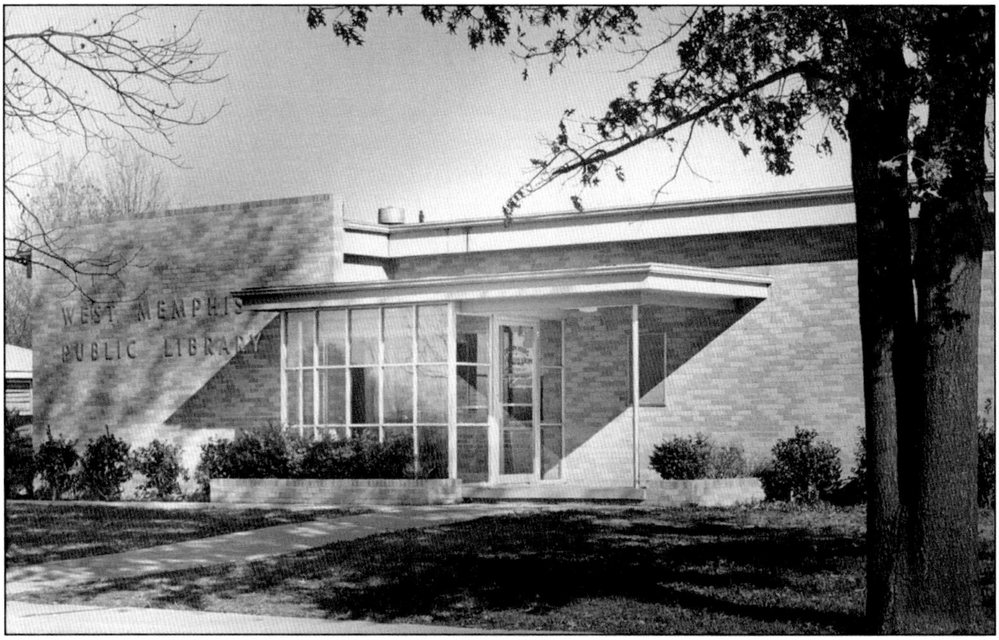

The first library in West Memphis came into existence in 1931, and it was located at various sites before a permanent building was constructed in 1958 on Avalon Street. A large addition was completed in 1975 that more than tripled the size of the original structure.

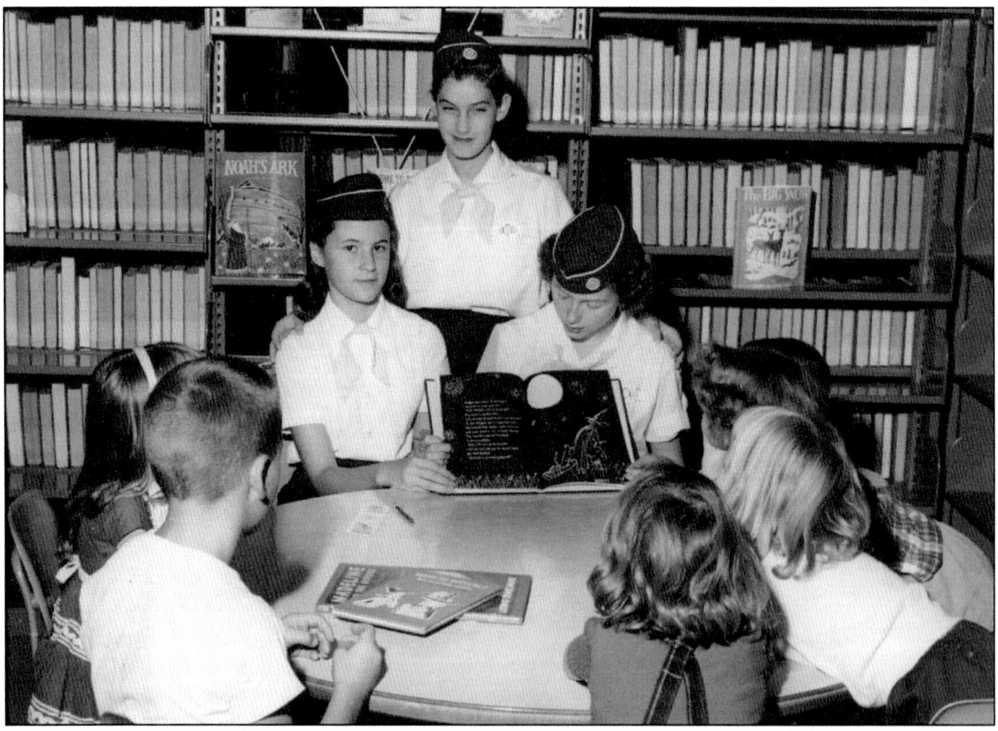

The West Memphis Library has been involved in local education and the promotion of literacy and reading comprehension since its beginning. Photographed here is a group of Girl Scouts in 1959 reading to younger children at the main library.

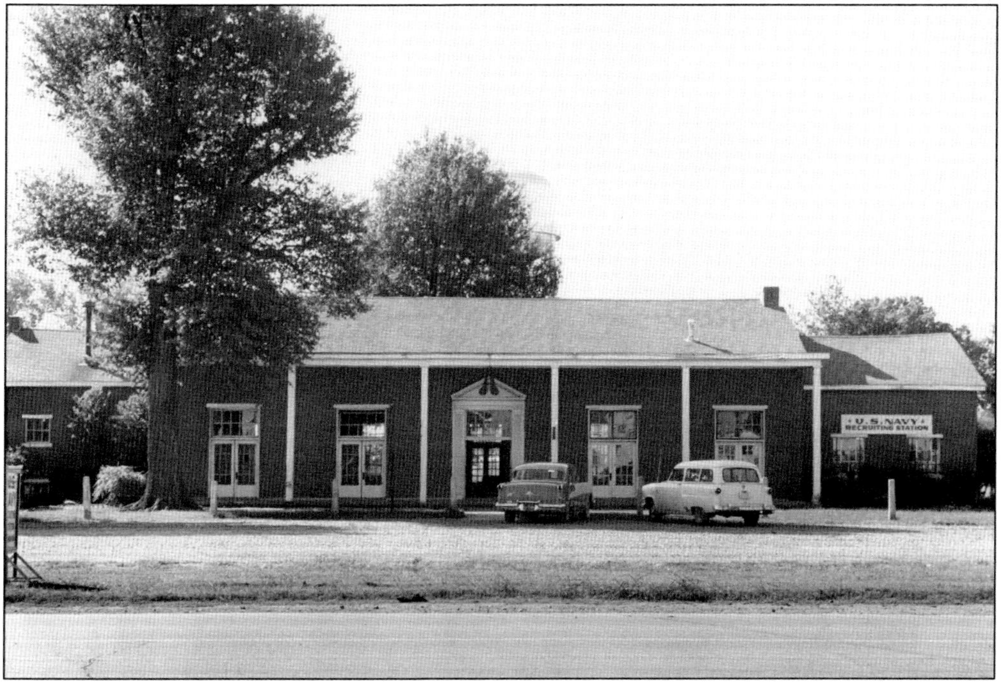

The West Memphis Community House was constructed in 1937 with a portion of the funds provided by a Works Progress Administration grant. The building consisted of a 500-person assembly hall, with meeting rooms located on the second floor. The building was torn down in 1964 and is currently the site of the West Memphis Boys Club.

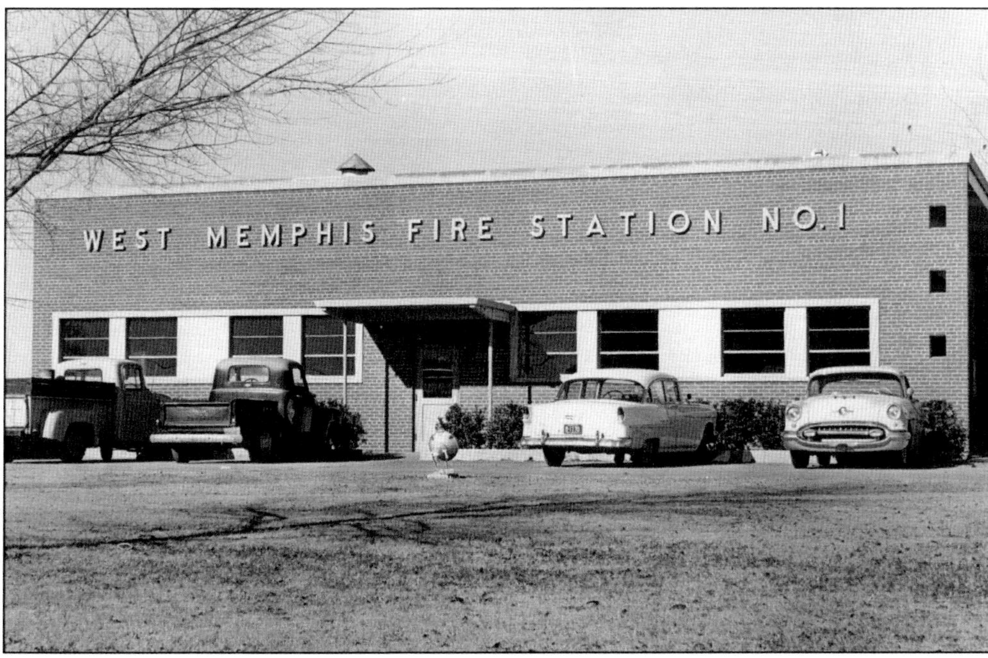

Fire Station No. 1 on Seventh Street was completed in 1955 and was the first firehouse in the city of West Memphis. Before its construction, fire equipment was stored in the rear of city hall. In 1961, two additional fire stations were completed on West Barton and East Barton Avenues.

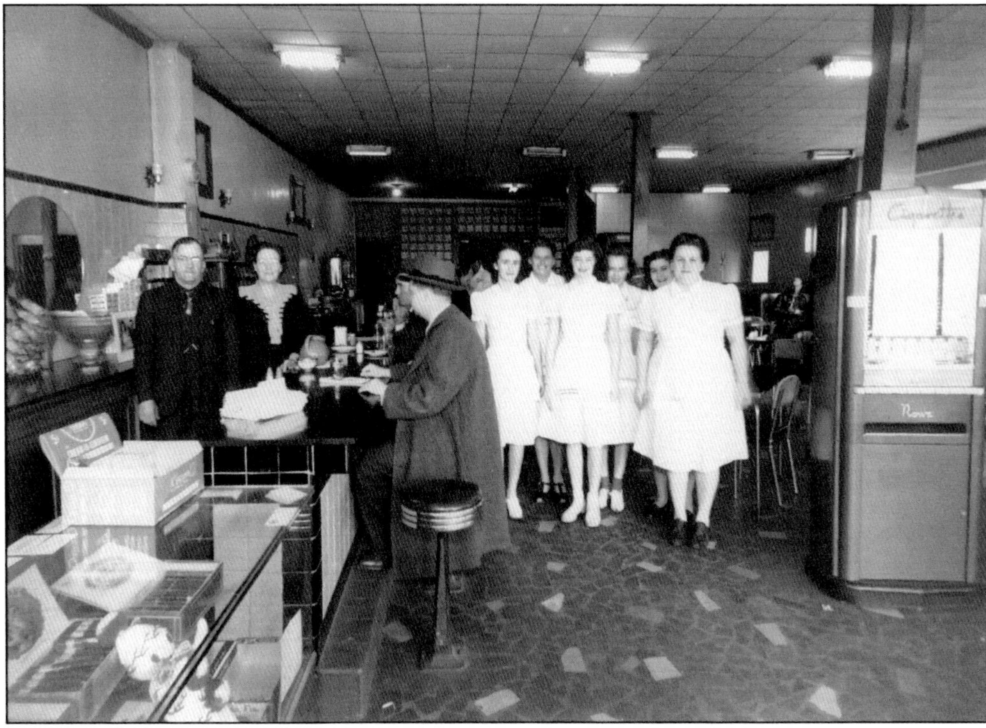

The Coffee Cup, located at 204 East Broadway, was one of the most popular cafés during the 1940s and 1950s. Photographed behind the counter in 1944 are owners Yancey and Ethel Sims, along with their staff. (Courtesy of Michael P. Sims.)

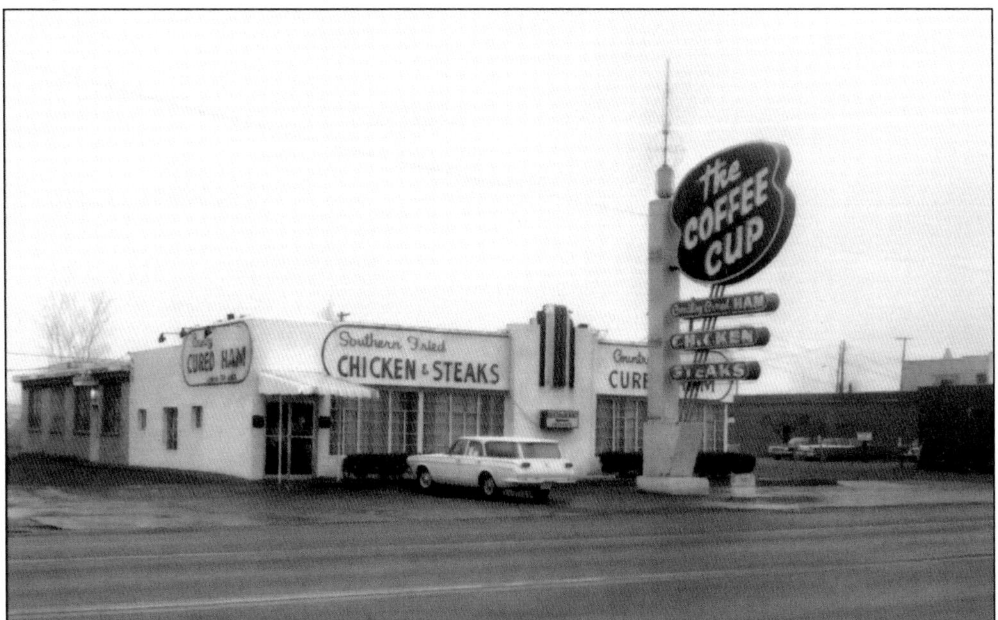

The Coffee Cup's iconic neon sign was a landmark along Broadway until the building was torn down in 1965. Elvis Presley patronized the establishment in the early 1950s and was served his first meal here after being inducted into the US Army in 1958 while en route to Fort Chaffee.

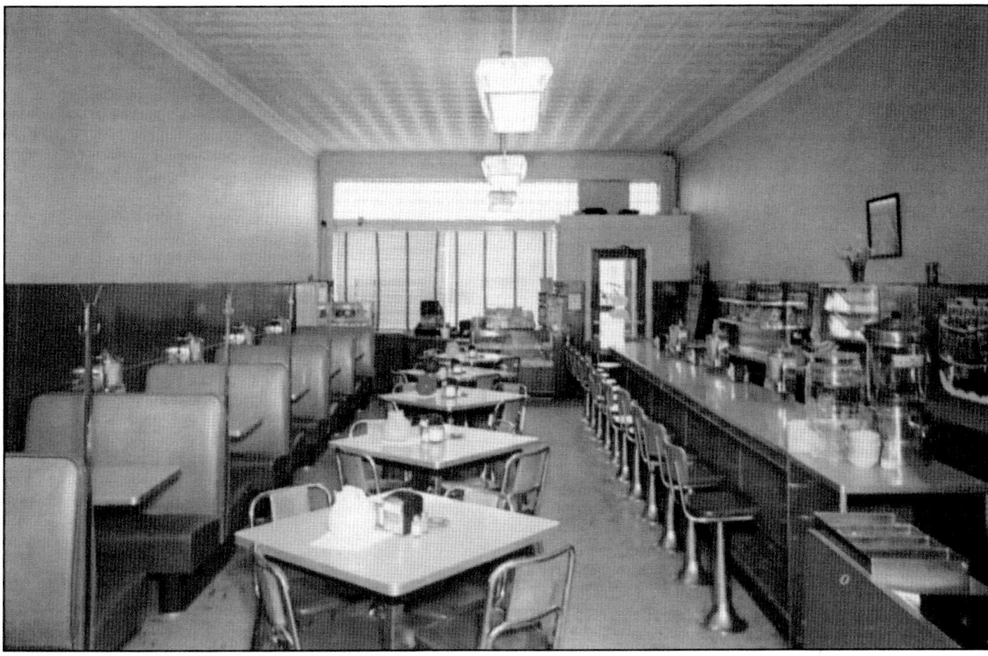

In 1937, John Carr opened the Wonder City Café, the name of which pays homage to the popular moniker for West Memphis. The café catered to the passing Broadway motorists and operated for over 60 years. The original 1950s-era sign has since been reworked to advertise the building's current businesses and to provide a remembrance of its nostalgic past.

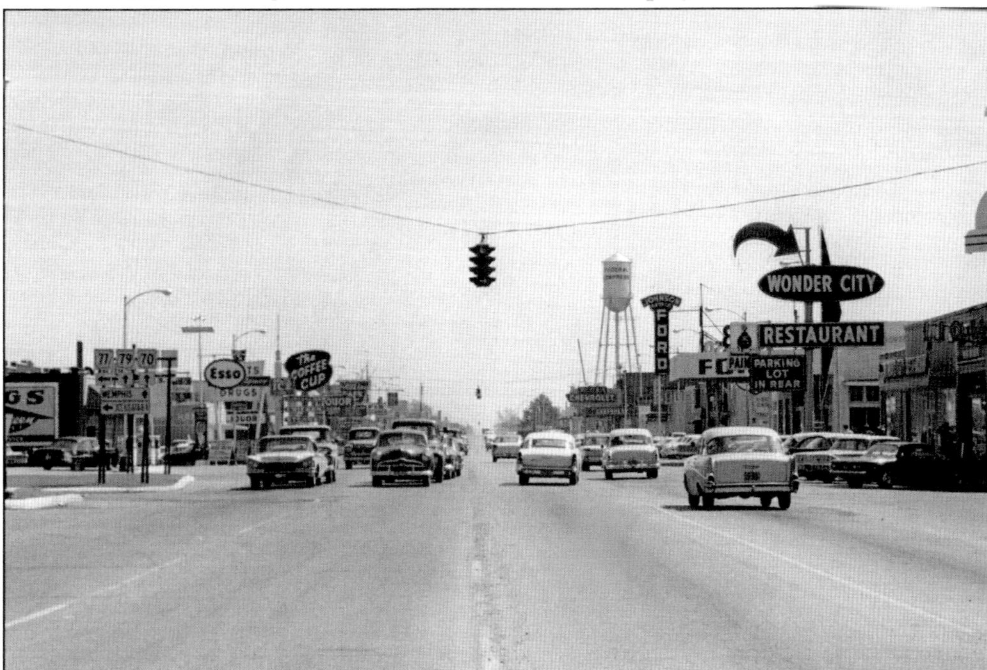

This photograph from 1961 shows Broadway at Missouri Street looking eastward. In December 1962, Interstate 40 opened from Missouri Street to Lehi, Arkansas, allowing eastbound and westbound motorists to completely bypass Broadway.

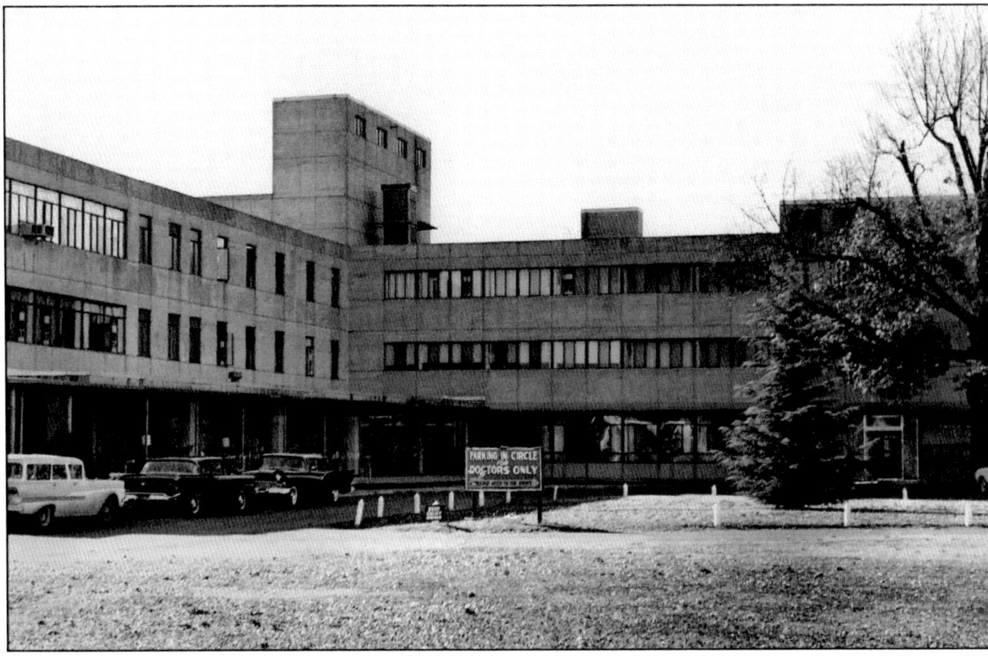

Crittenden Memorial Hospital opened in 1951 in West Memphis as the first hospital in the county. Originally, the $1.2 million structure had 88 beds; however, several expansions over the years have resulted in an increased bed capacity to 152. The hospital officially changed its name to Crittenden Regional Hospital in 2007.

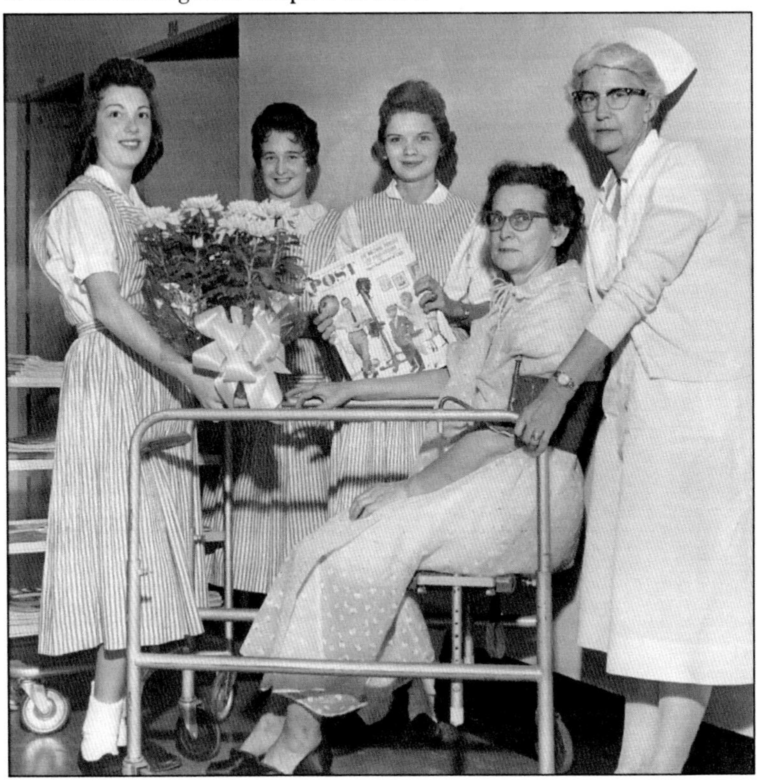

In the 1950s and 1960s, hospital volunteers, known as candy stripers, played an integral role at the hospital. Photographed here are a group of volunteers in 1959 assisting at Crittenden Memorial Hospital.

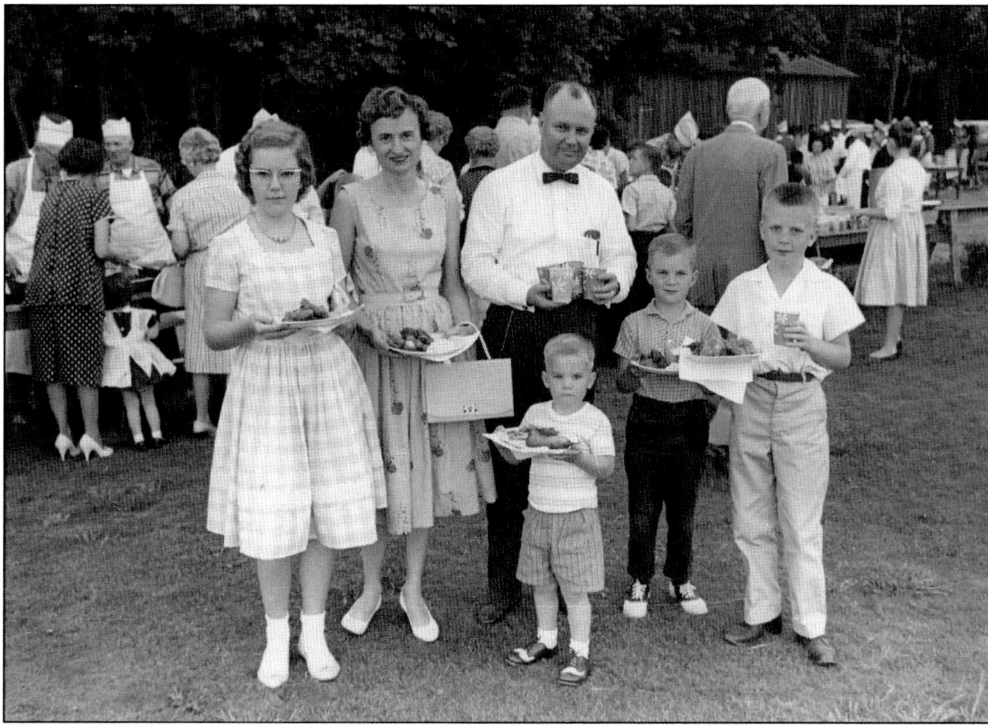

Richard F. Scruggs became the first administrator of Crittenden Memorial Hospital in 1950 and served in this capacity for 33 years. Scruggs was instrumental in the early years of the hospital's growth and expansion. Photographed here in 1961 are Richard and Margaret Scruggs with their four children during a hospital fundraiser.

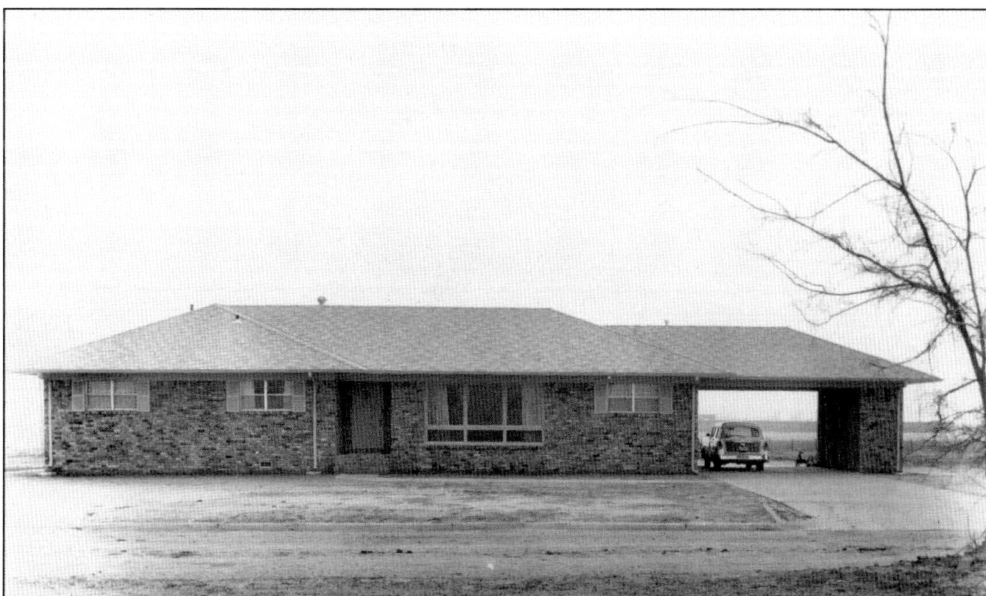

In 1961, the board of trustees at Crittenden Memorial Hospital commissioned this house at 500 Cooper Avenue to serve as the residence for the hospital's administrator. However, Richard Scruggs was the only administrator to ever receive housing from the hospital.

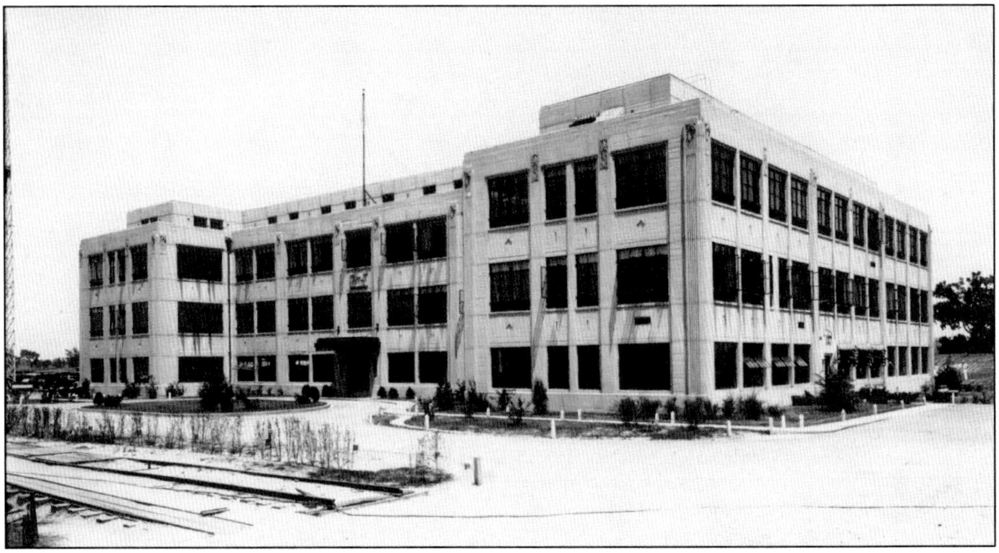

The Army Corps of Engineers constructed the Memphis district offices southwest of the Harahan Bridge in 1932. In 1963, the district's offices were moved to Memphis, and the old facility was developed for private industry.

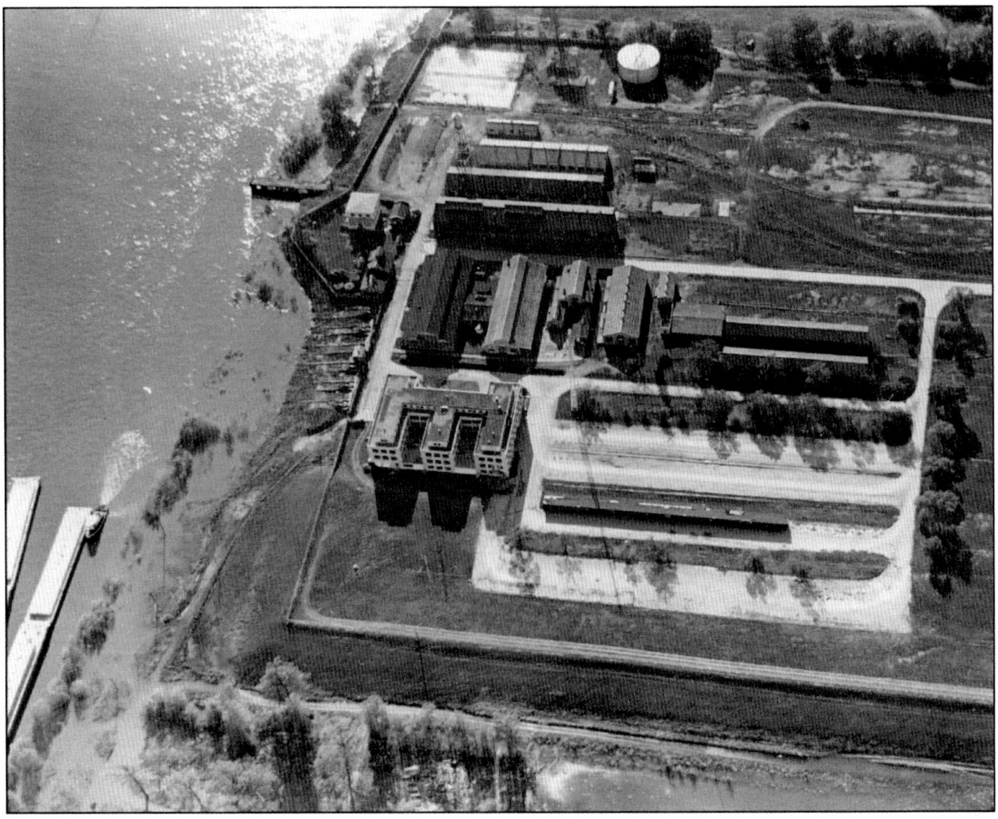

The Army Corps of Engineer's district office was built so that it was entirely surrounded by a levee to protect it from the floods of the Mississippi River. This site is currently the location of Bridgeport Industrial Park.

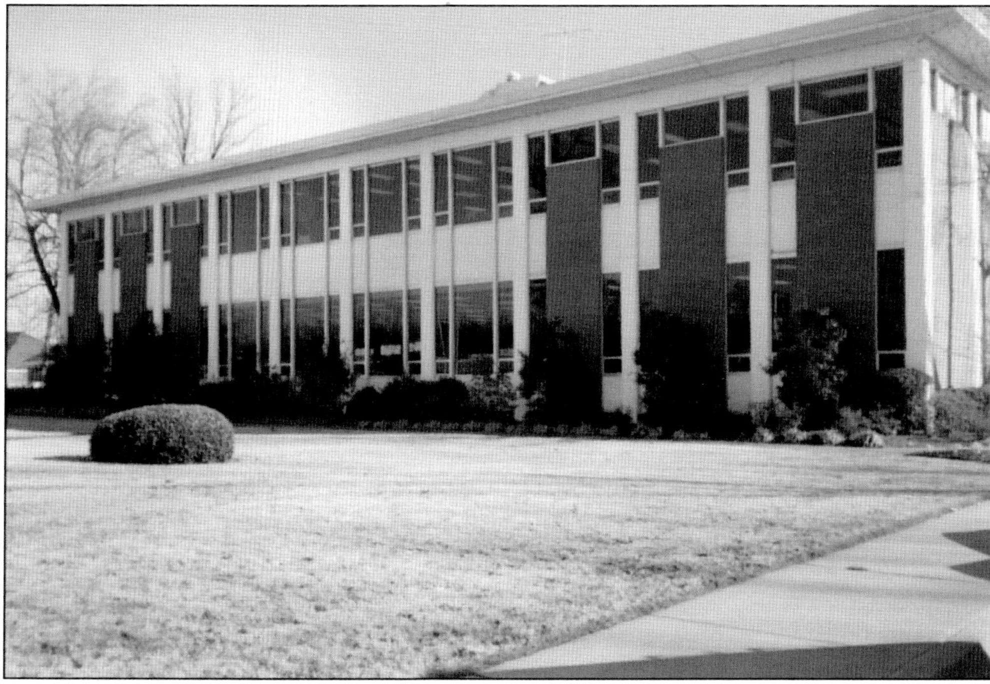

Fidelity National Bank was established in 1966 at 330 West Broadway. It is the oldest locally owned and operated bank in West Memphis and has been operating with its original name since its founding.

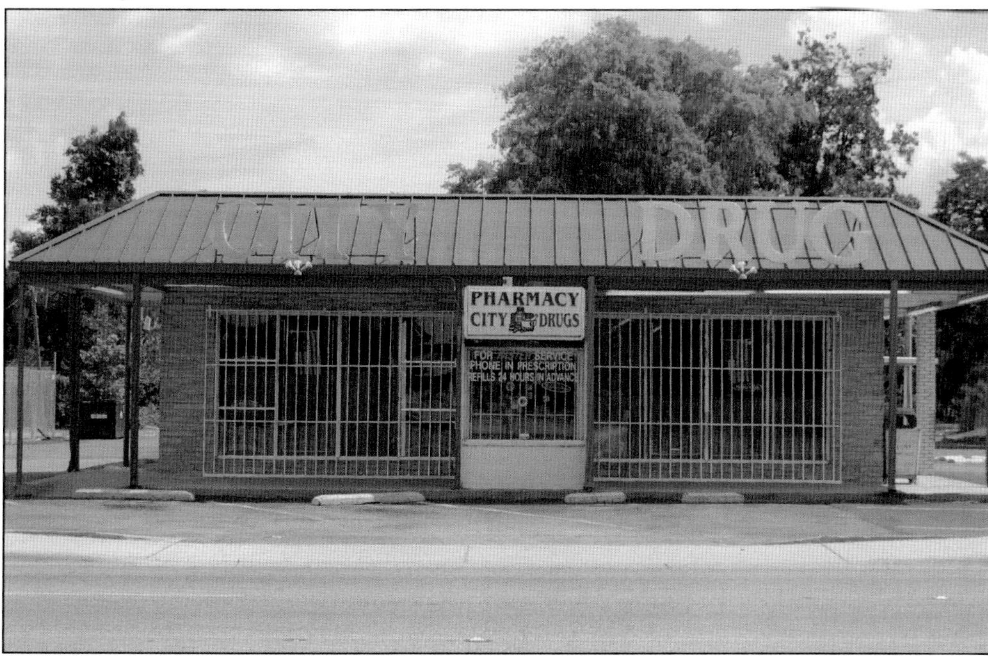

City Drug's original location was at East Broadway and Twelfth Street; it then was relocated to 1701 East Broadway in 1970 by store owner William Slaughter. This is the last independent drugstore still in operation in the city of West Memphis. At one time, there were five independently owned drugstores operating in the city.

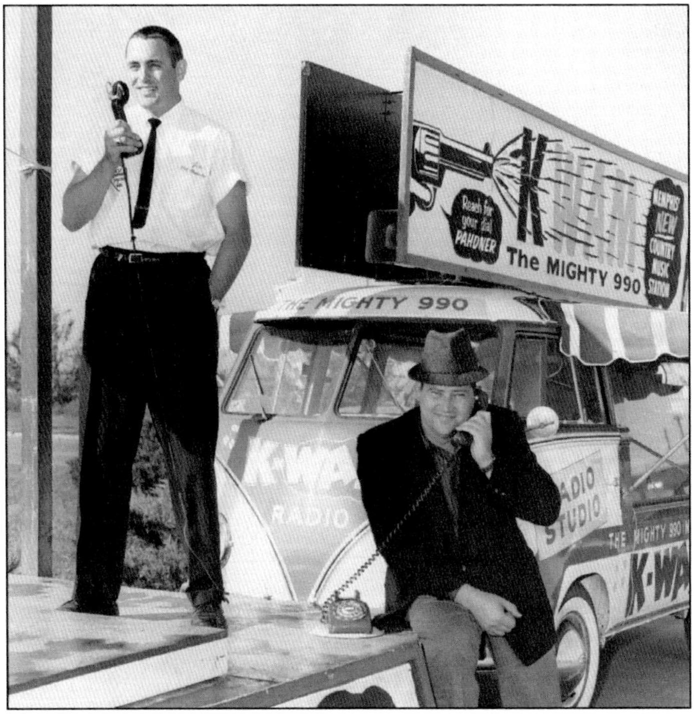

KWEM Radio in West Memphis was sold in 1960 and moved to Memphis with the call letters KWAM. Even though the station was relocated east of the Mississippi River, the Federal Communications Commission allowed for the call letters to begin with a *K* since its radio tower and transmitter remained in Arkansas.

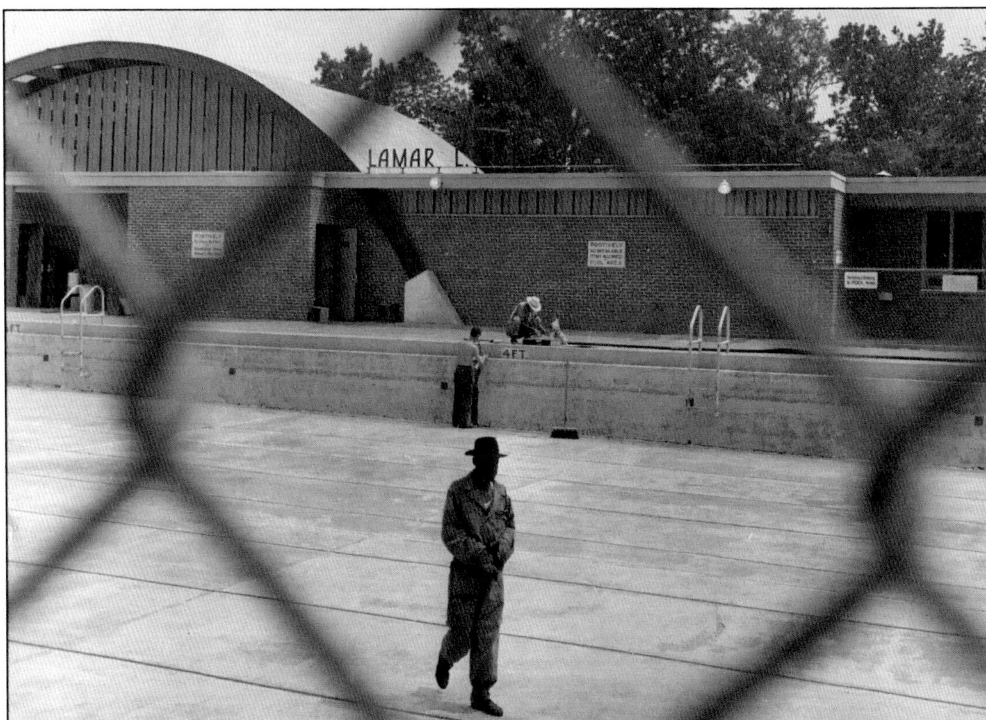

The Lamar L. Rogers Swimming Pool was located in Worthington Park along South Worthington Drive. The facility opened in 1955 and remained open for 21 years before being razed in 1977. The entire site was reworked in 1988 during a major renovation of Worthington Park.

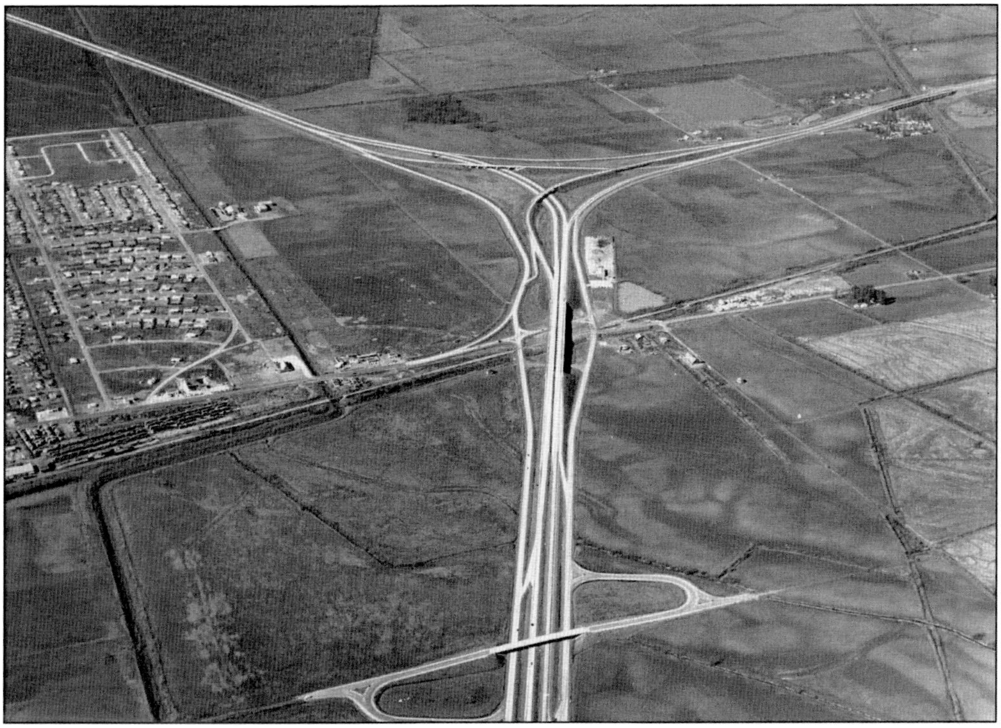

This aerial photograph from 1959 shows a western view of the interchange at Interstates 40 and 55, with this portion of Interstate 40 completed in 1962. The first major developments along the interstate in this area were a Holiday Inn in 1963, followed by the Holiday Plaza Mall in 1966.

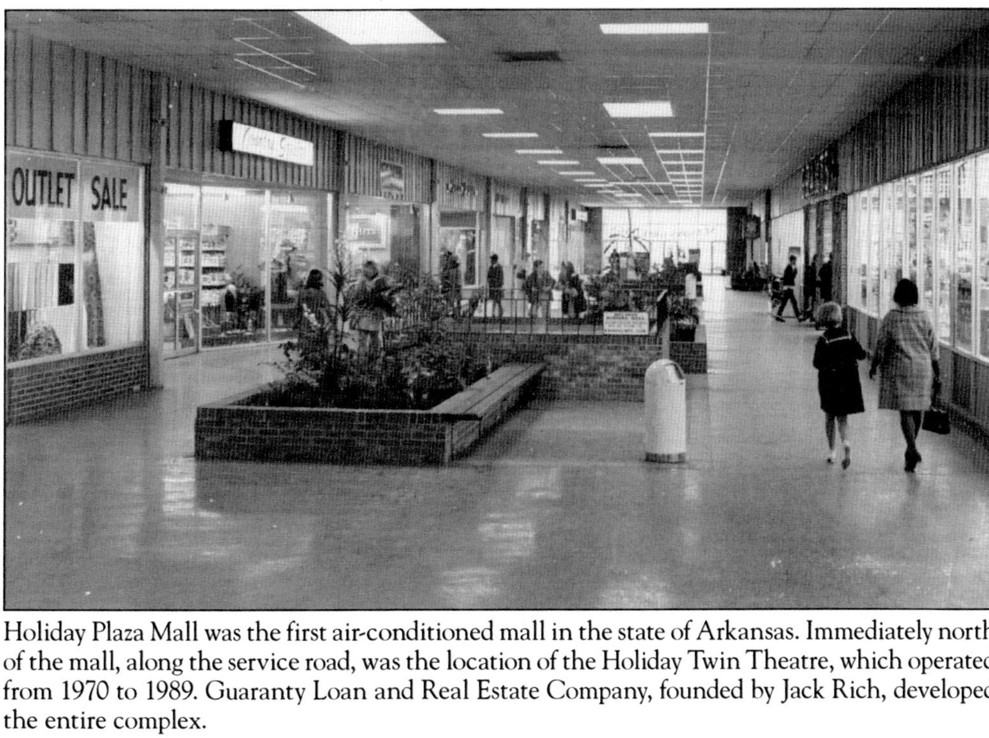

Holiday Plaza Mall was the first air-conditioned mall in the state of Arkansas. Immediately north of the mall, along the service road, was the location of the Holiday Twin Theatre, which operated from 1970 to 1989. Guaranty Loan and Real Estate Company, founded by Jack Rich, developed the entire complex.

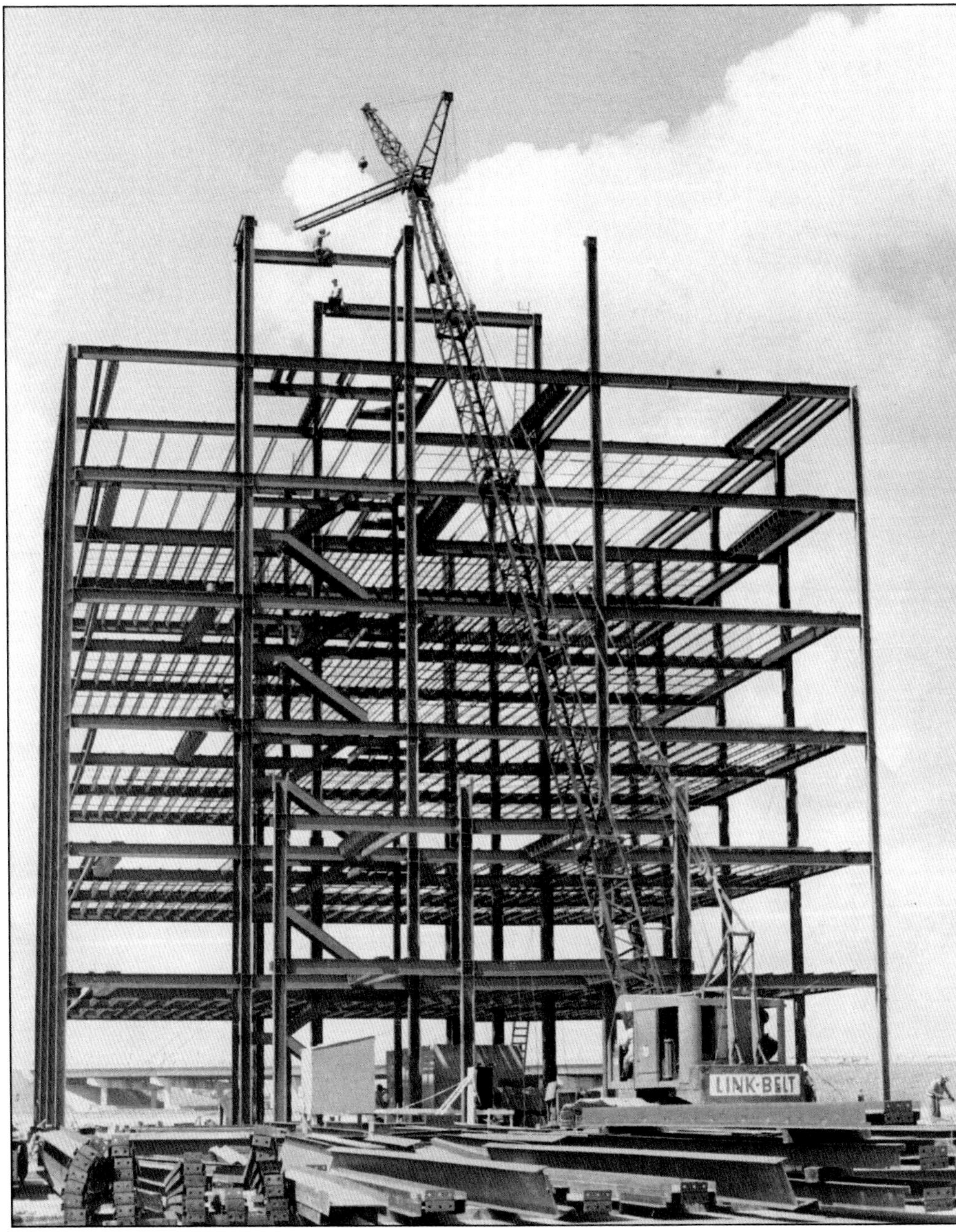

The Mid-Continent Plaza was completed in 1974 and, at six stories, remains Crittenden County's tallest building. The exterior deviated from the original plans due to a lack of funds, and the controversial style was not well received by the community. A leading architectural critic described the completed building as "a grotesque edifice of unspeakable ugliness."

Four

EDUCATION AND RELIGIOUS LIFE

Hopefield provided the earliest records of religious communities in the vicinity of West Memphis with two documented churches. A Methodist church and a Catholic church were known to have existed, but both disbanded soon after the Great Yellow Fever Epidemic of 1878. The earliest congregation in the city of West Memphis belongs to Old St. Paul Missionary Baptist Church, organized in 1905. Originally located adjacent to the railroad tracks on South Eighth Street, the congregation moved to a new site at 504 South Eighth Street in 1959. It continues to serve the community from this location.

The First Baptist Church was organized in 1924, after which the congregation acquired land on the corner of Missouri Street and Bond Avenue in the following year. In 1926, the congregation erected a small structure, which served the church until a new brick building was completed in 1944. The burgeoning congregation finished its current building adjacent to the original structures in 1966.

The First Methodist Church was organized in Hulbert in 1919, and a subsequent church building was constructed there in 1925. In 1933, the First Methodist Church of West Memphis was established as an outgrowth of the Hulbert church. Land was purchased on Pine Street, and the first sanctuary, which was a white clapboard structure, was completed in 1935. By the early 1940s, the Methodist congregation in Hulbert merged with that of West Memphis. By the end of the 1940s, West Memphis had congregations representing nearly all Christian faiths.

The public school system, which served both Hulbert and West Memphis, was originally named the Hulbert School District. Its only school, established in Hulbert in 1913, served grades one through twelve until a new structure was completed. In 1925, a large three-story brick building was constructed on the 1400 block of South Avalon Street. The new Hulbert School served all students in the vicinity until a new high school was constructed on West Barton Avenue in West Memphis in 1948. West Memphis students in grades one through six continued to attend Hulbert School until Bragg Elementary School opened in 1951. In 1940, the district's name changed to Hulbert–West Memphis School District, and in 1970, Hulbert was dropped as part of the official title.

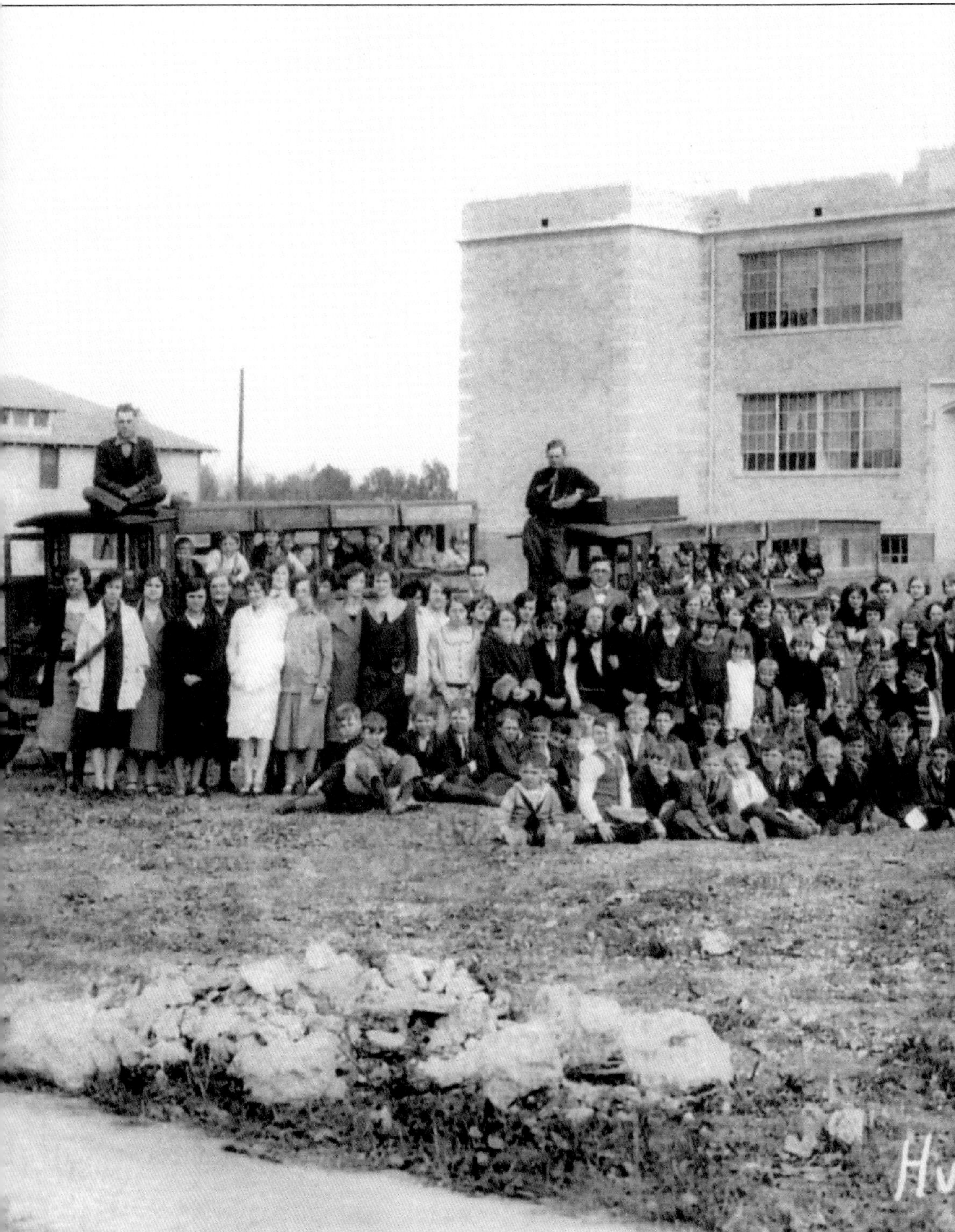

Hulbert School, which served grades one through twelve, was the only public school in the area for 35 years. This 1925 photograph shows the entire student body, faculty, and staff, including

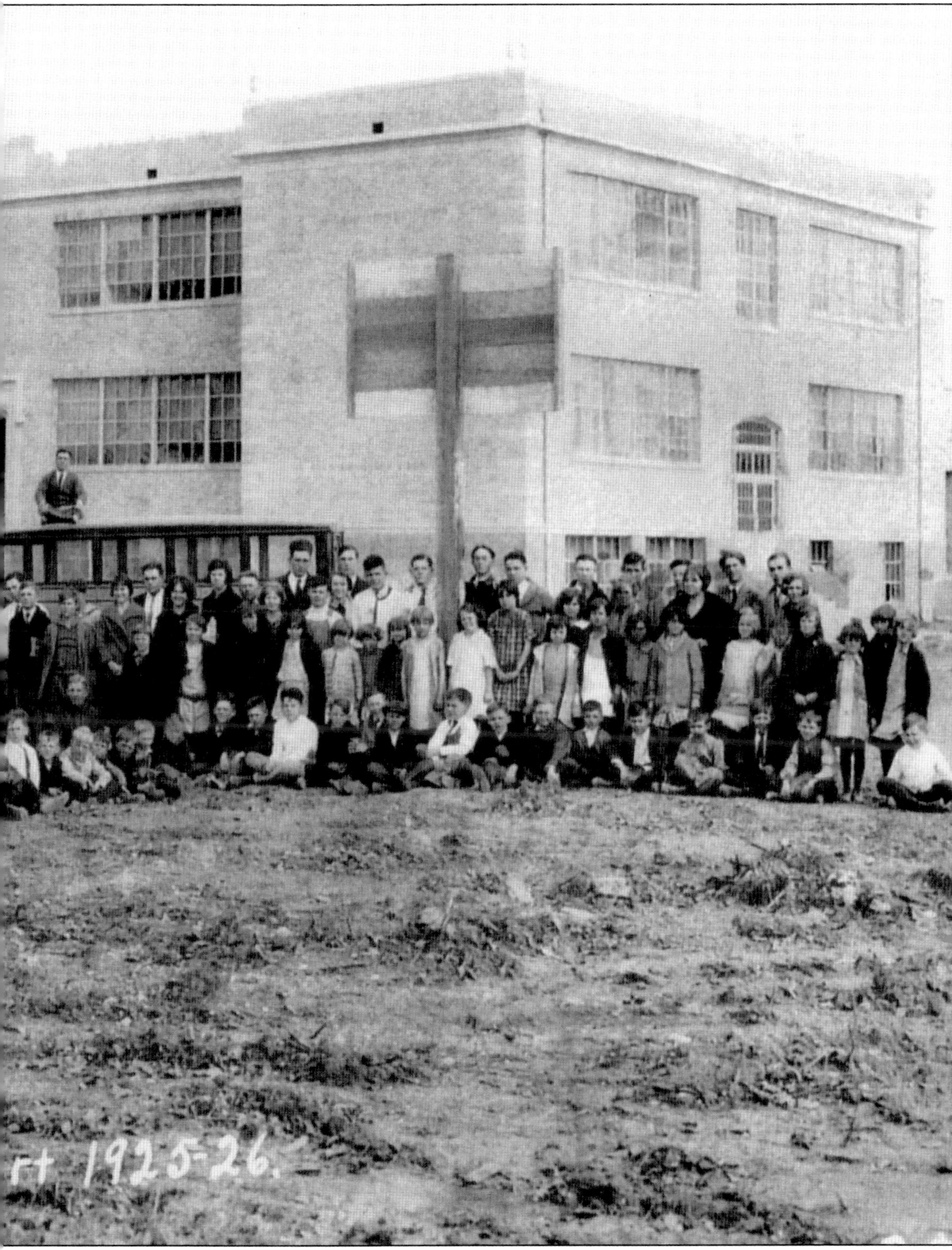

three bus drivers atop their privately owned buses. The school building was grievously damaged by a fire in 1992 after having been vacant for 14 years and was razed shortly thereafter.

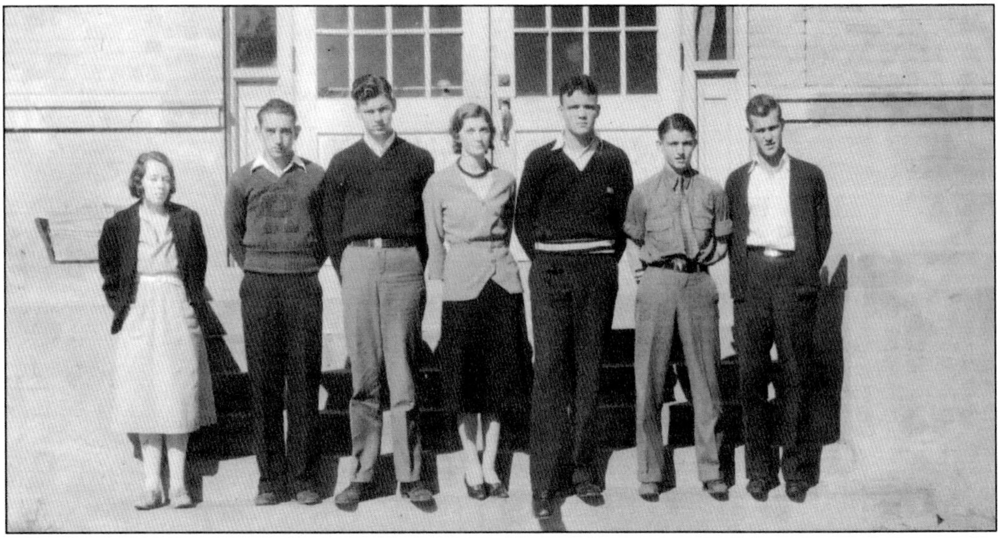

High school students at Hulbert are shown standing in front of one of the side entrances to the school in this 1927 photograph. Third from right is Otis Ball, who later became the fire chief in West Memphis for several years.

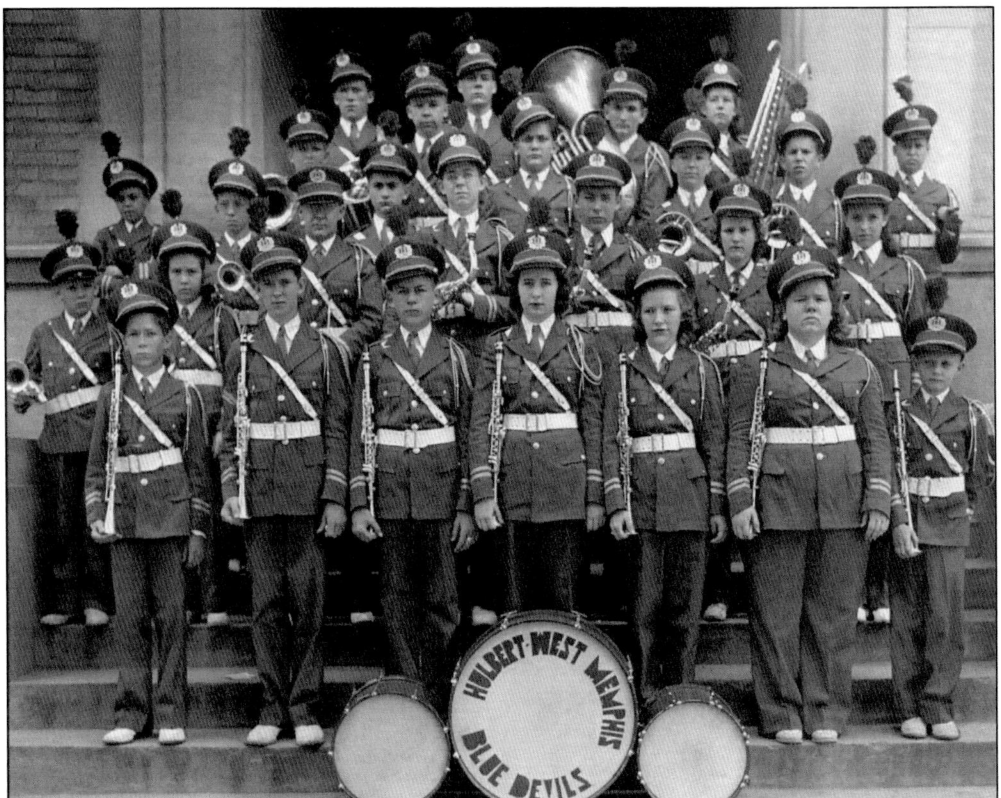

Members of the Blue Devils marching band pose on the steps of the main entrance to Hulbert School in 1942. During the early 1940s, Hulbert School was well known in the region for its athletic championships, at which the marching band proudly played.

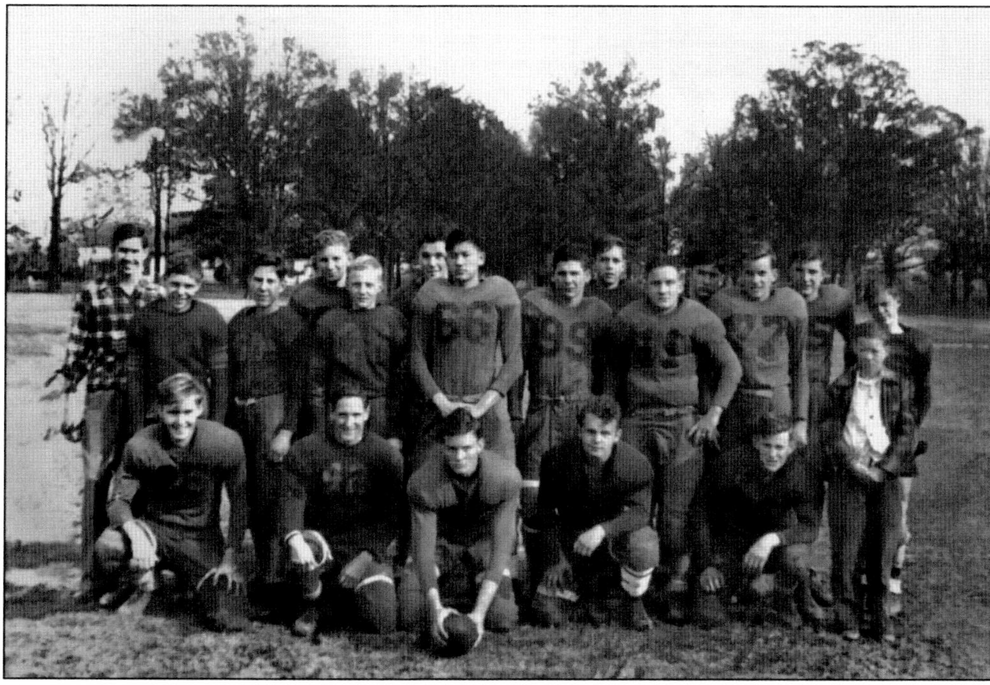

Photographed above is the Hulbert football team in 1945. Standing in the second row, third from left, is Lewis Carpenter, who later played professional football for the Detroit Lions, Cleveland Browns, and Green Bay Packers. After his playing career ended in 1963, Carpenter spent the next 31 years as an assistant coach for multiple NFL teams. (Courtesy of Danny Craft.)

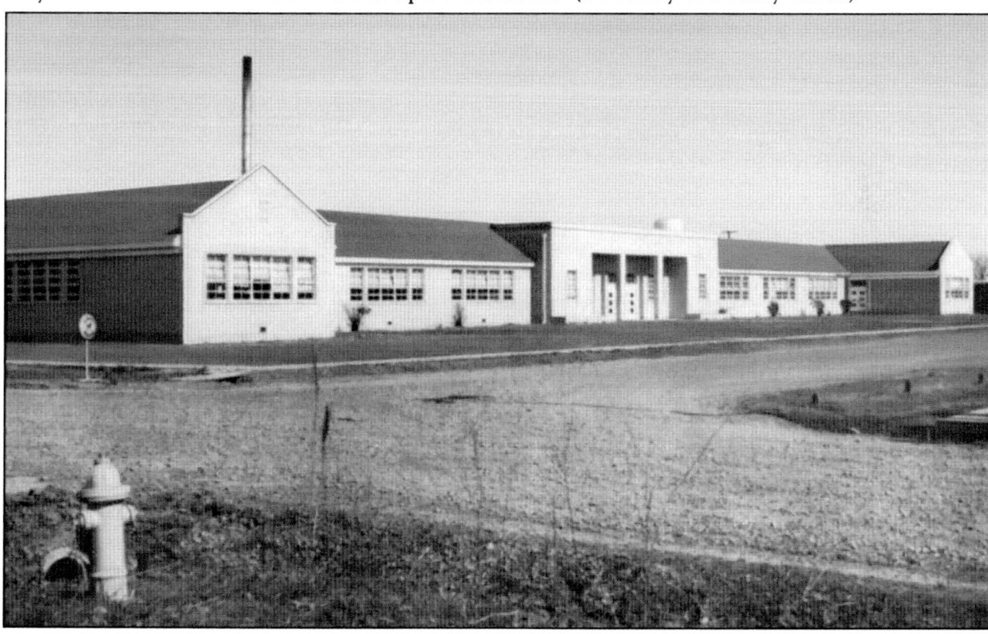

The first public school constructed in West Memphis was the high school built on West Barton Avenue in 1948 at a cost of $125,000. This school served high school students until a new building was constructed on West Broadway in 1960. Thereafter, the former high school has been used as a junior high school known as West Junior High.

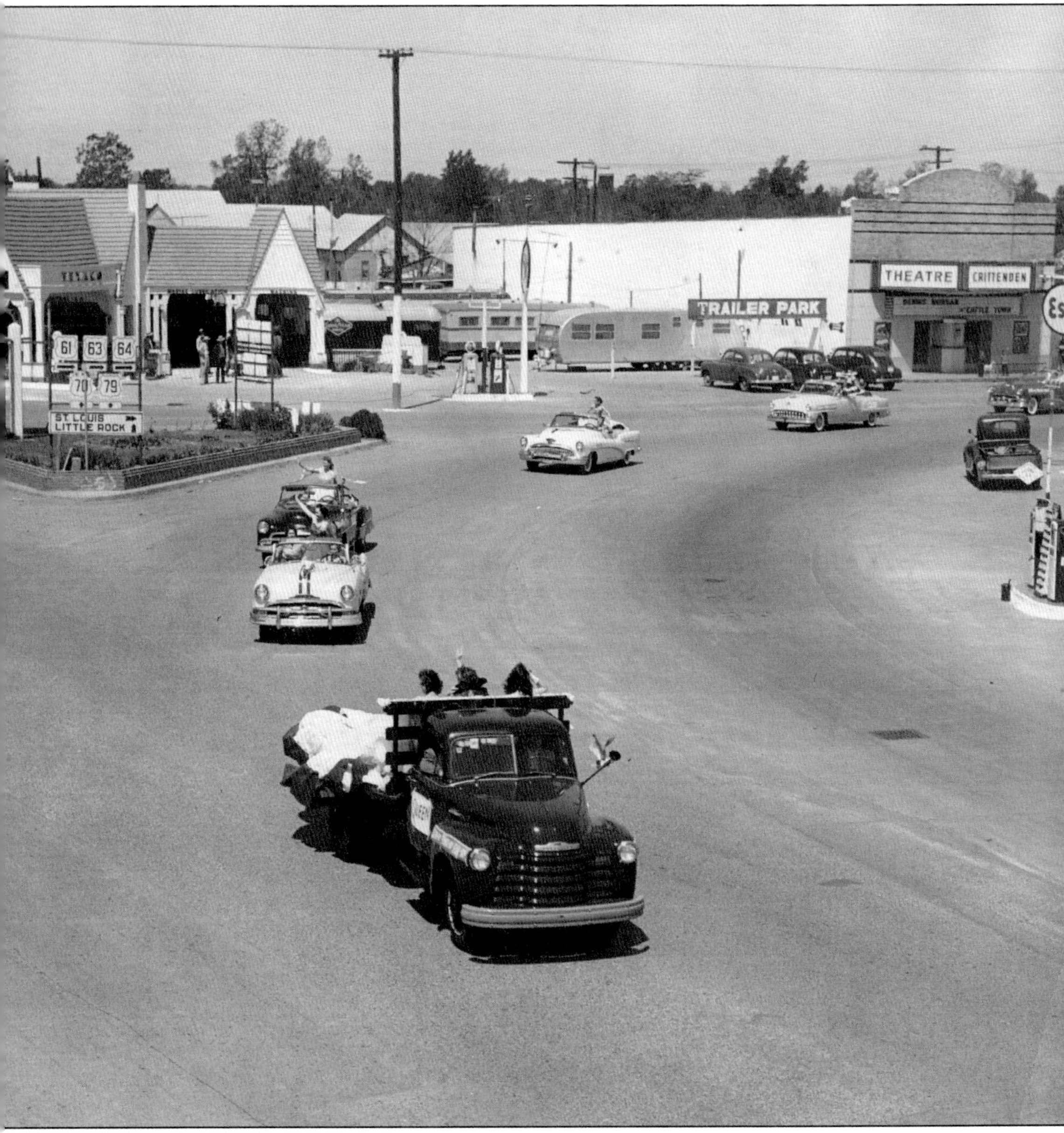

Taken from atop the Wonder City Café building on East Broadway, this photograph from 1953 shows the intersection of Broadway and Missouri Street during a football homecoming parade. The Crittenden Theatre, which closed the following year, is visible in the background. Before a football field was eventually constructed at the new high school, all football games were held at Friendship Field on the West Barton Avenue campus.

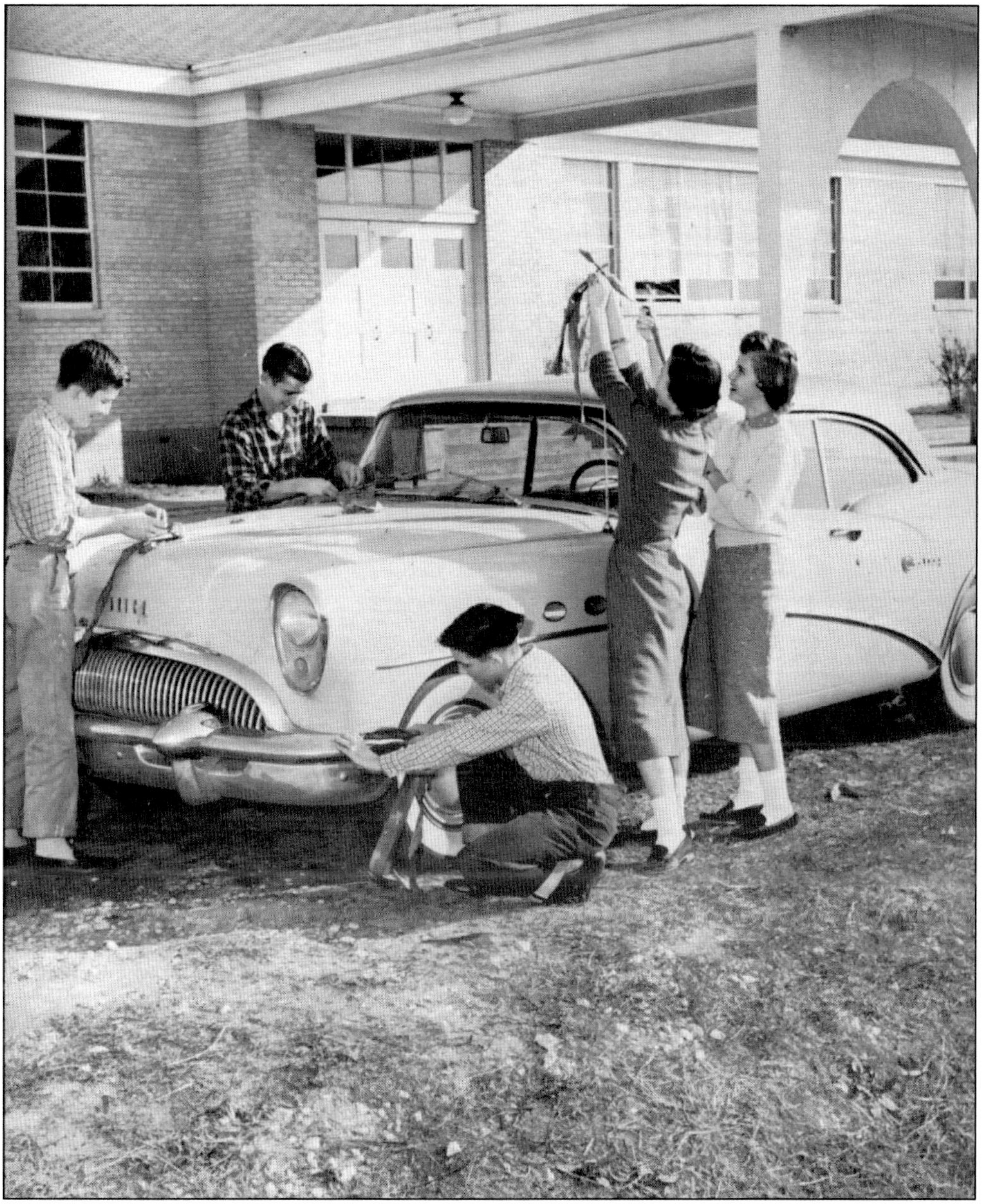

During the 1950s, the public schools in West Memphis witnessed a dramatic increase in enrollment. Between 1951 and 1963, a new high school and three new elementary schools were established. An additional elementary school and high school were also constructed to serve African American students. Pictured here preparing for homecoming celebrations in 1954 are, from left to right, Bill Weaver, Parker Eubanks, Donald Foshee, Martha Ann Bagwell, and Betty Sue Bledsoe.

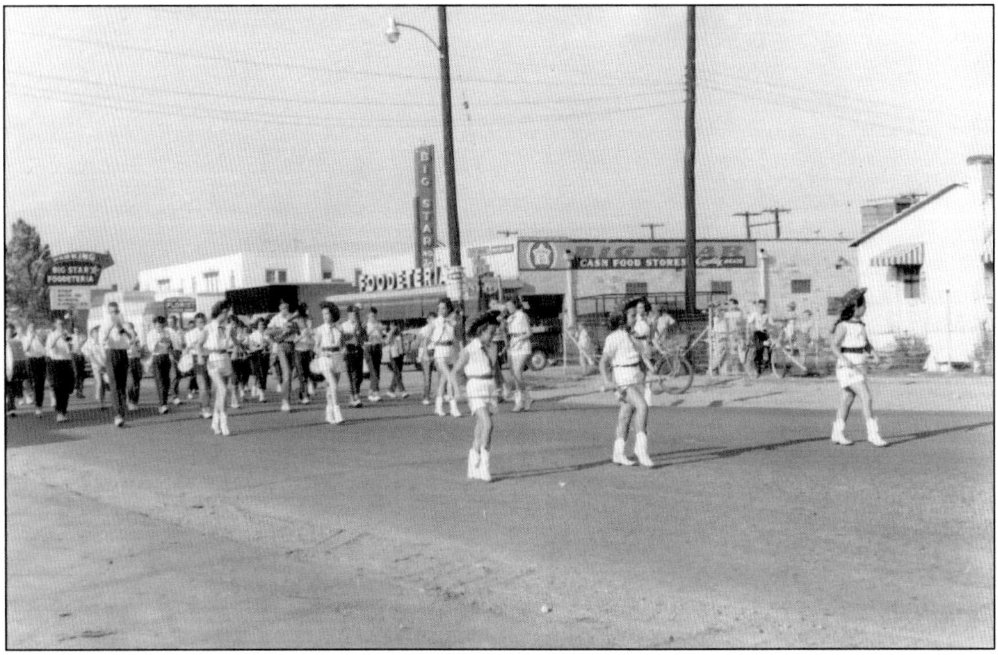

This 1955 parade on Missouri Street featured elementary students from Bragg and Hulbert Schools leading the procession. In the same year, Hulbert School was renamed Dabbs Elementary School in honor of Harry R. Dabbs of Hulbert.

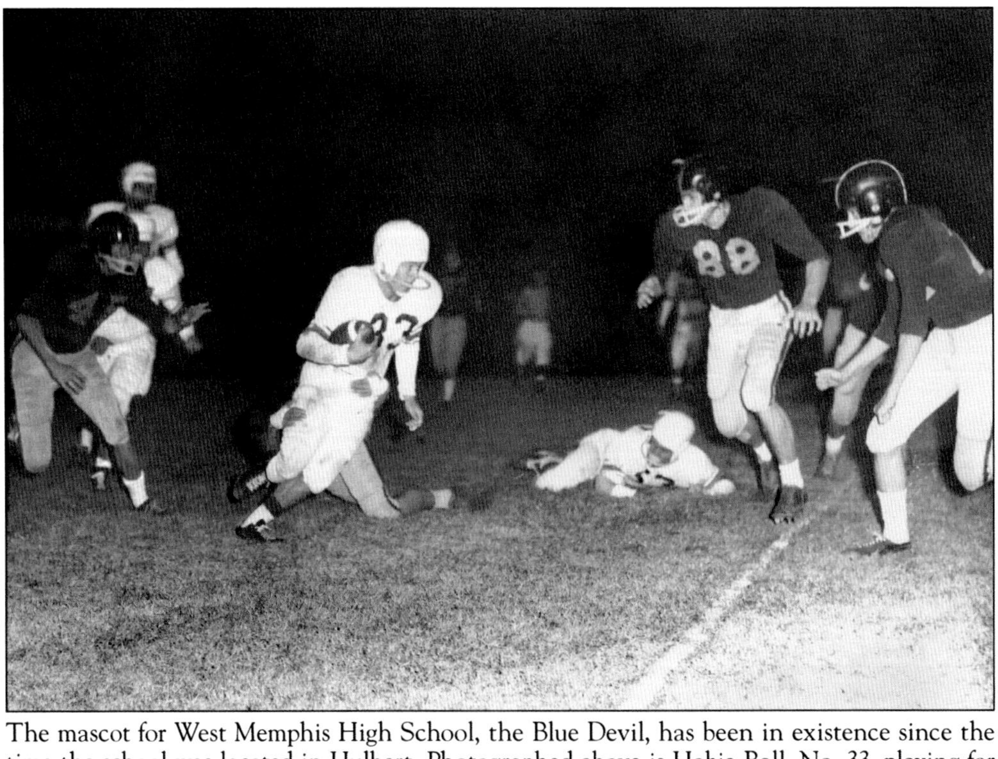

The mascot for West Memphis High School, the Blue Devil, has been in existence since the time the school was located in Hulbert. Photographed above is Hobie Ball, No. 33, playing for the West Memphis Blue Devils during the 1957 football season.

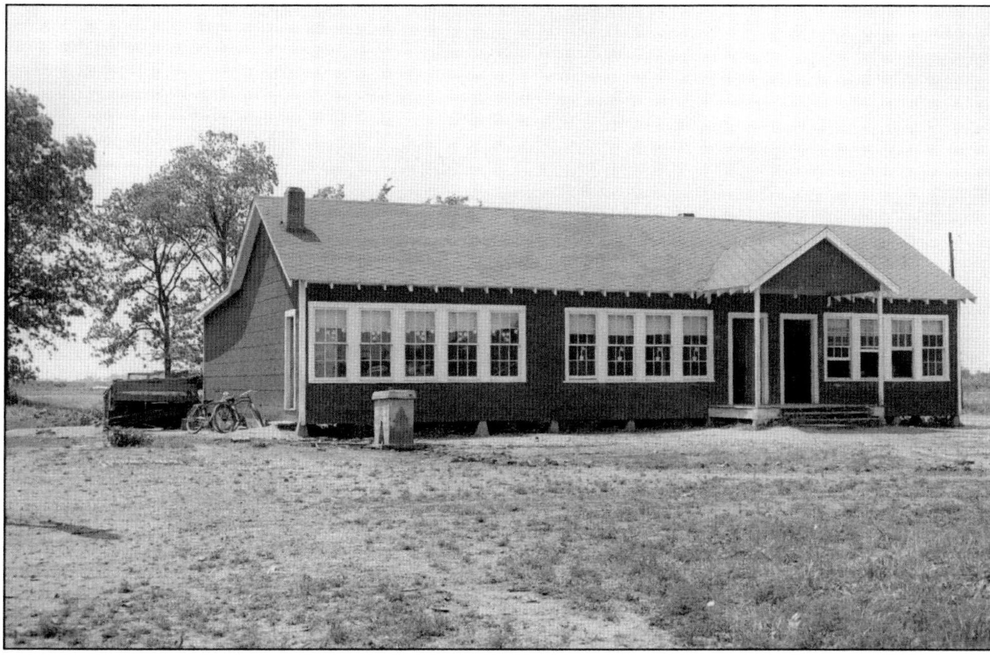

Shown here in 1948, the original Wonder School, located on the west side of South Eighth Street, near Jefferson Avenue, only served African American students. A new school facility was built at its current location on South Seventeenth Street in the early 1950s. The original structure was moved to the new site, serving as a band room for nearly a decade.

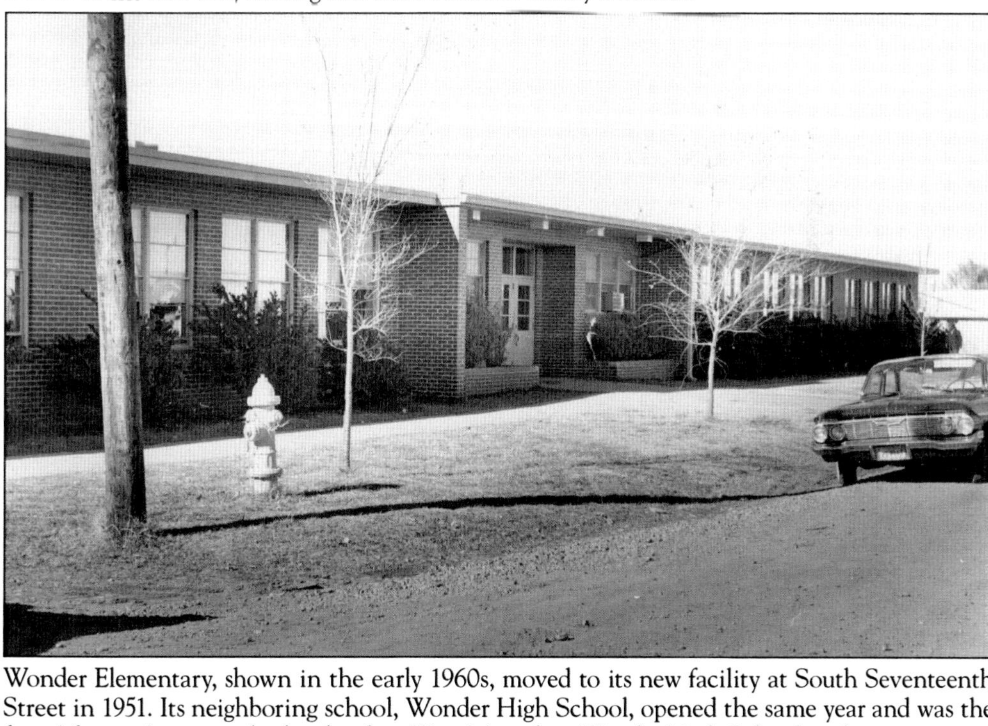

Wonder Elementary, shown in the early 1960s, moved to its new facility at South Seventeenth Street in 1951. Its neighboring school, Wonder High School, opened the same year and was the first African American high school in West Memphis. Wonder High School underwent several transformations after 1971 as a result of integration.

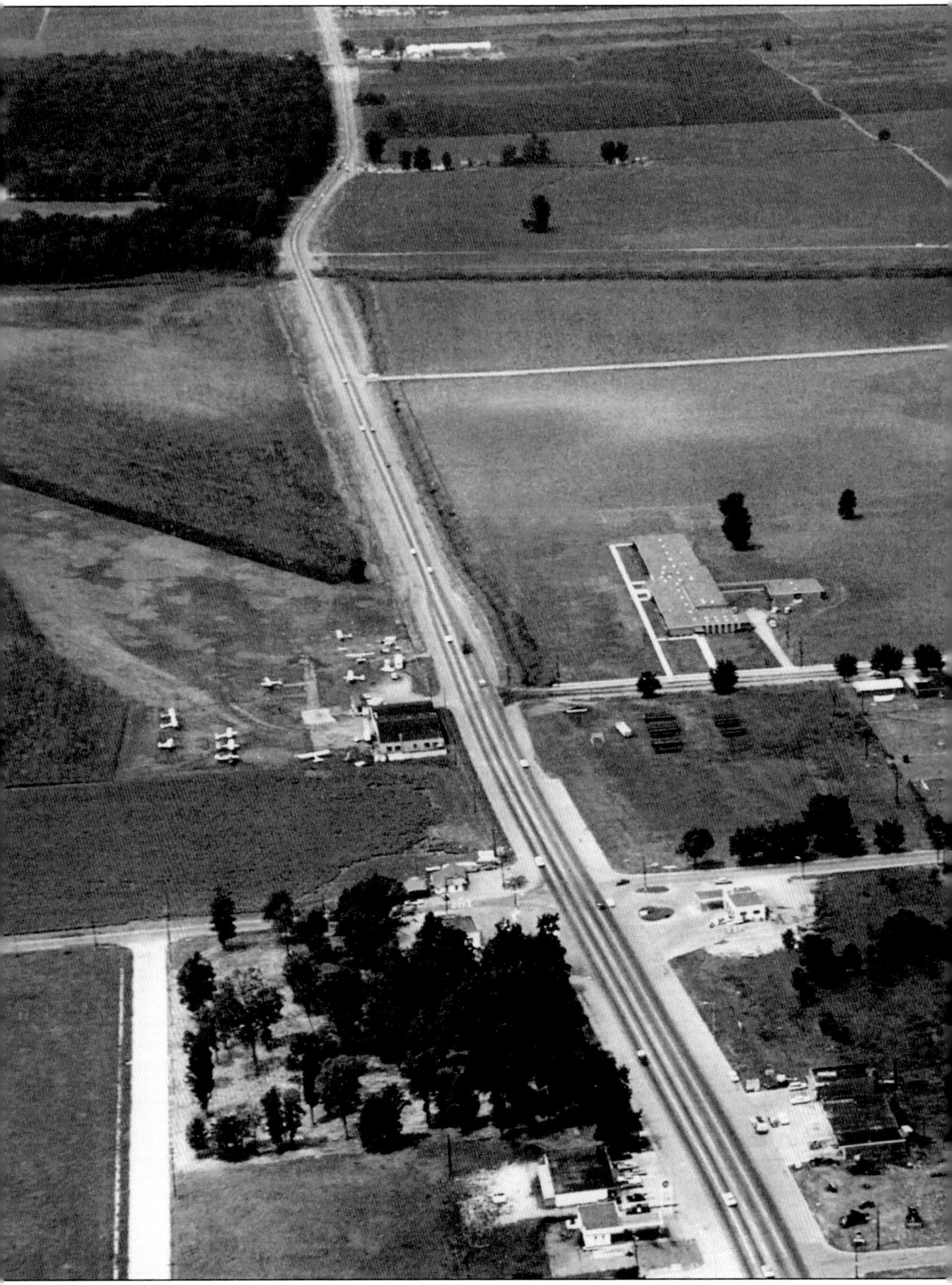

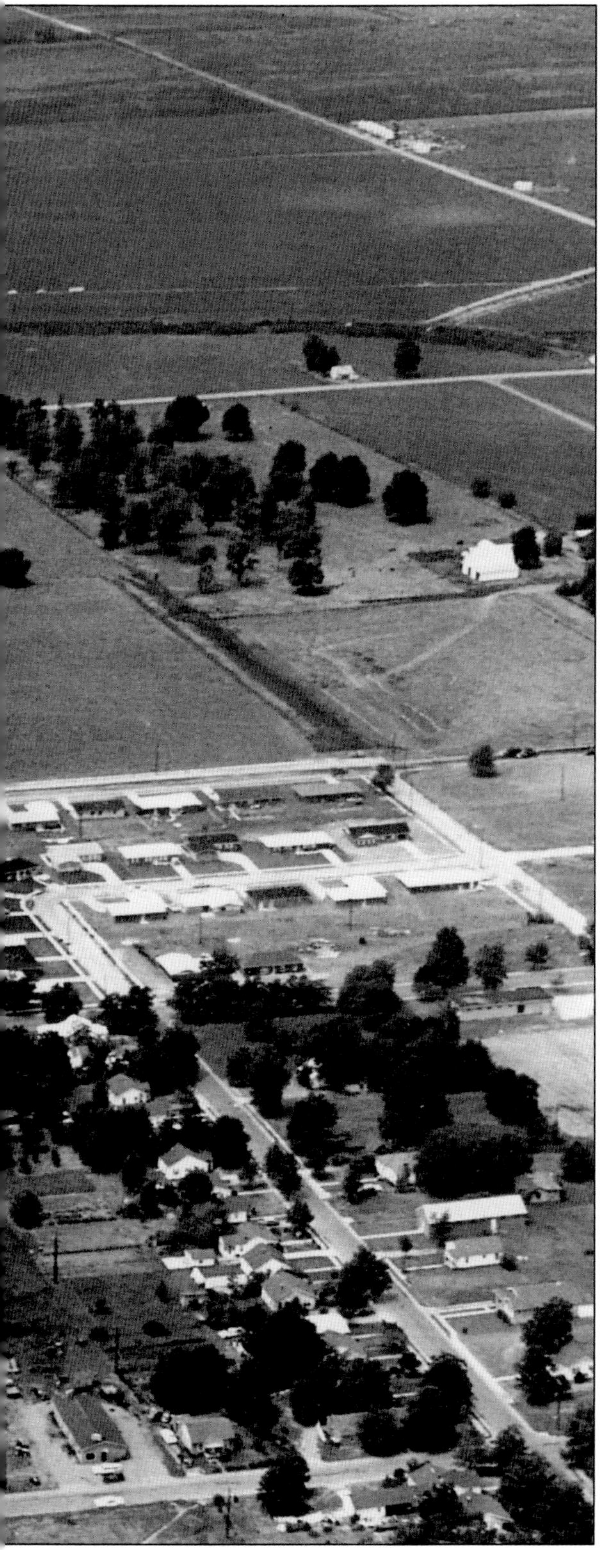

In the center of this 1961 aerial view is the newly constructed West Memphis High School on West Broadway. Immediately across the street is Bowen Airfield. The former airfield is the current site of the Meadowbrook Square shopping center.

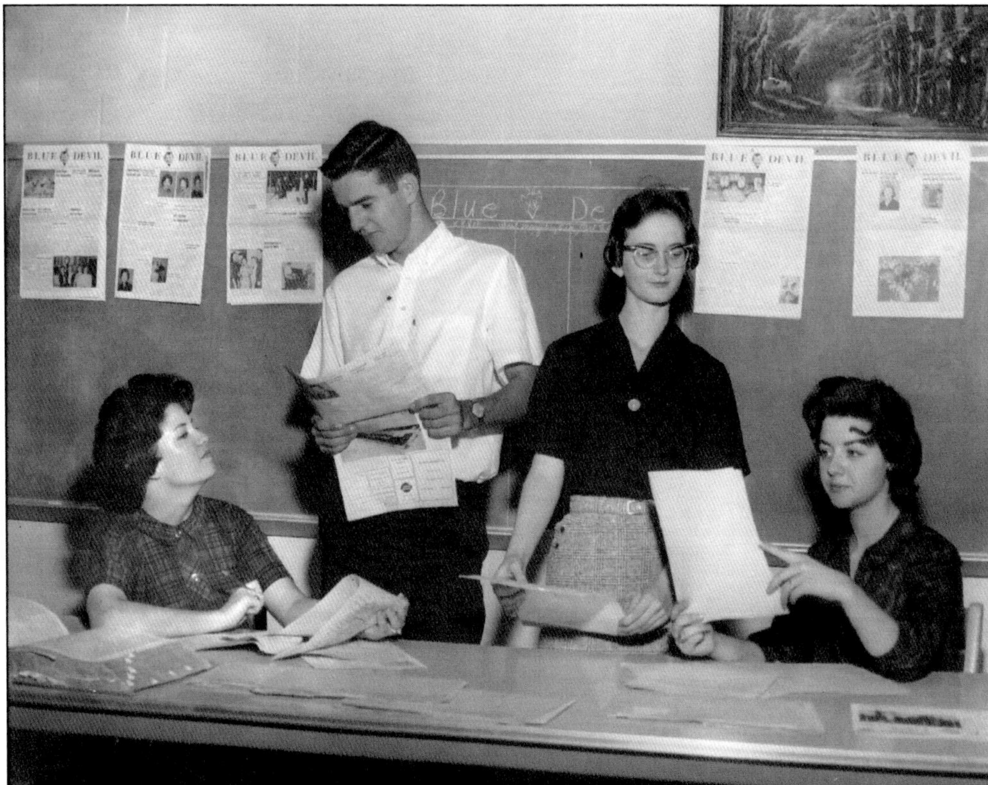

This group of West Memphis High School students is seen editing the first edition of the school newspaper in 1961. From left to right are Barbara Buchbinder, Thomas Propes, Virginia Chadwell, and Sally Edwards.

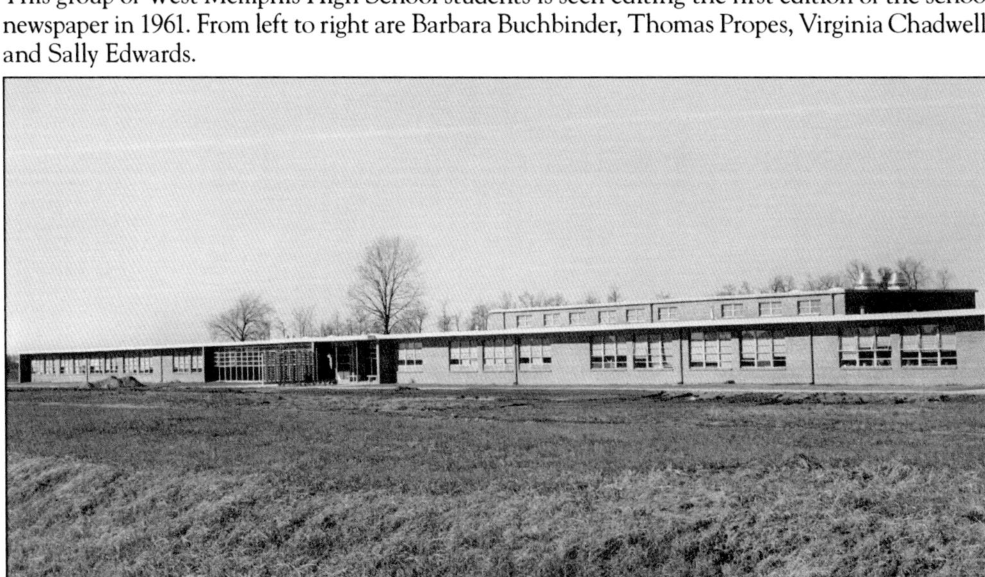

The new West Memphis High School was completed for the 1960–1961 school year for students in grades 10 through 12. The original location of the new high school had been planned for the 1000 block of West Barton Avenue in the late 1950s. Instead, that site was used to build Richland Elementary in 1963.

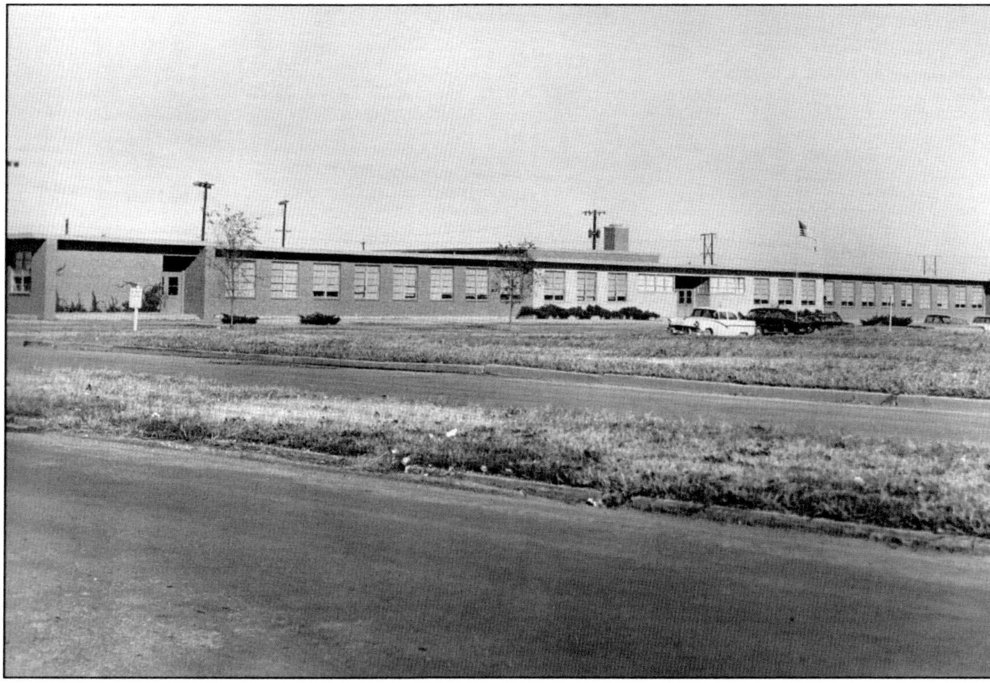

Maddux Elementary School, established in 1956, was named in honor of Alfred Maddux, who served as superintendent of schools from 1942 to 1953. The school's location at East Barton Avenue and Ingram Boulevard was chosen in response to the city's east side housing boom during the 1950s.

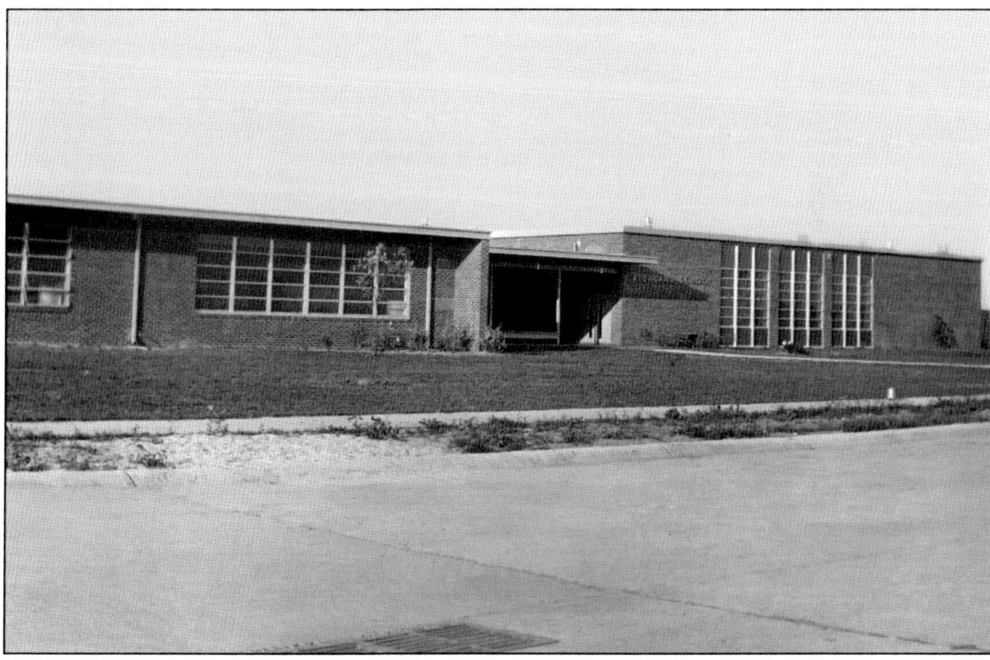

Richland Elementary School, photographed here on the school's opening day in September 1963, was named in honor of developer Jack Rich. It was originally the intended location of the new high school before land was acquired for that facility on West Broadway at a lower cost.

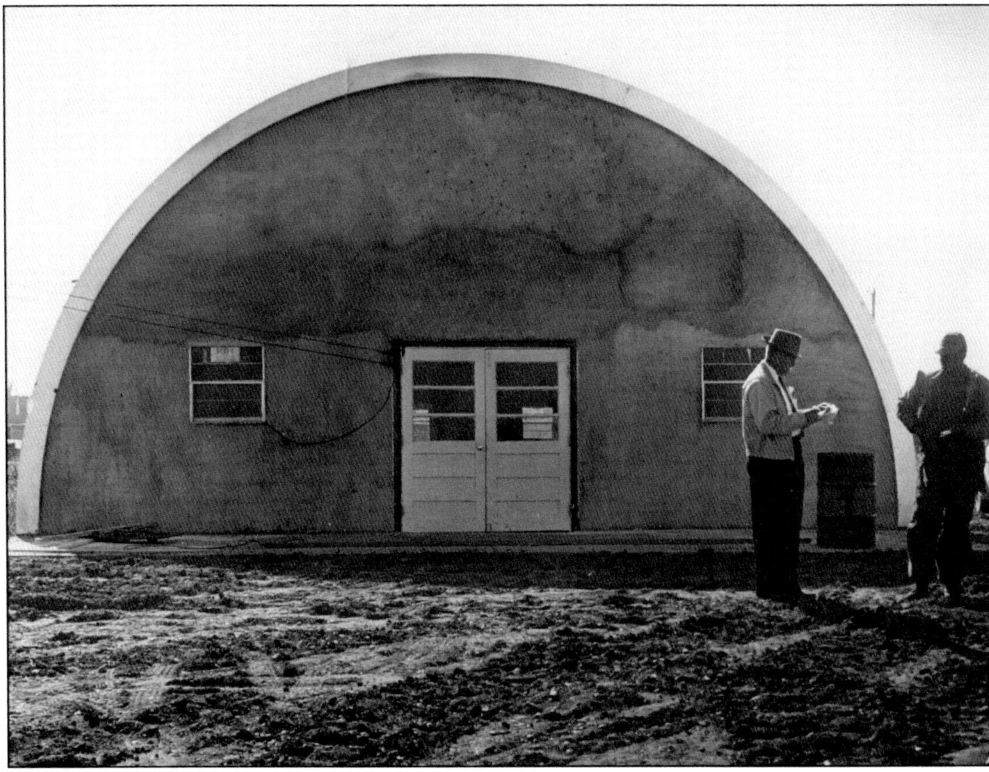

The West Memphis Boys Club, shown in 1962, was originally located in a Quonset hut near North Avalon Street. The club's present facility on Missouri Street was built in 1970 on the site of the former West Memphis Community House.

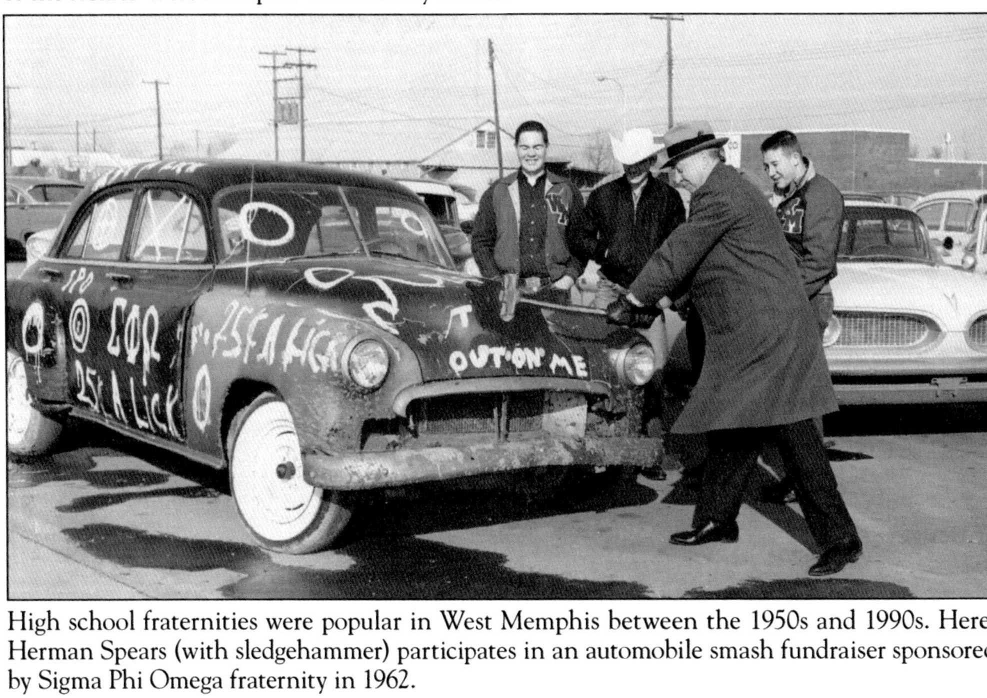

High school fraternities were popular in West Memphis between the 1950s and 1990s. Here, Herman Spears (with sledgehammer) participates in an automobile smash fundraiser sponsored by Sigma Phi Omega fraternity in 1962.

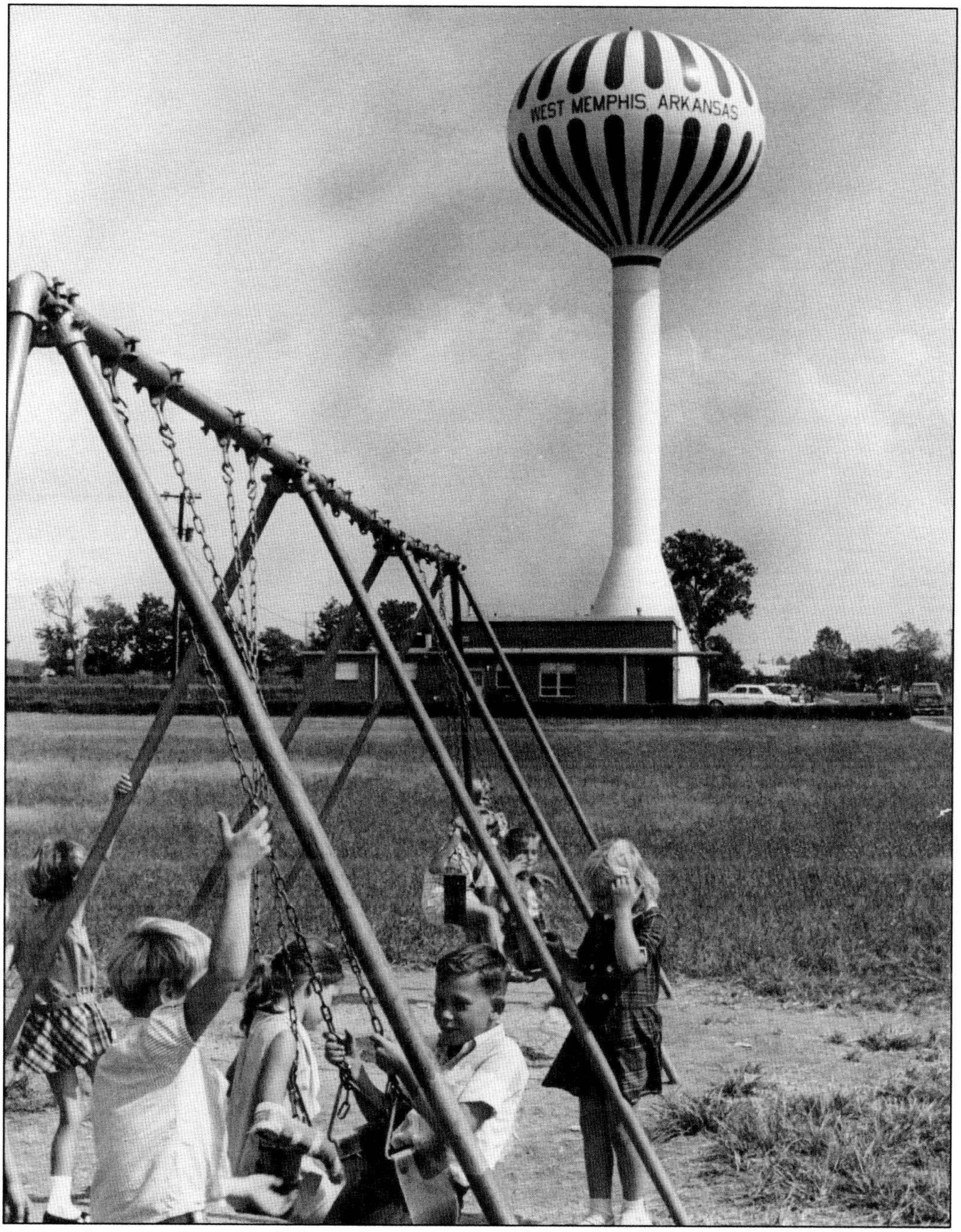

The student population in West Memphis public schools increased from 610 in 1945 to 2,800 by 1960. Pictured here are students at Maddux Elementary School playing at recess in 1968. Presently, the West Memphis School District has seven elementary schools, three junior high schools, and one high school.

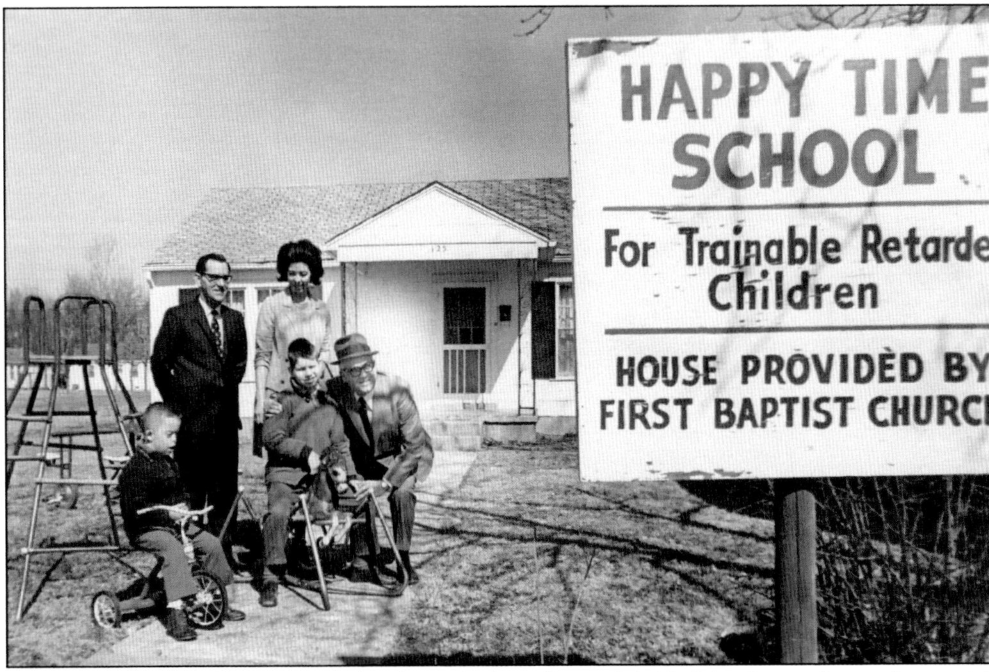

Happy Time School began in 1956, through the efforts of Adda Mae Jones, for students with special needs. In 1973, a modern facility was constructed on Balfour Road and later renamed Steudlein Learning Center in honor of Frank L. Steudlein. State senator William K. Ingram (right) is shown visiting the school in 1970.

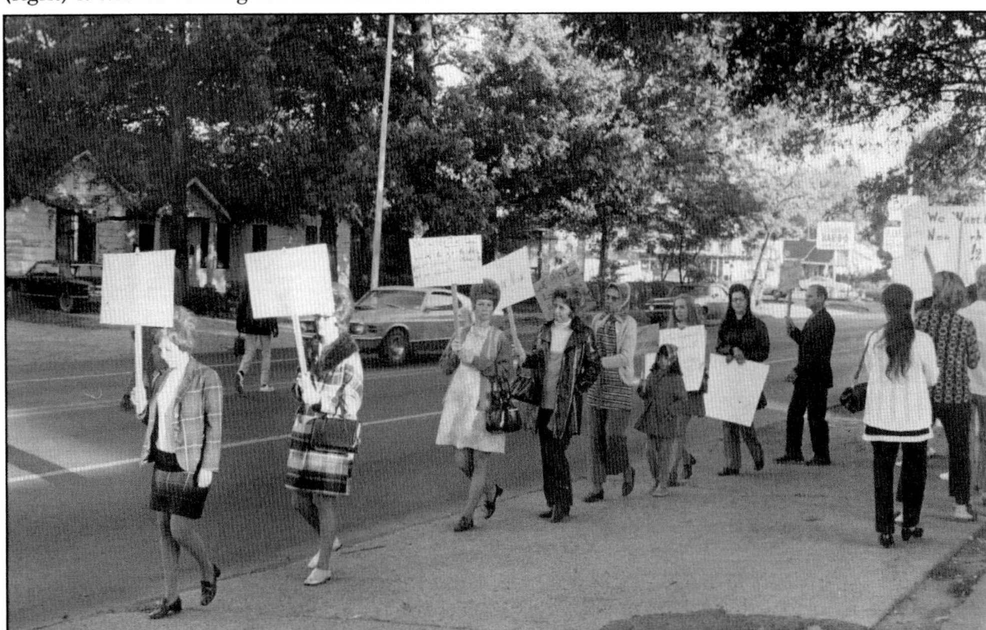

The West Memphis School District was fully integrated by 1971. While school integration occurred without incident, there was outrage over new busing policies. In September 1971, parents of students protested the new policy for several weeks outside the school district's office on Missouri Street.

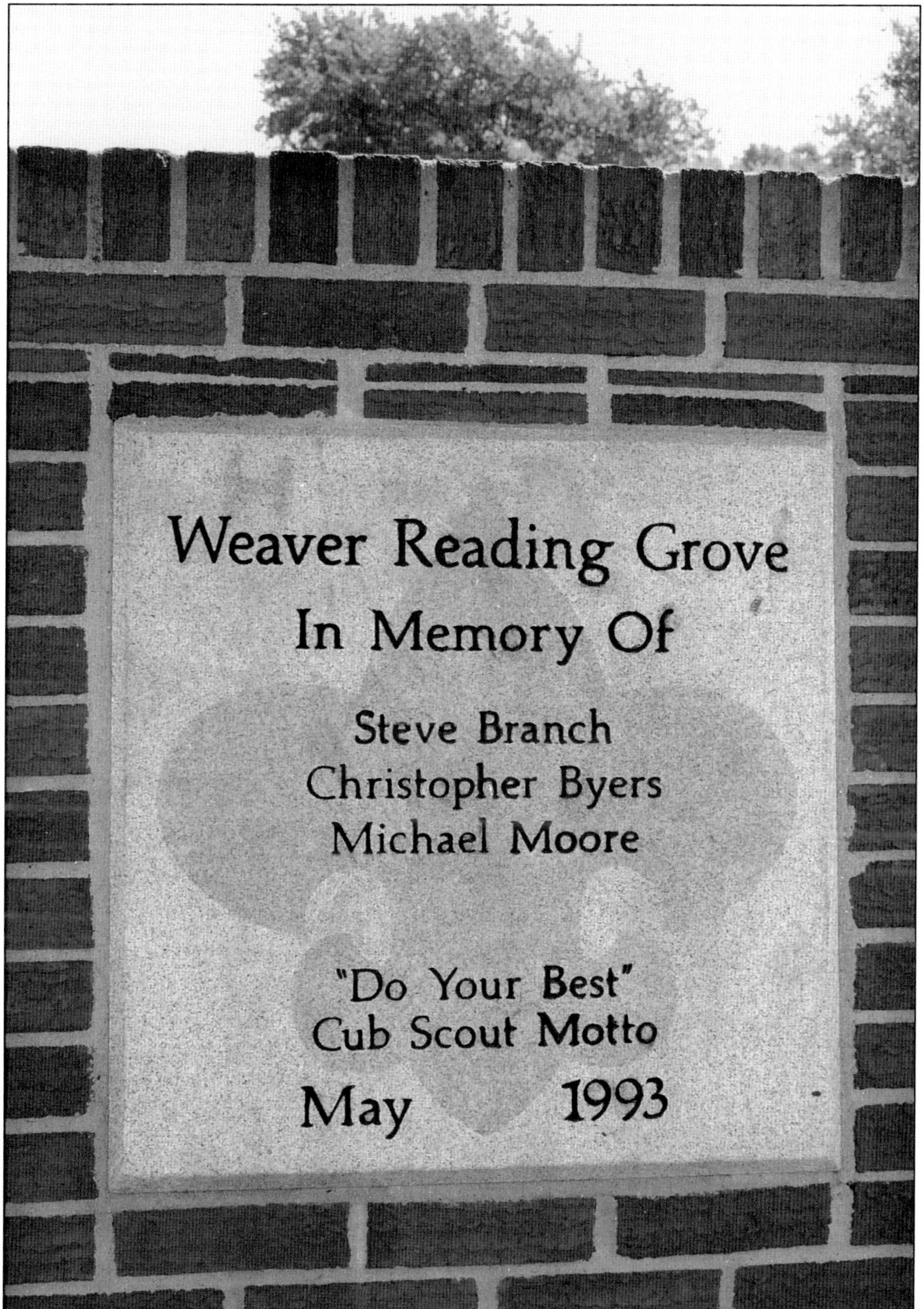

On the grounds of Weaver Elementary School is a reading grove memorial dedicated to three of its students, who were all Cub Scouts. The circumstances surrounding their murders on May 5, 1993, and the trials that ensued, have stirred international attention and debate.

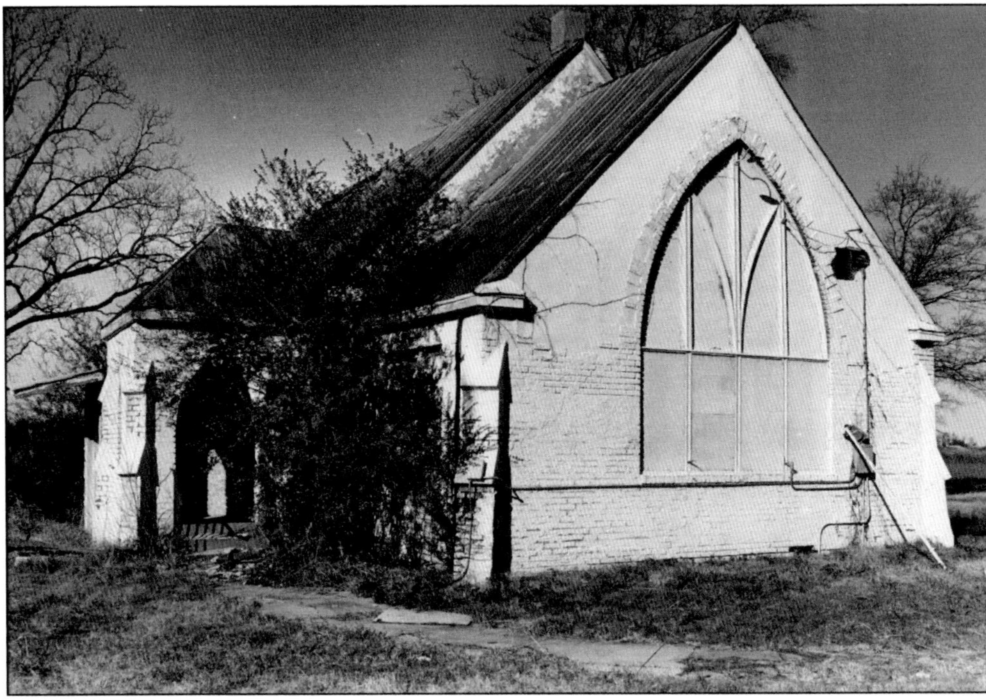

The Methodist Church in Hulbert was organized in 1919, and in 1925, a small, redbrick church was built on South Avalon Street. After merging with the congregation in West Memphis, the Hulbert church went through a series of ownerships. During the 1970s, the Crittenden County Little Theatre utilized the building for community theater performances until it burned in 1979.

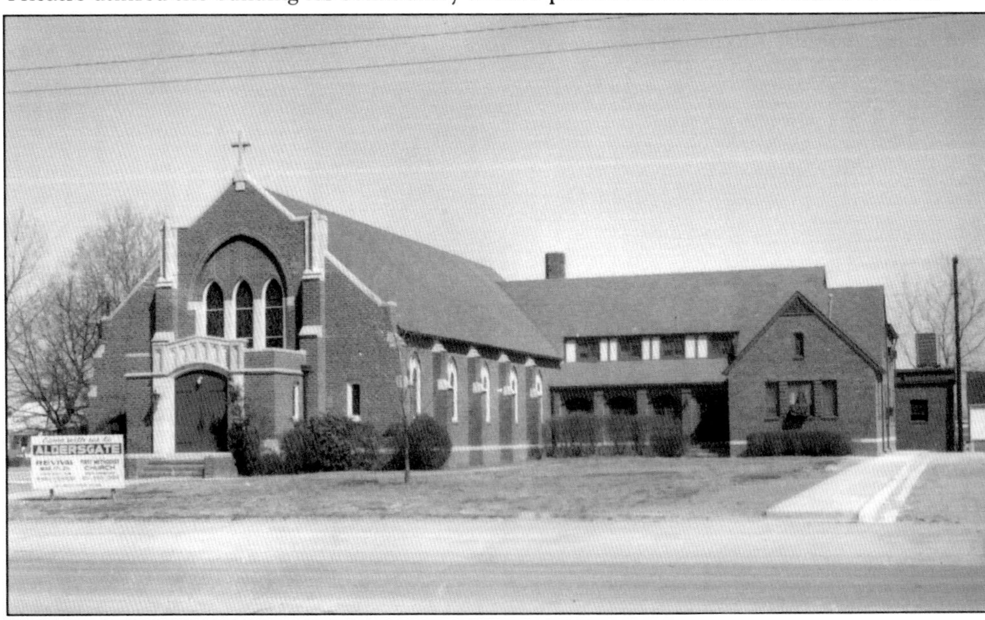

The First Methodist Church in West Memphis was an extension of the Methodist Church in Hulbert. Organized in 1933, its first sanctuary was built at 212 Pine Street at a cost of $5,000. In 1945, a new sanctuary, pictured here, was completed on Missouri Street. In 1990, this sanctuary underwent a major expansion, resulting in a reconfiguration of the original layout.

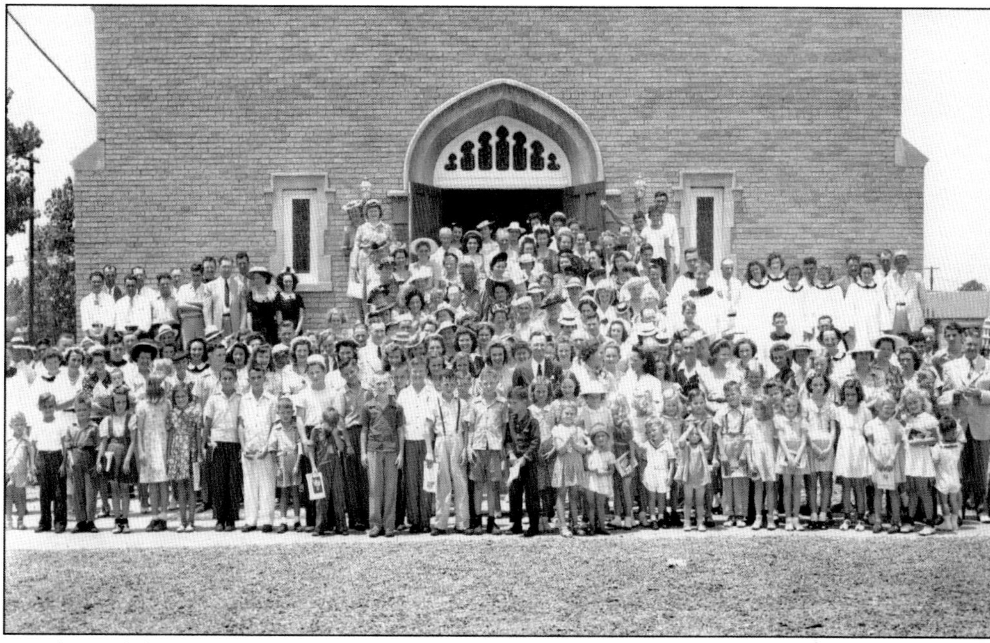

Members of the First Baptist Church pose outside the recently completed sanctuary on Easter Sunday 1945. Originally founded in 1924, the congregation began construction on a larger building in 1942 but was halted due to the war effort. To proceed further, the pastor appeared before the War Production Board in Washington to secure a high-priority building permit. The church was completed and dedicated in 1944.

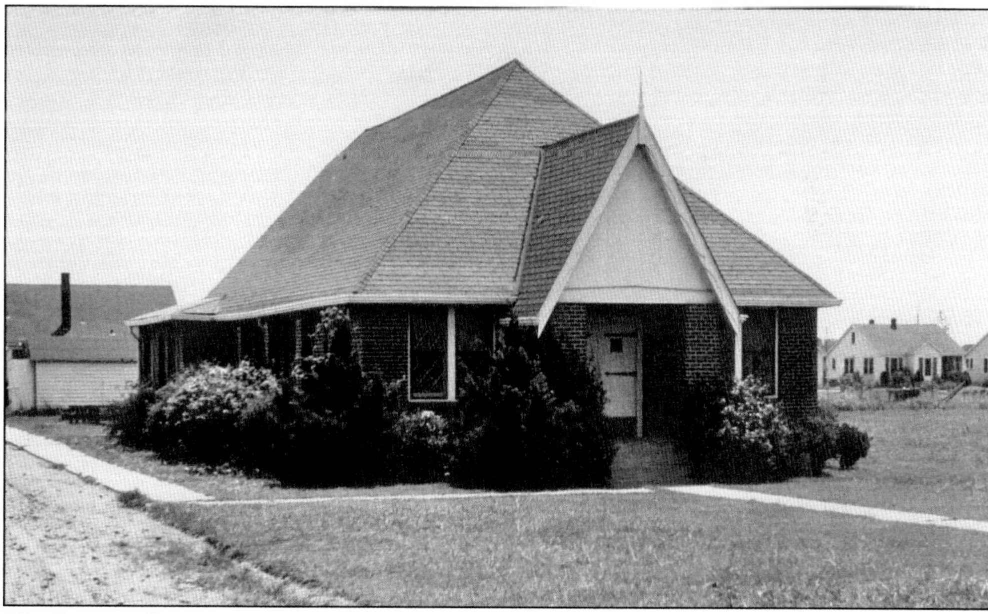

The First Presbyterian Church was established in 1936, and a small sanctuary was constructed the following year on the southeast corner of Missouri Street and Danner Avenue. In 1948, a new sanctuary was built, and in 1957, a vestibule and steeple were added to the facade. Although the exterior has been altered, the original structure, photographed above in 1938, still stands as the congregation's fellowship hall.

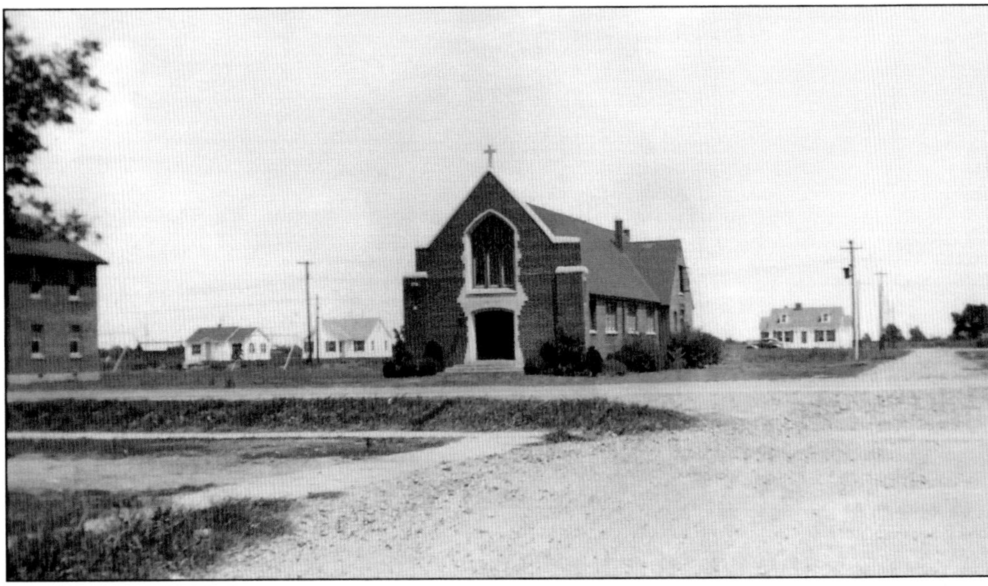

This photograph shows the original St. Michael's Catholic Church in 1939 on the northeast corner of Missouri Street and Danner Avenue. St. Michael's was established in 1936, with both its church and school being constructed in the same year. A new church was completed in 1959, and the original church structure was razed and replaced with a new school facility four years later. (Courtesy of Virginia Forman.)

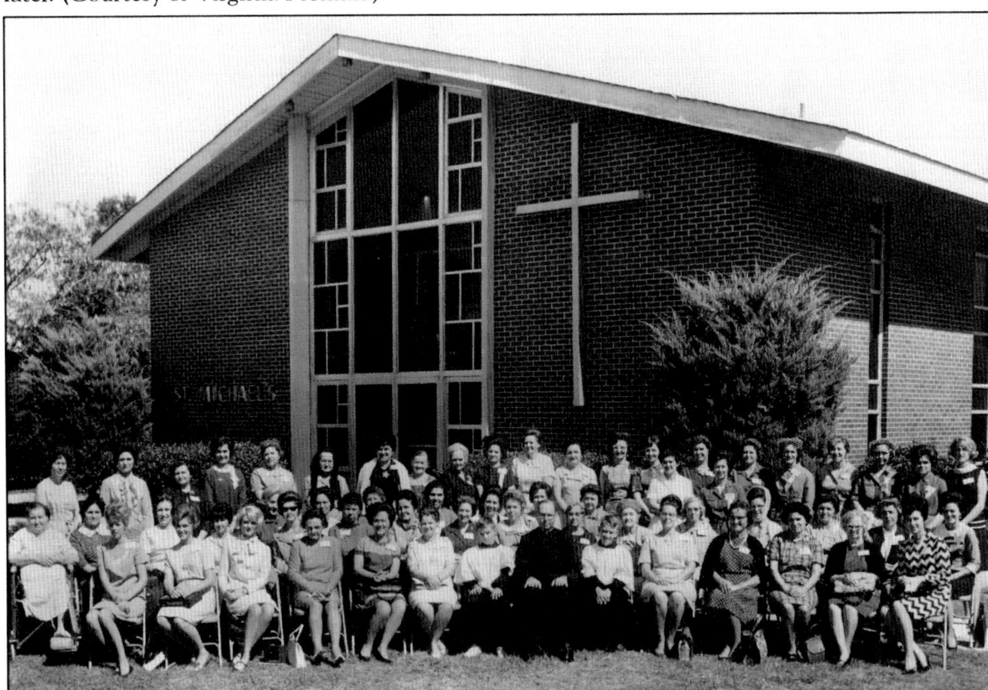

Members of the Infant of Prague Guild at St. Michael's pose during a day of recollection in 1967. The new modern church, shown here, was completed in 1959. The property around St. Michael's School was originally owned by gin operator Miles L. Thompson, who purchased the land in 1918. (Courtesy of Bonnie Waller.)

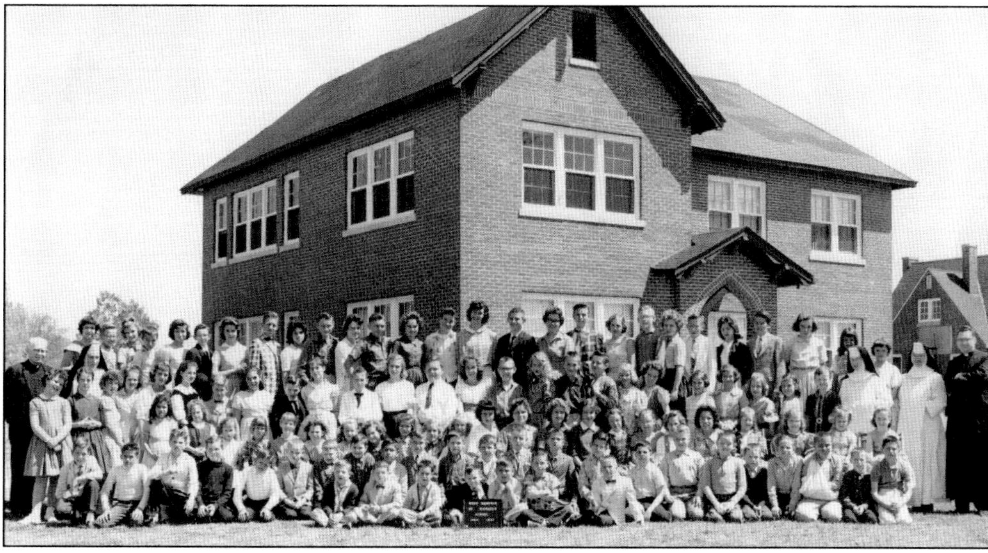

St. Michael's Catholic School was established in 1936 with an enrollment of 15 students. This photograph from 1960 shows the entire student body and faculty outside the original two-story school building. The school was first staffed by Dominican Sisters until 1952. Since 1954, the school has been served by the Olivetan Benedictine Sisters of Jonesboro, Arkansas.

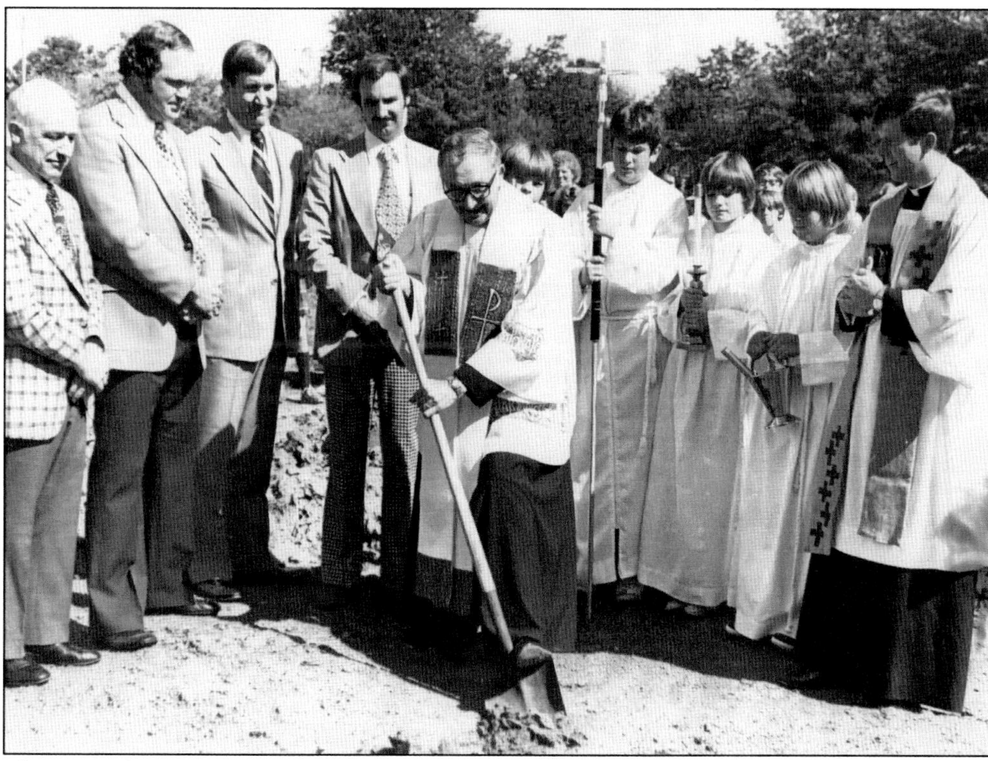

The original two-story school building at St. Michael's was razed in 1973, and the site was replaced with a church courtyard. Shown here in 1977 during the ground breaking for a new athletic facility are the Reverend John Barnes (center) and the Reverend Francis I. Malone (far right). School board members are, from left to right, Darby Henry, Jeptha Gates, Don Weis, and Jerry Hutchison.

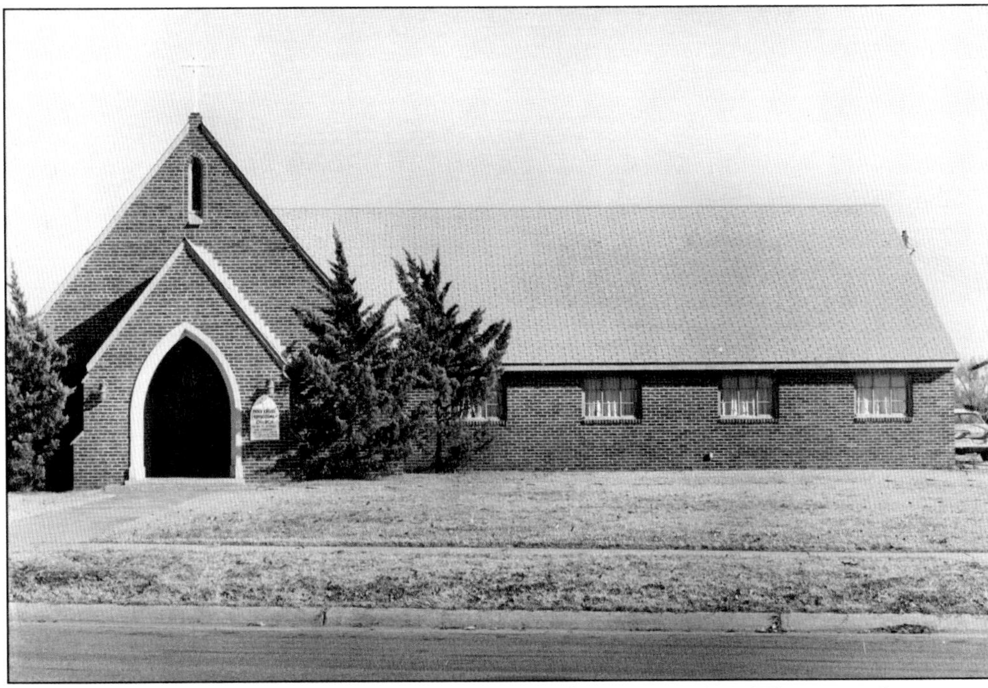

Holy Cross Episcopal Church was established on Park Drive in 1948. The original structure, which survived two fires during its history, still serves the congregation. This photograph from 1958 shows the church's original facade before it was altered and expanded in the early 1990s.

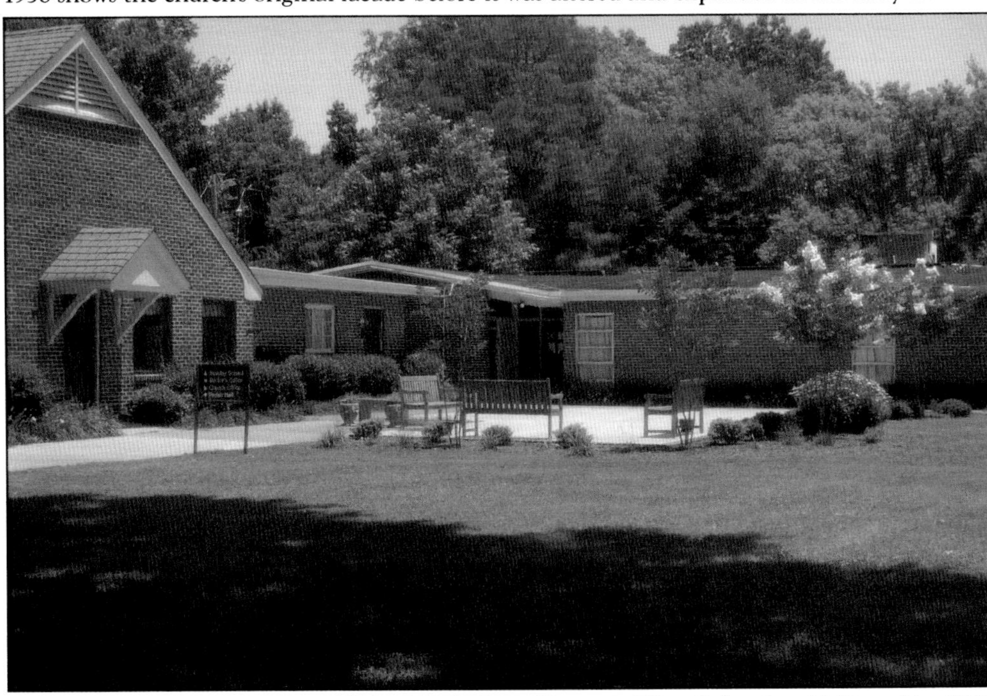

The Reverend Fred Kneipp established Holy Cross Episcopal Day School in 1959, and in 1971, a new school facility was dedicated to serve students in kindergarten through sixth grade until the school's closure in 1986.

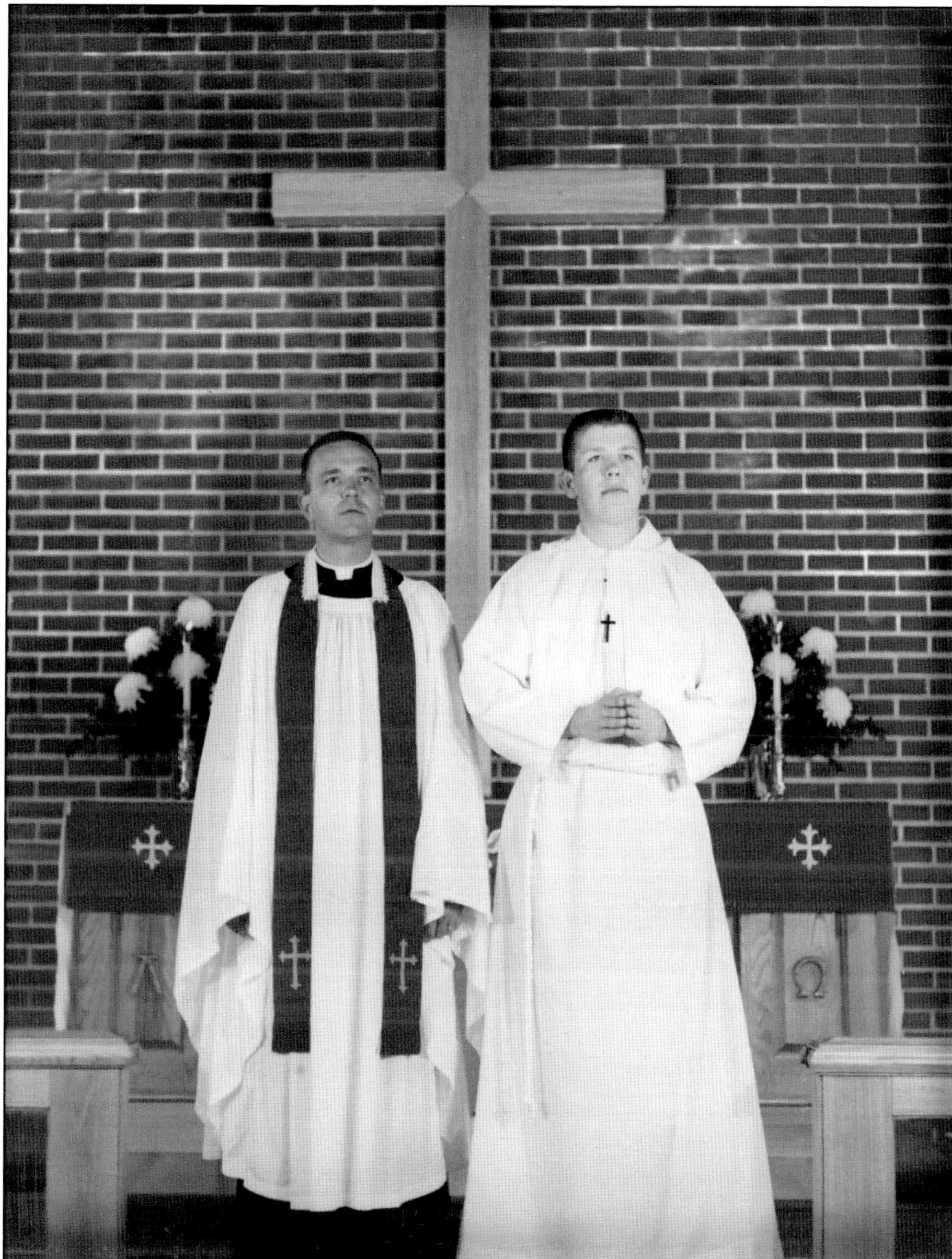

Holy Cross Episcopal Church was guided by the leadership of its rector, the Reverend Fred Kneipp, between 1953 and 1967. In addition to establishing Holy Cross Day School, he was instrumental in the acquisition of the church rectory, which was the former clubhouse of the West Memphis Country Club. This photograph from 1960 shows the Reverend Kneipp (left), with Frank Martin assisting as an acolyte.

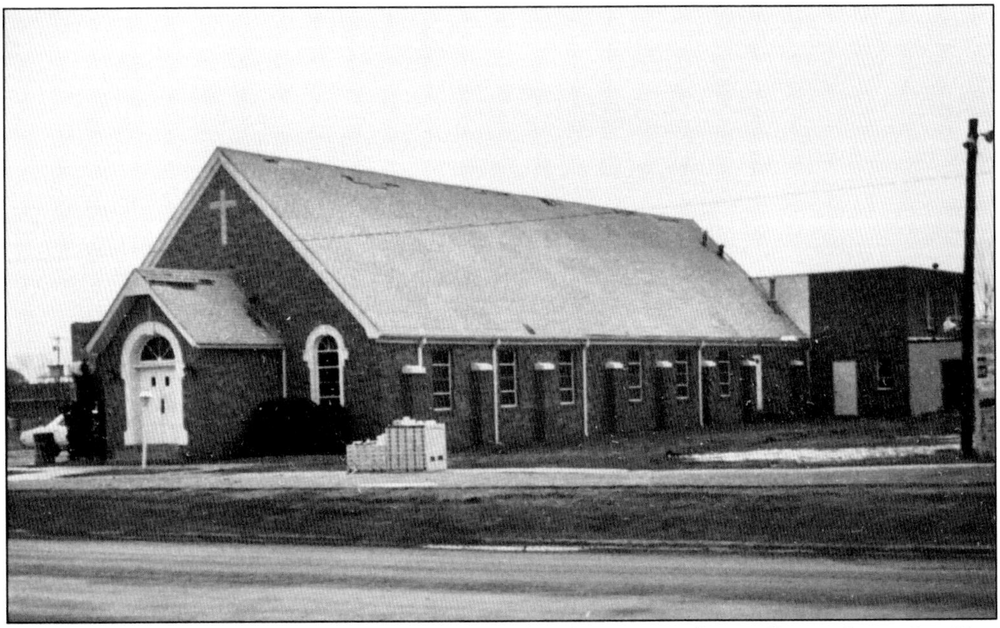

The first building of Trinity Missionary Baptist Church, organized in 1953, was located at East Barton and Hamilton Street on land donated by Jack Rich. The entire cost of the original church building, photographed above, was also provided by Rich as a gift to the young congregation. In 1995, the church relocated to the former Tabernacle Baptist Church on Graham Street.

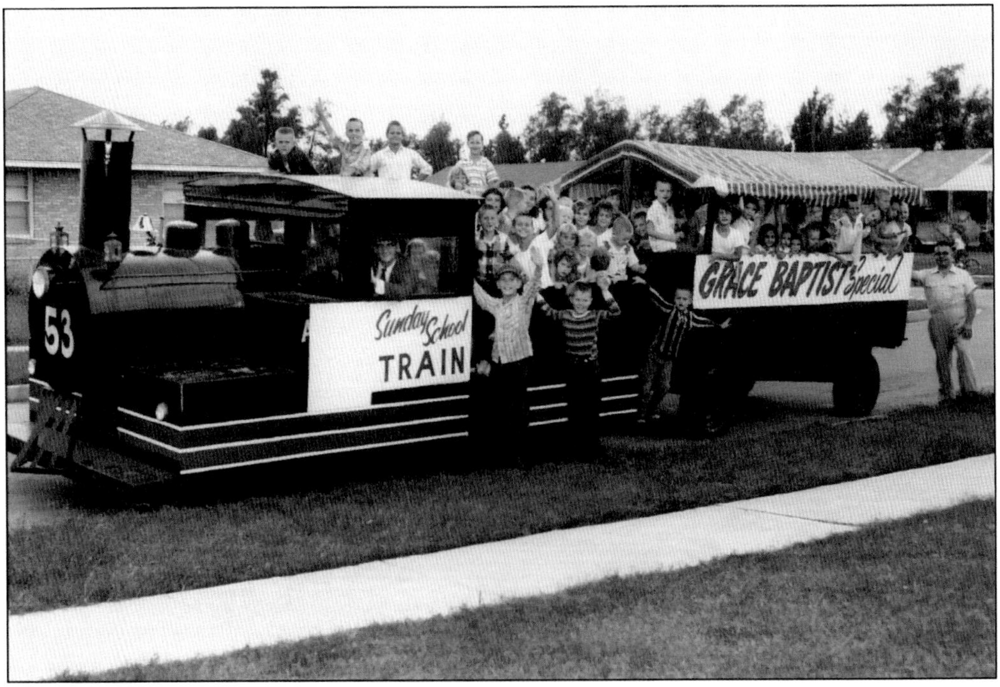

This photograph shows Grace Church's ingenious way of transporting neighborhood children to its Sunday school classes in 1957. Grace Baptist Church, organized in 1946, was originally a mission of the First Baptist Church in West Memphis. In 1957, the congregation purchased land on Ingram Boulevard, and the name was changed to Ingram Boulevard Baptist Church.

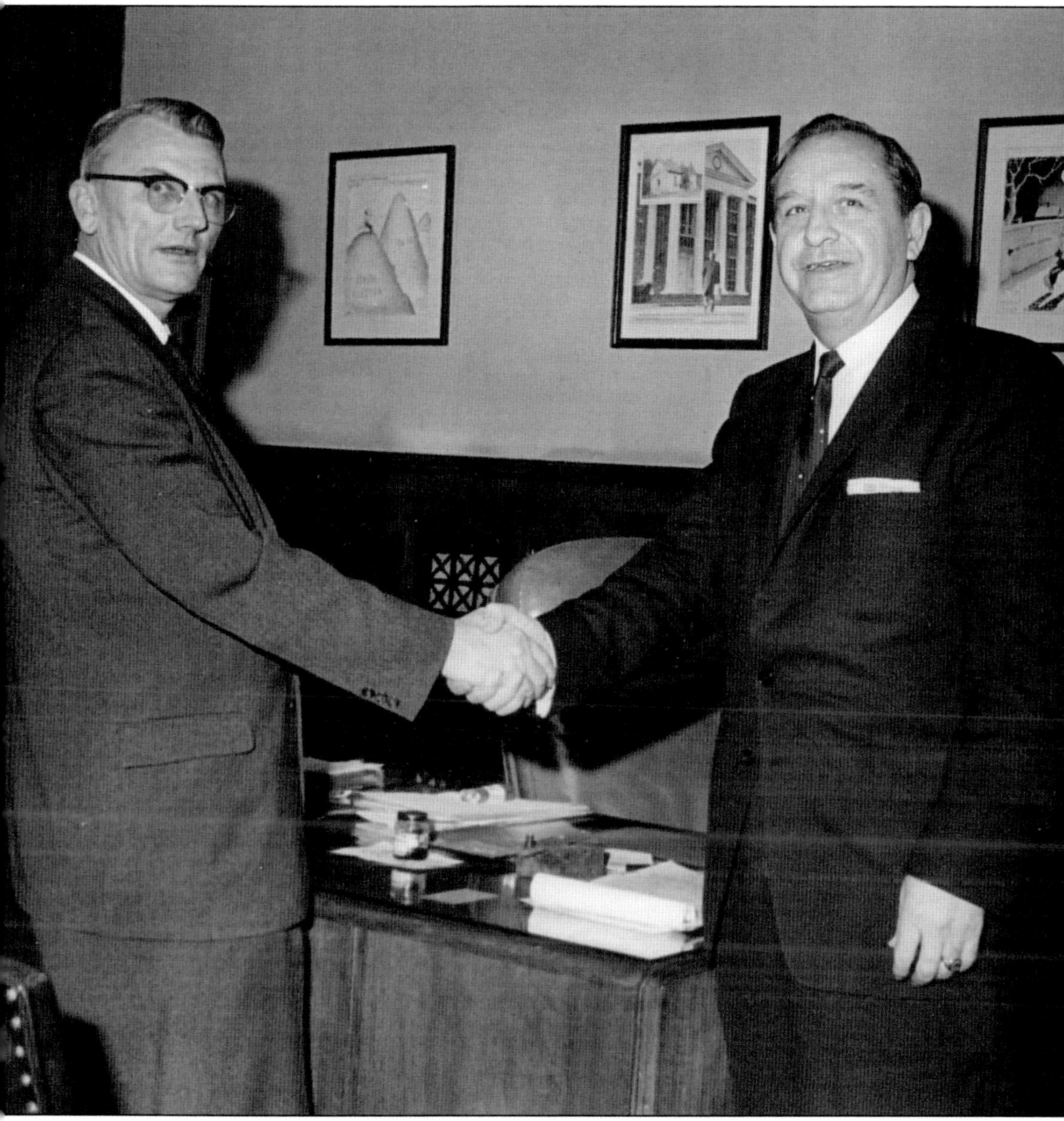

During the 1940s and 1950s, several congregations and religious leaders objected to the impropriety of the dozens of nightclubs and dance halls located in West Memphis. The reputation of these establishments, primarily located on Eighth Street, gained the attention of Memphians who campaigned for their closure. In late 1963, West Memphis mayor Robert Eden issued the final shutdown order. Photographed above in 1956 to discuss the situation is First Baptist Church pastor Walter Yeldell (left) meeting with Arkansas governor Orval Faubus.

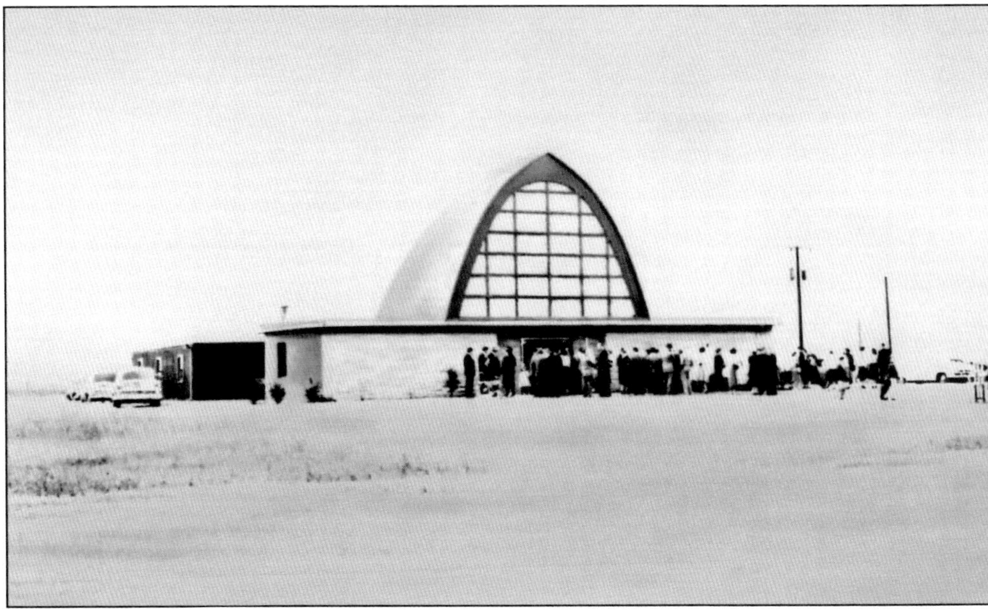

Missouri Street Church of Christ has been located at its present site since 1957. The original church building, shown above in the late 1950s, was eventually converted for use by West Memphis Christian School. Currently, the congregation is worshipping in its third church building.

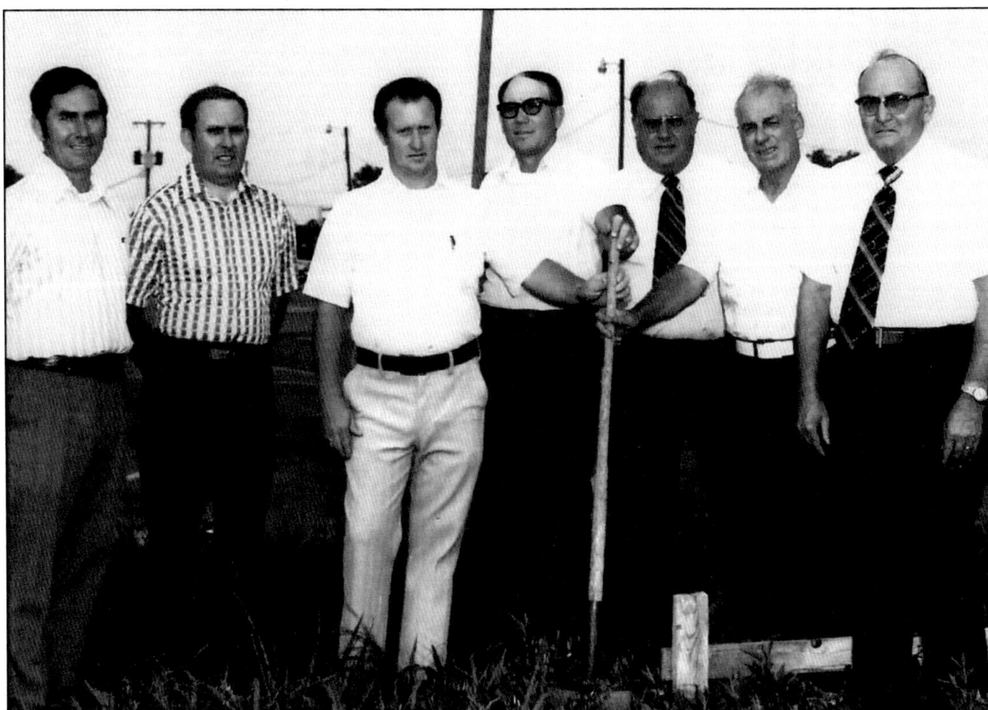

In 1970, Missouri Street Church of Christ established West Memphis Christian School, which began as a day care and kindergarten program and later expanded to a comprehensive elementary and high school curriculum by 1977. Photographed above are school board members breaking ground for a new building in 1972. (Courtesy of Loretta Dale.)

Mary Ann Pike and Lyndal Dale were instrumental in both the establishment and continued growth of West Memphis Christian School, where they served as administrators for several years. West Memphis Christian School is presently the largest private school in Crittenden County.

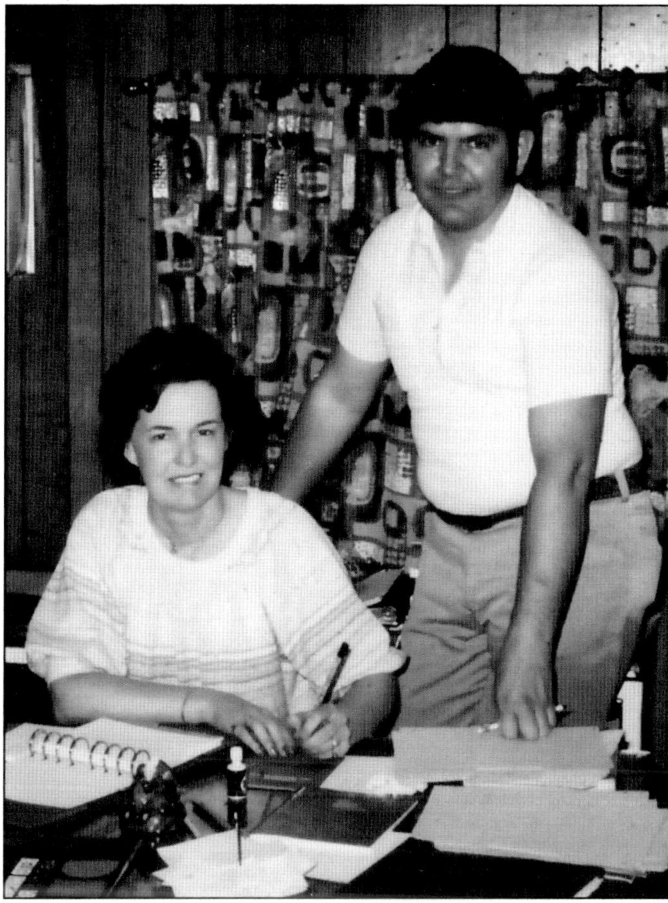

The elementary campus of West Memphis Christian has remained adjacent to the Missouri Street Church of Christ complex since its founding. The high school campus was originally located on Avondale Circle beginning in 1975 and relocated in 2006 to the site of a former Kmart building on Missouri Street. Photographed below is the school's Black Knight football team in 1977.

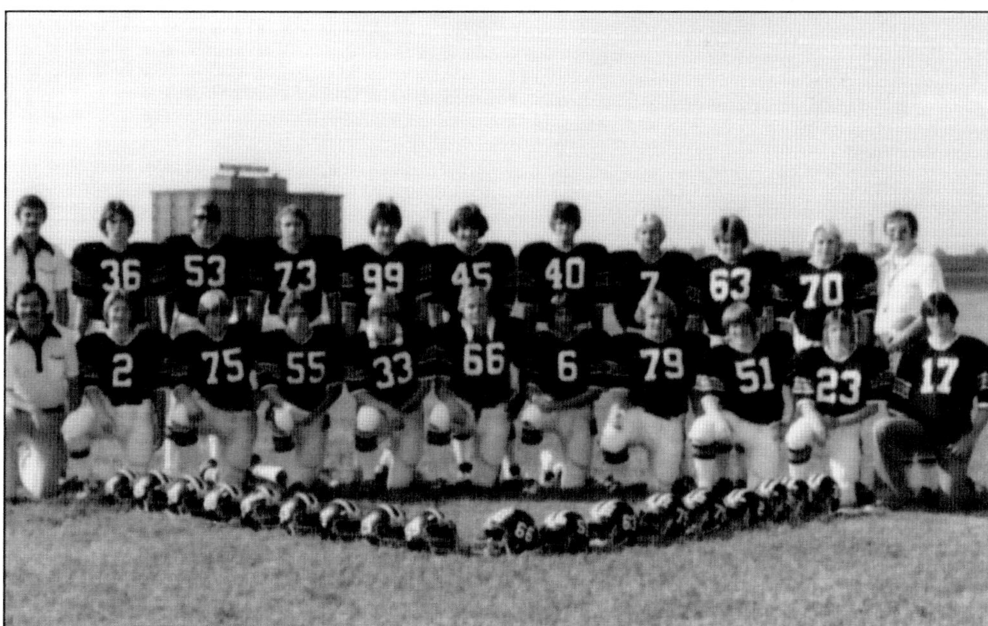

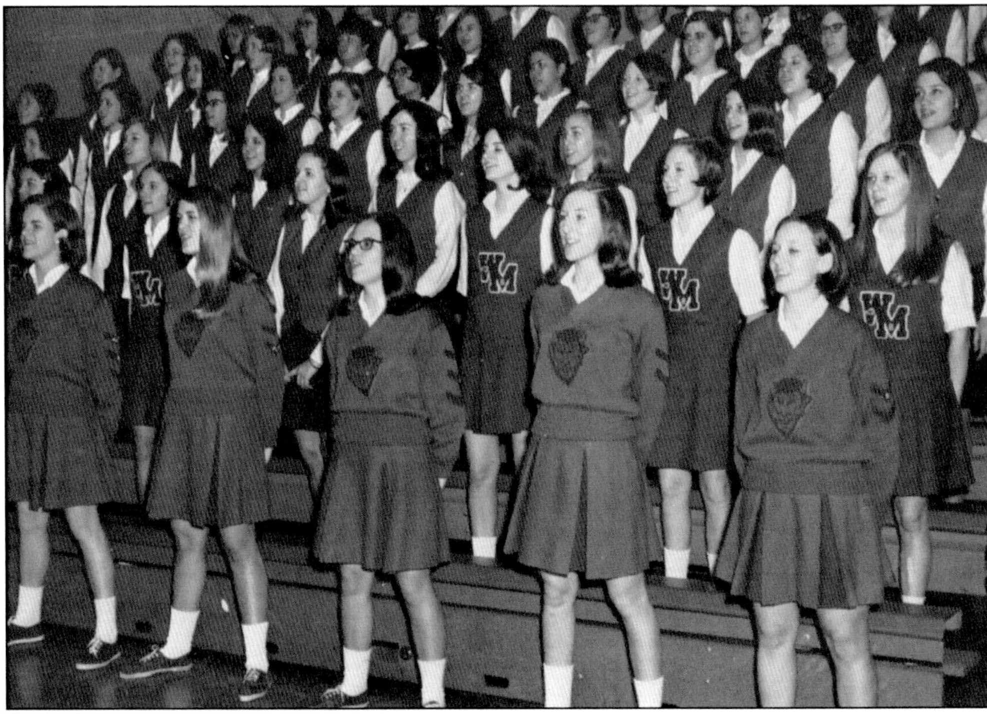

The pep club at West Memphis High School is photographed here during a 1968 pep rally for the West Memphis Blue Devils. The Blue Devils basketball team has won multiple state championships, and the 1980 and 1981 teams set a combined state record of 60 consecutive wins.

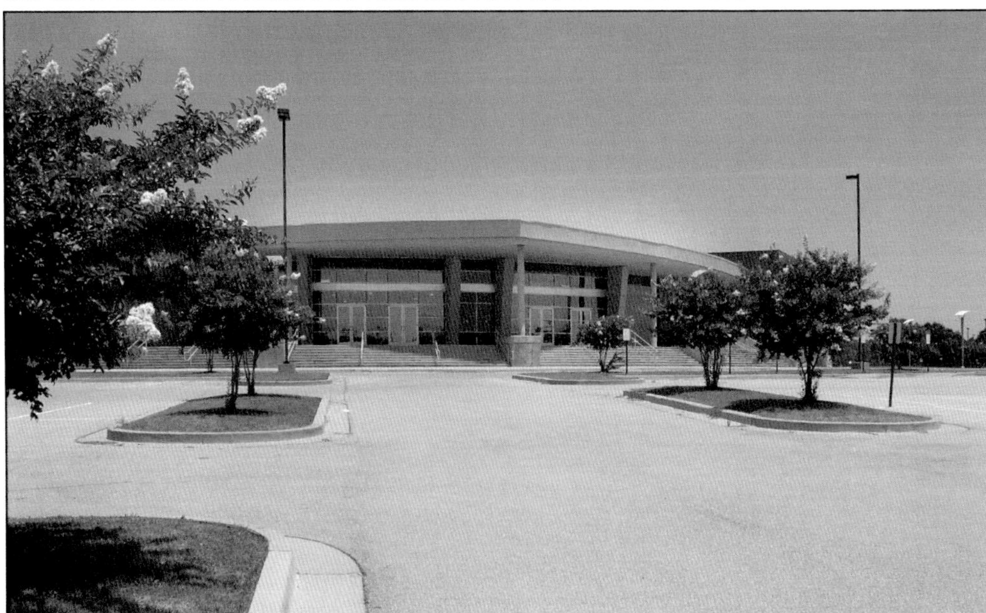

In 2008, Lehr Arena was dedicated at West Memphis High School. The arena replaced the school's gymnasium for basketball games and is also used for extracurricular events and civic functions. The arena was named in honor of the Lehr family, who originally owned the land where the high school is located.

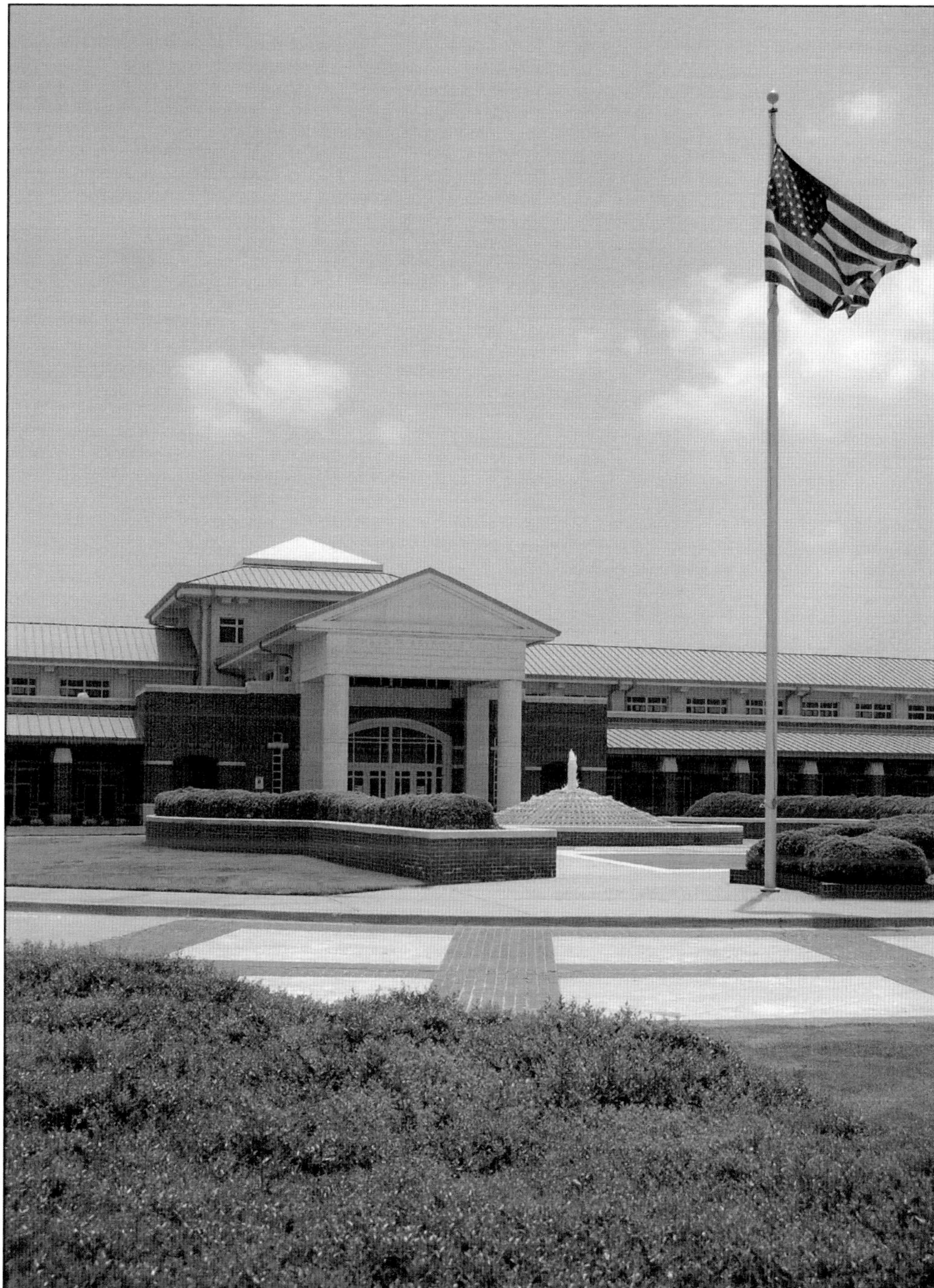

In 1979, local civic leaders were instrumental in establishing a vocational-technical school in West Memphis. The school was converted to a community college in 1993 and renamed Mid-South Community College. Presently, the college enrolls approximately 2,000 students annually at its 90-acre campus.

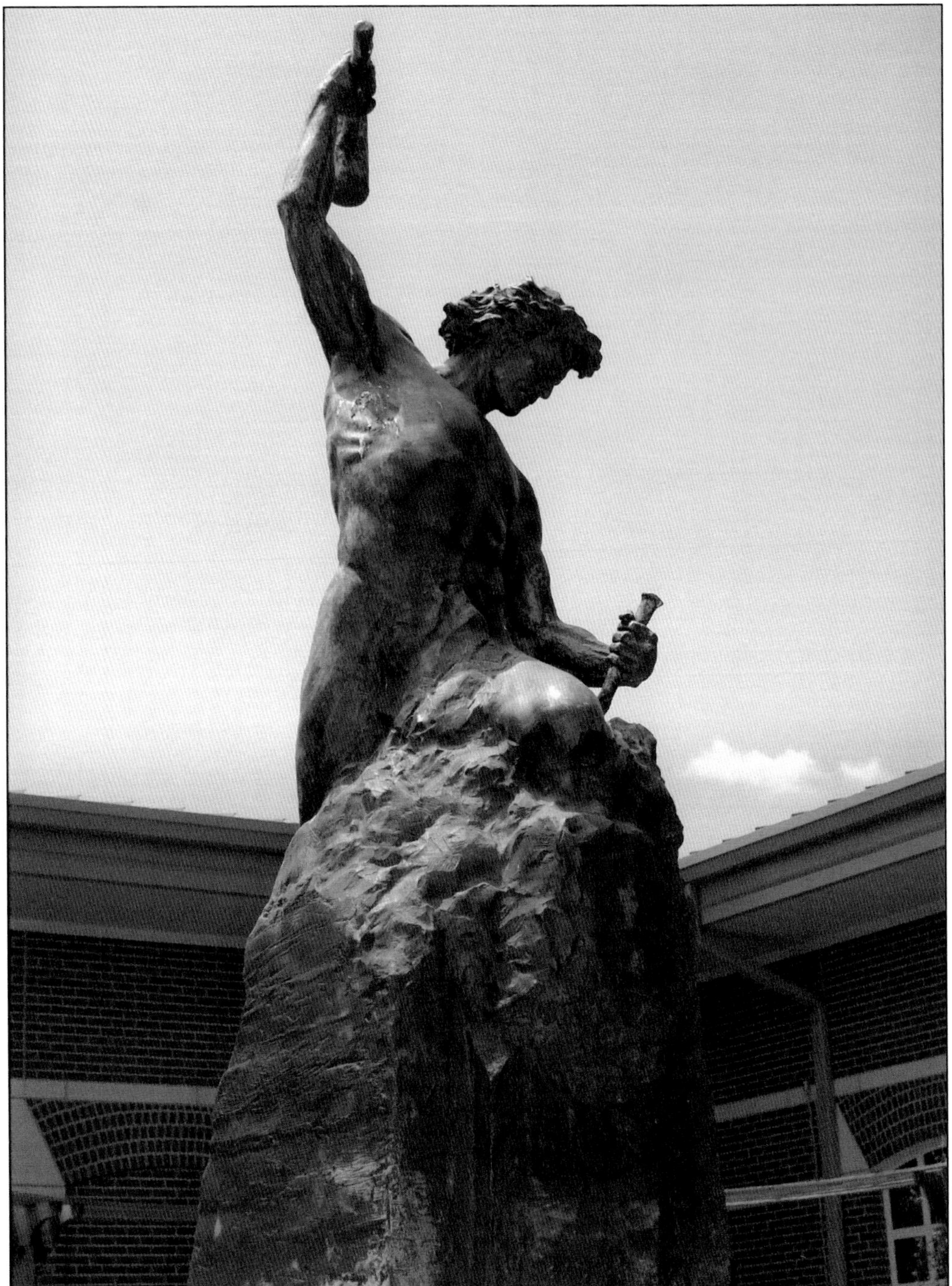

This bronze statue, located on the grounds of the Mid-South Community College campus, depicts the self-made man in his struggle to create himself out of common stone. The statue serves as an illustration to students that they can achieve economic success pending hard work and ingenuity. It also personifies the hardships overcome by the first settlers of West Memphis who forged a community out of the unsettled, forested lands of the early 20th century. (Courtesy of Jeannie B. O'Toole.)

Time Line

1797: The Spanish establish Campo de la Esperanza along the Mississippi River.

1803: The Louisiana Purchase is made between France and the United States.

1825: Crittenden County is created from territory separated from Phillips County.

1836: Arkansas is admitted to the Union.

1859: Hopefield becomes an incorporated town.

1863: Union troops burn the town of Hopefield.

1892: The Frisco Bridge is completed over the Mississippi River.

1914: Zack Bragg begins his lumber operation on Missouri Street.

1915: William H. Hundhausen Sr. establishes Bolz Cooperage Plant.

1925: Final improvements to the Mississippi River levee system are completed.

1927: West Memphis becomes an incorporated city, with Zack Bragg elected as its first mayor.

1930: City council members select Marshall B. Currie as the second mayor following Zack Bragg's resignation.

1932: William H. Hundhausen Sr. is elected as the third mayor.

1935: West Memphis reaches a population of 2,225.

1940: The City of West Memphis acquires the utility company.

1944: Melvin Dacus is sworn in as the fourth mayor.

1949: The Memphis-Arkansas Bridge is completed.

1950: West Memphis reaches a population of 9,112.

1952: William Fordyce is sworn in as the fifth mayor.

1954: Howell B. Price is sworn in as the sixth mayor.

1960: West Memphis reaches a population of 19,374.

1962: Interstate 40 is completed from West Memphis to Lehi.

1963: Robert Eden is sworn in as the seventh mayor.

1970: Tilden Rodgers becomes the eighth mayor.

1973: The Hernando de Soto Bridge is completed.

1975: Joyce Ferguson becomes the ninth mayor.

1980: The population of West Memphis reaches 28,138.

1983: Leo Chitman becomes the 10th mayor.

1987: Keith Ingram becomes the 11th mayor.

1987: A deadly F3-rated tornado severely damages West Memphis.

1995: Al Boals becomes the 12th mayor.

1999: William H. Johnson becomes the 13th mayor.

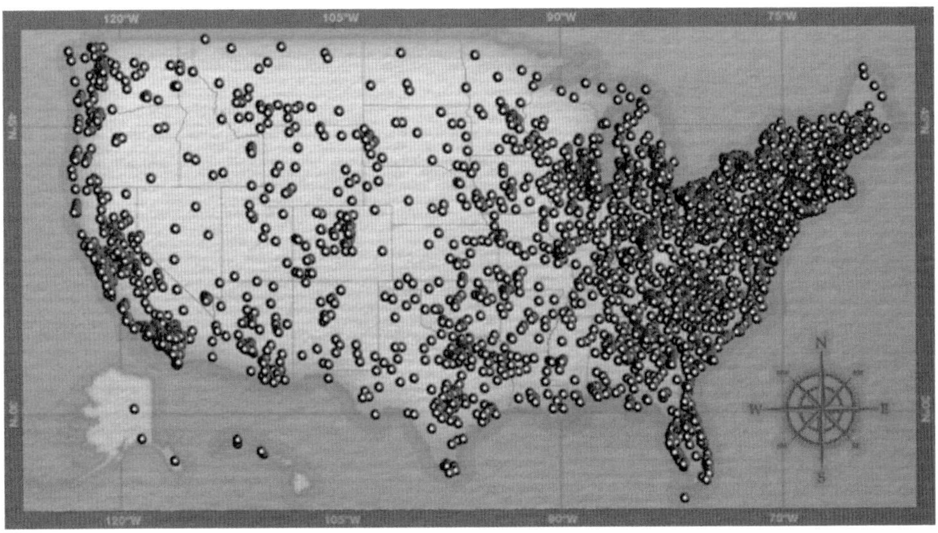

Consistent with our mission to preserve history on a local level, this book was printed in South Carolina on American-made paper and manufactured entirely in the United States. Products carrying the accredited Forest Stewardship Council (FSC) label are printed on 100 percent FSC-certified paper.

MADE IN THE USA